DATE DUE

Forbidden Books in American Public Libraries, 1876–1939

RECENT TITLES IN CONTRIBUTIONS IN LIBRARIANSHIP
AND INFORMATION SCIENCE
SERIES EDITOR: PAUL WASSERMAN

EVELYN GELLER

Forbidden Books in American Public Libraries, 1876–1939

A STUDY IN
CULTURAL
CHANGE

CONTRIBUTIONS IN
LIBRARIANSHIP AND
INFORMATION SCIENCE,
NUMBER 46

GREENWOOD PRESS
WESTPORT, CONNECTICUT
LONDON, ENGLAND

Copyright Acknowledgment

Grateful acknowledgment is made for permission to
reprint from "Speech to Scholars," by Archibald
MacLeish, *Saturday Review of Literature,* 16
(June 12, 1937), 12. Reprinted by permission of
Houghton Mifflin Company.

Library of Congress Cataloging in Publication Data

Geller, Evelyn.
  Forbidden books in American public libraries, 1876–
1939.

  (Contributions in librarianship and information
science, ISSN 0084-9243 ; no. 46)
  Bibliography: p.
  Includes index.
  1. Public libraries—United States—Censorship—
History.   2. Censorship—United States—History.
3. Library science—United States—History.   4. Books
and reading—United States—History.   5. Freedom of
information—United States—History.   I. Title.
II. Series.
Z711.4.G44   1984   025.2'1874'0973   83-12566
ISBN 0-313-23808-1 (lib. bdg.)

Library of Congress Catalog Card Number: 83-12566
ISBN: 0-313-23808-1
ISSN: 0084-9243

First published in 1984

Greenwood Press
A division of Congressional Information Service, Inc.
88 Post Road West, Westport, Connecticut 06881

Printed in the United States of America

10 9 8 7 6 5 4 3 2 1

To my Mother
and in memory
of my Father

CONTENTS

ILLUSTRATIONS

Figures

Tables

Documents

ACKNOWLEDGMENTS

I am particularly indebted to Professor Sigmund Diamond of Columbia University for his painstaking readings, perceptive criticisms, and constant encouragement in all stages of my research. Professors Bernard Barber and W. Phillips Davison were most instrumental in refining my work. The theoretical orientation of this study has been strongly influenced by the work of Professors Robert K. Merton and Harriet A. Zuckerman, in whose seminars on the sociology of science I received constant inspiration, insight, and perspective. I would like also to thank Professor Phyllis Dain of the Columbia University School of Library Service for her careful reading and comments, and Professors Richard L. Darling and Kathleen Molz of the library school for their interest.

I am pleased to thank the librarians at Columbia University and the New York Public Library for their always courteous and competent assistance, and Arlene Belzer of Greenwood Press for her sensitive editing of the manuscript.

When some oppose the ideal society to the real society, like two antagonists which would lead us in opposite directions, they materialize and oppose abstractions. The ideal society is not outside of the real society; it is a part of it. . . . For a society is not made up merely of the mass of individuals who compose it, the ground which they occupy, the things which they use and the movements which they perform, but above all is the idea which it forms of itself. It is undoubtedly true that it hesitates over the manner in which it ought to conceive itself; it feels itself drawn in divergent directions. But these conflicts which break forth are not between the ideal and reality, but between two different ideals, that of yesterday and that of today.
—Emile Durkheim, *The Elementary Forms of Religious Life.*

INTRODUCTION

This study traces the way in which the ideal of the freedom to read came to replace a quite different ideology between 1876 and 1939. In 1876, when the American Library Association was formed, its leaders avoided controversial literature and endorsed the librarian as moral censor. In 1939, when the association adopted its first Library Bill of Rights, the librarian was defined as guardian of the freedom to read.

Two sets of questions are suggested by these changes. First, why did the idea of the freedom to read become dominant at a given time and not another? Why did censorship policies once seem to be consonant with our liberal political traditions and First Amendment freedoms? Second, how does a profession choose the values that justify its existence and social contribution? How do its concepts of the public interest change?

Today, as censorship efforts increase, and issues long thought resolved become controversial once more, the historical comparison of these competing ideologies becomes especially urgent. A long-term perspective is needed to shed light on the changing meanings of censorship and the shifting boundaries of permissible expression. Every society, however liberal, imposes its taboos, explicit and implicit. The ideas and values it forbids reflect its deepest fears and commitments, and their defenses and challenges define its cultural frame.

Equally complex is the relationship between First Amendment freedoms and academic freedom, freedom of the press, and the freedom to read. Academicians, journalists, librarians all have codes of freedom, but all have censored themselves and operate within overt and tacit limits. All have had their freedoms challenged by others and defined by court decision.

Librarians now opposing censorship in and out of court may be taking the opposite side in an old debate. Yet they have always had to defend their criteria for choosing books, as well as their professional authority, vis-à-vis the lay community to which they are accountable. The content of these disputes and even the values invoked may change, but the dilemmas that librarians have faced show remarkable parallels over time. By exploring the way librarians have justified their policies in terms of the public interest, this study sheds light on the complex background of policy alternatives that seem to spring from contemporary situations.

The study is divided into three major sections. After a prologue describes the origins of the first major public library in 1853 and the concept of freedom it embodied, Part I, "Missionaries of the Book: 1876–1900," explores the early years of library development and the first professional culture, which embodied the values of populism, neutrality, and censorship. It traces the first literary disputes and censorship controversies and describes the impact of the 1890s depression on librarians' sense of mission and direction. Part II, "Structures of Ambivalence: 1900–1922," covers the period in which censorship as a professional value was reflected in closed-shelf policies that attempted to resolve competing demands for restriction and for controversial books. The erosion of the value of censorship and the special problems that arose in World War I are delineated here. Part III, "From Secular to Sacred: 1923–1939," discusses the emergence of an ideology of freedom as a value central to the goals of libraries.

In line with the sociological and structural approach of this study, the shift in ideology is traced against a backdrop of major social and literary change: the moral crusades of the late nineteenth century; the challenge of literary naturalism; the peculiar mix of political liberalism and moral conservatism of the Progressive years; the book-burning crusades of World War I; the Boston bannings and nativist eruptions of the 1920s; the revolutionary impact on all professions of the Depression, Soviet communism, and German Nazism. Underlying these changes were processes of secularization and of nationalization—the emergence of a national economy and communications network.[1]

Within this context, the ideals of censorship and freedom are treated as part of an occupational ideology that was affected by these broader social forces. Ideology is defined in Talcott Parsons' terms as a system of truth-claims (empirical statements) and values in terms of which a group explains and justifies its existence. This definition allows for the possibility that ideologies may be, but are not necessarily, masks for economic self-interest. They may also be genuine statements of commitment.[2]

The distinction between genuine ideals and "ideological" rationalizations is especially important in analyzing professional ideologies. Sociologists do not agree on whether "profession" is a theoretically distinct type of occupation. Presumably, its unique characteristics are: *specialized expertise* based on university training in a body of theoretical knowledge; an *ethical* or public interest orientation that is distinguished from the profit motive of business and from the narrow group interest of unions; and, perhaps most important, *independence* of lay, bureaucratic, or political control—since no one lacking the specialized training is competent to evaluate the profession. In return for their autonomy and the privilege of regulating themselves, professions are expected not to abuse that privilege. They promise to provide impartial service, remaining free of political involvement or partisan identification.

In daily life, of course, professions fall far short of these standards. Even more important, as sociologists recognize, value conflict and ambivalence are built into professional cultures and into the relationship between the expert and the client. A critical school of sociologists, however, goes further, arguing that "profession" is an ideological label that helps elite occupations justify their material interests—monopoly on prestige, jobs, and unfair fees and salaries.[3]

The issue of professionalism bears on the subject of this study in several ways. First, librarians have invoked the values both of censorship and of freedom in the name of precisely the three central features of professions: professional *expertise*, professional *ethics*, and professional *autonomy*. They have often done so, moreover, in claiming professional status.

Second, sociologists have used the librarians' code of freedom to illustrate different aspects of professionalism. Robert K. Merton uses the librarians' code of freedom to show how professional norms can reduce community conflict:

Professional codes . . . are designed to state in advance what the socially supported behavior of the status-occupant should be. . . . Social support is provided by consensus among status peers as this consensus is recorded in the code or is expressed in the judgments of status peers. . . . Thus, thousands of librarians sparsely distributed among the towns and villages of the nation and not infrequently subject to censorial pressures received strong support from the code on censorship developed by the American Library Association in conjunction with the American Book Publishers Council.[4]

In this study, censorship and freedom were historically specific values that both functioned in such a manner.

William J. Goode has taken the librarians' 1939 code of ethics to illustrate how librarianship falls short of professional status. "A code reflects the peculiar genius of the profession that writes it. How lacking is this code in any sense of drama, of moral urgency! How absent is a sturdy awareness that the profession has a task, a destiny, a set of issues about which it is concerned!" Its major drawback, for Goode, is its concern for giving people what they want rather than trying to educate. He criticizes especially its handling of censorship:

The code urges fairness and wisdom in book acquisitions, a pale and watery exhortation, but does not assert the simple ethical duty to follow professional principles in this central matter and to ignore lay opinion as irrelevant and incompetent. Few clearcut cases of censorship arise; the librarian avoids the risk. In a high but unknown percentage of instances, the librarian does not buy the books which might arouse local critics. There is a wide discrepancy between values and practices, and here again librarianship fails to attain the moral stature of a profession, in which the practitioner must risk unpopularity by serving the larger interests of society.[5]

Ironically, as this study will show, the posture of censorship showed precisely the attributes of professional superiority that seem to be absent in the 1939 code of ethics. That code, in fact, signified a *retreat* from the tradition of censorship, just as the 1939 Library's Bill of Rights expressed a commitment to freedom.

These references show the close bearing of the values of censorship and freedom on issues of professionalism, ideology, and autonomy. Just as the value of academic freedom has been used to study professionalization in the social sciences,[6] the values of censorship and freedom are used here to shed light on librarians' claims to professional status autonomy, and their changing concepts of ethical service.

The values of censorship and freedom have a particularly strong resemblance to the values of freedom of the press and academic freedom. Journalists, scientists, teachers, university faculty all assert the freedom to choose the content of their work in the face of pressure from outside—to publish what they see fit, to engage in the disinterested pursuit of science, to choose books. These professions are faced with similar conflicts between values, between their own values and interests and those of laymen, and between their professional identities and other important commitments, such as political affiliations.[7] For them, autonomy from outside interference becomes crucial to resolving their dilemmas in terms of their professional culture or ideology.

The dispute over professional ideology is approached in this study in terms of analogous problems in the sociology of science. These problems include the functions and internal conflicts of a professional culture—for example, the code of science—and the conditions under which professional values may change; the question of problem selection in science and its determinants, inside and outside the scientific community; and the issue of scientific autonomy as professional ideology. As a result, the following conceptual scheme has guided the analysis of the data:

First, freedom and censorship are treated as components of a professional culture or code—a complex of norms and values—that determines their meaning. All libraries are constrained by their values and by their budgets to exclude some books. In its broadest sense, censorship implies the definition of boundary lines in book selection. These boundary problems, in turn, are multidimensional, involving three major sources of potential value and role conflict:

The first is the *populist-elitist* dilemma. It involves the conflict between elite and popular culture, between the tastes of professionals and sponsors and the more popular taste for bestsellers of little literary value or lasting interest. Herbert Gans's distinction between supplier-oriented and user-oriented concepts of library service points up analogous conflicts.[8]

The second is the *neutrality-advocacy* dilemma. It involves the librarian's posture with regard to partisan conflict in the community and the efforts of dominant groups to impose their views on the library. The librarian, as a civil servant responsible to the entire community, is required to be neutral in such disputes. Yet the librarian's own social responsiblities can cast the value of neutrality into question.

The third is the *freedom-censorship* dilemma. It involves the attitude toward deviant ideas outside the framework of conventional debate, ideas that seem to threaten the moral or the social order.

Another issue in the sociology of science involves the questions: Does science pursue its own intellectual agenda or is it affected by external forces? Can science be influenced by social values without sacrificing its norms of disinterestedness and objectivity? How does it reconcile these potentially competing influences? One answer is proposed in Max Weber's notion of *Wertbeziehung*. The problems chosen for scientific study are influenced by social and economic factors as well as by the stage of development of a discipline or what its schools deem important; however, scientific evidence itself is not necessarily distorted by these factors. Critics of this distinction contend that science and social science avoid controversial problems, answering trivial questions with meticulous precision.

The choice of scientific problems and orientations is also affected by elites who stake their careers on particular paradigms and modes of analysis. These paradigms become hard to uproot until they clearly lose their explanatory power, engendering intellectual crises. Thomas Kuhn adopted this perspective in his landmark *Structure of Scientific Revolutions* and opened up a new area for scholarly research. Applying it to the history of sociological theory, Schmuel Eisenstadt in *The Form of Sociology—Paradigms and Crises* explores competing paradigms, research programs, and role orientations among sociologists.[9]

In this study, three processes are identified as analogous to problem selection in science. The first is *client selection*: that is, out of the many types of users and potential users of the library, whom does the library emphasize as important? The second is *status selection*: out of the many identities in terms of which users may be defined—age, class, political affiliation—which are seen as relevant to library service? The third is *issue selection*: what problems of book choice and service capture professional attention? The choice of certain issues and user definitions, and the neglect of others, explains how librarians can retain their autonomy and integrity of purpose yet avoid role definitions that are too controversial.

Thus, scientific and professional roles are not given but are debated by outsiders and insiders, and they change in response to crises that challenge old roles and assumptions. The role orientations that emerged among librarians in the 1890s and 1930s, for example, are analogous to paradigm shifts, or changes in research programs, in science—especially social science, in which problem-selection is highly vulnerable to external influence.[10]

Third, the claim to professional freedom or autonomy is treated in terms of still another question often overlooked: Autonomy from whom? From that question, two forms of professional autonomy are derived: *institutional autonomy* and *status autonomy*. Institutional autonomy unites professionals and administrators or sponsors against outside control—for example, by laymen or politicians. Status autonomy, by contrast, asserts the independence of professional decisions from administrative or bureaucratic control, from control from above. It may align the professional with outsiders—with clients or laymen—against superiors. Implicit in this distinction is a triangular relationship between professional, sponsor, and client, rather than a simple relationship of opposition.

These concepts provide the theoretical framework for a detailed qualitative content analysis. The major sources are the national library journals and American Library Association conference proceedings from 1876 to 1939. Scanned page by page, these documents provide a continuing record of statements of high intentionality that reflect changing values. They are supplemented by relevant articles in state library publications, reviews, legal cases, autobiographies, and textbooks of the time. The major professional booklists published between 1893 and 1940 are also analyzed for their inclusion or omission of significant works. For background, inference, and comparison, a variety of secondary sources have been used, including biographies, general histories and special histories of literature, publishing, censorship, and academic freedom.

The approach adopts some aspects of quantitative content analysis. The sampling and analysis of documents is systematic, and an effort is made to examine ranges of opinion rather than to rely on illustrative data. The emphasis, however, is on the qualitative analysis of the documents in terms of the conceptual scheme outlined above.

Substantively, this study fills a gap in the history of libraries and of censorship. Its conceptual scheme, however, should have broader applicability in the sociology of professions. The major trend in sociological analysis has been to examine professions in terms of relative prestige and rewards and in terms of a unilinear professional "development." In terms of this perspective, a study of professionalism in libraries would have dictated analogies with other "semiprofessions"—social work, nursing, or teaching. Instead, I chose professions that resemble librarianship in function, and I set up a different set of questions.

What distinguishes my model is that features generally accepted as givens for a profession, or as goals for an aspiring profession—specialized knowledge, a public service orientation, autonomy, a professional culture or ideology—are studied here as variables. They embody alternatives that involve conflict and that require decisions at each stage of professional change. Thus, professional change or development is multidimensional, with each component varying independently of the others. Concepts of the public interest change over time, or are defined differently and disputed by various groups; there is thus no one definition of ethicality. Notions of expertise also assume certain role-definitions. And ideology performs a broad range of functions, from the selfish to the sacrificial. The linear perspective often adopted in studies of professions does not deal adequately with these changing dimensions of professionalism or with the range of alternatives that require decisions and affect the direction a profession takes.

The approach adopted here avoids the normative definitions and issues and their refutations that have preoccupied students of professions at the same time that it illuminates their implications. By providing a different set of problems for analysis, this alternative model may bring to the sociology of professions a set of concepts, perspectives, and insights relevant to the structure of professions and their changes over time, and to the comparative analysis of professions and other occupations with similar structures and functions.

Forbidden Books in American Public Libraries, 1876–1939

1.

PROLOGUE: KNOWLEDGE AS A PUBLIC UTILITY: THE MOVEMENT FOR FREE LIBRARIES

"It will be second only to the introduction of water," wrote Josiah Quincy, mayor of Boston, in his journal on January 17, 1848, about his hopes for a projected public library.[1] Implicit in his statement was the notion of the library as a public good and a sense of startling innovation. Libraries were hardly new to the continent. Since the earliest colonial days, a variety of libraries had sprung up to meet the need for sharing scarce and costly books and for preserving a culture that had been transplanted to a wilderness. Two massive research libraries, the Astor and the Smithsonian, were being planned for free public use, and tax-supported libraries had been established on a small scale. Yet when the Boston Public Library opened its doors in 1854, it heralded a new concept, the popular library.

As agencies for the communal ownership of books, libraries are the products of social activities, shaped by the goals of their founders and users and by existing agencies for book distribution. The first public libraries were marked by their precursors' traditions and conflicts, as well as by their own special role in the diffusion of knowledge. Their democratic function and the freedom that they represented differed sharply from what they would come to mean in a later day.

BOOKS IN THE NEW ENGLAND

The first libraries were partisan, even propagandistic in nature, attesting to the dominance of religious ideology in their culture. The little collection accompanying the Massachusetts Bay Company settlers in Salem in 1629 served to carry out the plantation's official goal: the conversion of the Indians. John Harvard's 1638 bequest of his library, along with half his estate, was for a religious institution in a community "dreading to leave an illiterate ministry to the churches, when our present ministers shall lie in the dust." In several colonies, the Anglican tradition was spread through parish or missionary libraries set up by Reverend Thomas Bray and his Society for Propagating the Gospel in Foreign Parts. By the eighteenth century, colleges and college libraries, largely denominational, existed in a majority of the colonies.[2]

In the eighteenth century, the social or subscription library became popular. The first one was Benjamin Franklin's Library Company, patterned after the London taverns, coffeehouses, and social clubs, which he formed in 1731 for his junto, a group of artisans who met to discuss philosophy, science, and politics. Catering to the secular and scientific interests of the junto, the books and journals, largely imported from Britain, included the *Philosophical Transactions of the Royal Society* and books on science, as well as the works of the liberal Abbé de Vertot and works on uprisings, revolutions, and the "subversion of established monarchies." Among the most important liberal writings were the *Spectator*, the *Tatler*, and *"Cato's" Letters*, the radical work by John Trenchard and William Gordon that provided much of the ideological underpinning of the American Revolution.[3]

Franklin, claiming priority for "the mother of all the North American subscription libraries," praised social libraries for having "improved the general conversation of the Americans, made the common tradesmen and farmers as intelligent as most gentlemen from other countries, and perhaps contributed in some degree to the stand so generally made throughout the colonies in defense of their privileges." Whatever the truth of his claim, the voluntary library became one symbol of the American craving for books and its emphasis on literacy. The "coonskin library" in Ames, Ohio, so called because subscriptions could be paid for in raccoon skins, was one part of that myth.[4]

From 1762 on, circulating or rental libraries also became popular, especially as the novel, an eighteenth-century literary innovation, came into vogue. The novel was a controversial genre, both to Puritan moralists and to rationalists adhering to faculty psychology, whose theories warned of overstimulating the imagination. In Sheridan's *The Rivals*, Sir Anthony Absolute called the circulating library "an evergreen tree of diabolical knowledge." In England, the Society for the Suppression of Vice advocated its regulation. Even the liberal Thomas Jefferson deplored the "inordinate passion for novels" as a poison that infected the mind, turning it against factual, "wholesome reading. The result is a bloated imagination, sickly judgment, and disgust toward all the reason of life."[5]

Although some social libraries circulated such popular titles as Sir Walter Scott's works, Fanny Burney's *Evelina*, and James Fenimore Cooper's *The Deerslayer*, others either excluded all fiction, drama, and poetry, or purchased them with a small fraction (e.g., 10 percent) of the book budget, or required a two-thirds membership vote. Many also excluded controversial partisan literature. The Union, Rhode Island, social library prohibited "religious and political dissertations favoring one party or sect more than another." Neutrality achieved through exclusion was common among early libraries.[6]

Women were often excluded from social libraries, a policy that made book selection easier. The Boston Athenaeum allowed only two women, Hannah Adams, a relative of the president, and Lydia Maria Child, to use the library. (Mrs. Child was later excluded, she charged, for her forthright antislavery position.) When in 1849 some trustees advocated accepting women as readers and as employees, the librarian, Charles Folsom, objected that the policy would embarrass male users. Nor was it desirable that a modest young woman be exposed to "the corrupter portions of the polite literature. A considerable portion of a general library should be to her a sealed book."[7]

THE LOOM OF LOCKE

> Bacon & Newton, sheath'd in dismal steel, their terror hang
> Like iron scourges over Albion [England]: Reasonings like vast serpents
> Infold around my limbs. . . .
> I turn my eyes to the Schools & Universities of Europe
> And there behold the Loom of Locke, whose Woofe rages dire,
> Wash'd by the Water-wheels of Newton: black the cloth
> In heavy wreathes fold over every Nation: cruel Works
> of many Wheels I view, wheel without wheel, with cogs tyrannic
> Moving by compulsion each other. . . .
> William Blake, "Jerusalem," Part I, 15 (c. 1804)

Blake's nightmare vision of a union of schools, science, and technology joined in exploitation had its bright counterpart in the hopes of the new society. For Washington, Jefferson, and other Revolutionary thinkers, the "diffusion of knowledge" had meant equal opportunity that would prevent the monopolization of learning by a tyrannical elite. With the spread of mass suffrage and the decline of apprenticeship, which had provided rudimentary literacy in the master's home, the training of citizens and workers became even more critical. Elementary schools were established to provide basic literacy. A highly varied and polemical press enhanced political consciousness and political education. New agencies were needed to replace the family as apprenticeship declined and the factory system developed, to provide technical information to farmers and workers, even for leisure during lonely evenings in the city. Joshua Bates, the banker whose $50,000 donation helped launch the Boston Public Library, remembered his lonely youth in that city: "Having no money to spend and no place to go, not being able to pay for a fire in my own room," or for books, he had spent his evenings in a local bookstore.[8]

Among the agencies that attempted these tasks were mercantile and mechanics' libraries, factory libraries established by employers, and public libraries housed in schools. Mercantile libraries were organized by aspiring clerks and other workers as means of self-education and often provided lectures as well as reading matter. Mechanics' libraries, patterned after the workingmen's institutes of Glasgow, Liverpool, and Birmingham, were sometimes set up by trades unions themselves. Others, however, were sustained by philanthropic factory owners who sought to provide their workers with technical education and keep them from bad company.[9]

Among the best-known efforts were the "boarding house towns" constructed for the young women coming from farms who sought alternatives to domestic labor. In this early, paternalistic phase of factory development, the women lived under the careful guardianship of employer and minister. For whatever scant leisure they enjoyed after a twelve-hour day, they were provided with a variety of cultural facilities: mutual improvement societies, libraries, evening classes, lyceum lecturers, and, in Lowell and Chicopee, literary magazines. The mill girls' literary efforts in the *Lowell Offering* and their many memberships in circulating libraries were admired and publicized by Harriet Martineau and Charles Dickens.[10]

Men could enjoy the ambitious "palace of culture" in Lowell, Massachusetts, housing the Middlesex Mechanics' Institute, a museum, library, and lecture hall. Abbott Lawrence, a director of the Boston Society for the Diffusion of Useful Knowledge, and donor of $50,000 (then an impressive sum) to Harvard College for a scientific school to train mechanics, miners, and engineers, also took an interest in the Lowell library. In 1847 he donated $1,000 for the purchase of "valuable French books on mechanical subjects."[11]

The sponsored institutions were highly restricted. In the evangelical Sabbath School libraries, fiction and drama were forbidden—even the works of Shakespeare and Sir Walter Scott. The more daring mill girls, as a result, joined circulating libraries and borrowed novels by Scott, Bulwer-Lytton, and Dickens, which were "read with delight and secretly lent from one young girl to another." The literary magazines were deferential to their sponsors. Avowing freedom from a "party spirit," the *Lowell Offering* and *The Olive Leaf* opposed labor's demands and published no more than a few unrebellious laments at the noise and tedium of the girls' work.[12]

Yet women struck as early as 1834 in Lowell and in Dover, New Hampshire, joined a female Labor Reform League in 1844, moved for a ten-hour day, and repeatedly petitioned the Massachusetts legislature to study their working conditions. They saw themselves as wage slaves. A poem about the death of a factory girl from overwork expressed that identification in its slap at the easy Abolitionist sentiment of sheltered ladies:

> Their tender hearts were sighing
> As negroes' woes were told;
> While the white slave was dying
> Who gained their fathers' gold.

While corporation agents sponsored talks on useful knowledge, Sarah Bagley, a labor leader, set up her own lectures on such subjects as abolition and the Free Soil movement.[13]

Workers' libraries developed differently in America and Britain. In Britain, working-class literacy was feared, and radical tracts like Tom Paine's *Rights of Man* were officially censored. There the workingmen's institutes, initially launched by the Socialist Thomas Hodgskin, were taken over by the "liberal" middle-class Society for the Diffusion of Useful Knowledge. It advocated education as an alternative to government suppression of unions and the press, and it stressed useful knowledge (science and classical economics). But it excluded radical politics, "works subversive of the Christian religion," and imaginative literature.[14]

The consequence of censorship was defection. For where the society or other movements from "above" controlled institute activities, the workers dropped out. However, where the institutes retained their autonomy, as in Edinburgh, or formed new organizations, as in Leeds, their libraries held far more political and literary controversy: Byron's works, Shelley's *Queen Mab*, George Eliot, Ruskin, and Howitt's anti-Anglican *History of Priestcraft*. Sometimes the censorship of "dangerously controversial" theology and politics helped in the formation of a militant class culture—of Owenite, Chartist, Socialist, and Trades halls, where the works of radicals were discussed.[15]

How is it that the same consequences did not mark the American experience? Mechanics' libraries did not last, Ditzion observes, because mechanics were a marginal class who would eventually be differentiated into middle and working classes. Other factors, however, were at play. Some of the goals of British workers, such as suffrage, which they would win in 1877, and free public education, had already been achieved in America. Moreover, the doctrines of Paine and other radicals, censored in Britain, were part of the dominant American culture. In America, the ideology of mobility pitted achieved status against hereditary privilege. In terms of that ideology, the American worker could not be distinguished from his employer. That ideology, and the phenomenon of mobility, observed by Tocqueville, and illustrated in the lives of some of the mill girls, militated against class consciousness. The mill girls were replaced by immigrants; mechanics' training by schools; factory libraries by public libraries.

SCHOOL-BASED COMMUNITY LIBRARIES

Community libraries based in schools were a last transitional form of library, spreading as the free elementary school movement spread. In 1835 the National Trades' Union urged its affiliates to agitate for the establishment of public libraries in cities, towns, and villages "for the use and benefit of mechanics and workingmen." Educators like Horace Mann and Henry Barnard promoted community libraries as part of their free schools. After the new generation was taught to read, argued Mann, what would they read? Social libraries reached only a fraction of the population and besides were filled with "trash," novels, "bubble" literature. For Barnard, libraries would provide books for all classes and "both sexes" (a significant innovation), while the "more wealthy and intelligent" would resort there to "bear testimony of their presence and participation."[16]

These tax-supported libraries, administered by school districts, provided the logic for the free provision of books at public expense. They rested on a strongly educational rationale. No concession was made to popular taste, and county and state school superintendents strictly limited the options of local trustees. Novels, with their often undemocratic concern with rank and wealth, were discouraged. Libraries were carefully censored. Although they were intended for adults, they could not contain matter unsuitable for children. "Improper books" were excluded, whether they were adventures like *Captain Kidd* or exaggerated histories and biographies that failed to teach American institutions and provide models of behavior. Expurgated editions were required for Shakespeare, Smollett, Fielding, Dryden, Pope.[17]

Finally, works on "all sectarian and controversial subjects" were also prohibited on pain of removal of state funding for the library. Following state laws forbidding books that favored any Christian sect, Horace Mann prohibited religious books that advocated or attacked the views of any sect. The ban extended even to biographical and historical works and novels that by allusion showed religious bias, criticism, or exposé; in one county, *The Vicar of Wakefield* and *Children of the Abbey* were excluded on that score. These strictures applied also to the more general attacks on religion by writers like Godwin, Shelley, Paine, Lessing, and Voltaire.

The reason, paradoxically, was democratic tolerance. As Henry Randall, a New York County superintendent, put it: "The common school and its library are neutral ground, on which those professing different, and antagonistic creeds, can meet together in peace; and this neutrality must be preserved, if we would preserve the utility of these educational institutions." With scrupulous consistency, he specified that "the rule of exclusion should be equally and inflexibly applied to each; otherwise all must be permitted to enter the arena." Horace Mann, too, fighting for the secular school in an age of religious and political partisanship, raised it above conflict by stressing useful knowledge and maintaining a rigorous impartiality in the names of religious toleration and church-state separation.

Similar criteria obtained for political literature. Standard works on political issues were acceptable, as were impartial treatments of the aims of political parties, discussions of "what may be legitimately termed politics—that is, the science of government"—works like the *Federalist* and *Democracy in America*. But political weeklies and other sectarian literature were out of bounds.[18]

Public libraries departed from this early, what Jesse Shera calls "abortive," form, and social libraries are regarded as the main precursors of public libraries. However, school libraries had extremely important consequences for public library development. Proponents of public libraries would promise benefits strikingly similar to those for schools: for youth, innocent leisure; for parents, assurance that their children would acquire culture and knowledge; for merchants, farmers, and workers, the best information to make them successful; for employers, the benefit of intelligent and efficient workers; for the community, a force "favorable to all the moral reforms of the day, by leading to more domestic habits of life" that would reduce the circulation of "low and immoral publications."[19] Thus school libraries provided the first rationale for the free provision of books through tax support.

BOSTON AND THE POPULIST IDEOLOGY

Between 1830 and 1850, other influences produced pressure for a public library. Among them were assorted education and self-education movements, like the lyceum movement; a publishing industry that burgeoned with expanding reading markets, a protective tariff, and technological advances; and the demand for a native scholarship and literature that might rival Europe's. Scholars who studied abroad—Henry Wadsworth Longfellow, George Bancroft, George Ticknor—were impressed by the immense German and French libraries. Bookmen promoted library legislation, and in 1853 Charles Norton, publisher of *Norton's Literary Gazette*, called a conference of librarians.[20]

What kind of library would best serve the people? That question had been hammered out in the Congressional debate over the Smithsonian bequest for an institution that would aid in "the increase and diffusion of knowledge among men." Arguing for a research library that would be open to all, Rufus Choate, the Whig Senator from Massachusetts, had asked, rhetorically, if it would be "exclusive and of the nature of a monopoly," and had answered himself: the people would benefit indirectly from the efforts of the studious men who wrote for them.

Robert Dale Owen, son of the British manufacturer-socialist, had called the library plan "aristocratic, designed for a few local and wealthy bibliophiles." The same issue arose with the private Astor Library, which, said its librarian, Joseph Cogswell, would serve "the lasting welfare and progressive improvement, and not the momentary gratification of the community."[21]

The Boston Public Library departed from this scholarly orientation, largely through the efforts of George Ticknor, a Harvard scholar and founder-trustee of the library. Ticknor developed a populist rationale that he defended against the objections of other trustees, including Edward Everett. Written into the first report of the Boston Public Library trustees, which is now known as the "Ticknor report," it is a classic statement of public library philosophy.

Ticknor's main contention was that a public library could be useful even to elites only if it sparked popular interest as "a great and rich library for men of science, statesmen, and scholars, as well as for the great body of the people," whose struggle for distinction was always to be encouraged. As an agency promoting equal opportunity, the library could not confine itself to those few with extraordinary ambition and ability. Books were to be brought "into the homes of the young; into poor families; into cheap boarding houses; in short, wherever they will be most like to affect life and raise personal character." Thus the library's function was linked to both the "benign form" of the ideology of mobility and the humanitarian function of alleviating the distress of the poor.[22]

The notion of civic education was raised only briefly. In a democracy, Ticknor held, it was essential that information be widely diffused, so that the largest possible number of people would be induced

to read and understand questions going down to the very foundations of social order, which are constantly presenting themselves, and which we, as a people are constantly required to decide, and do decide, either ignorantly or wisely. That this *can* be done—that is, that such libraries can be collected—there is no doubt.

To achieve that end, however, one had first to create the desire for reading by "following the popular taste—unless it should ask for something unhealthy." Gradually, taste would be refined, and "the older and more settled works" would be demanded.[23]

Ticknor did not deal with the issue of doctrinal controversy, but at the 1858 dedication of the library Robert Winthrop, president of the board of commissioners, did. Praising the library as virtually the only public agency that was truly designed for all, he explained:

> Even the old Cradle of Liberty [Faneuil Hall] itself is far less frequently and uniformly devoted to the uses of the whole people, than this new Cradle of Literature and Learning will be. A political canvass, or a patriotic celebration, or an anniversary festival, may fill that hall . . . thirty times, in a year;—but even then, the free discussion which justly belongs to all such occasions involves an element of division and strife, of party, of sect, or of section. But this hall will always be open, and always be occupied, and the free reading which is to find a place in it, involves neither contention nor controversy. Those who entertain the most discordant opinions may here sit, shoulder to shoulder, enjoying their favorite authors as quietly and harmoniously as these authors themselves will repose, side by side, when restored to a common shelf.[24]

Unlike the rules of censorship, neutrality through exclusion was the earmark of the nonsectarian state, standing above faction to promote peace among adversaries. It implied disengagement from party politics, from the working class press, and, even more significantly, from abolitionist literature. That frail effort to preserve tolerance was the symbol of a peace that could not be kept.

PRIVILEGE, POPULISM, AND FREEDOM

The freedom to read as it has come to be perceived had little to do with the aspirations of the founders of the first public libraries, for the knowledge relevant to their goals was linked to quite different preoccupations. In a period that predated widespread secondary and higher education, the diffusion of knowledge meant certified knowledge of value to elites. That tradition stemmed from the colonial revolt against English discrimination, which had kept religious dissenters out of professional schools and hence out of elite occupations. The result was an emphasis on self-education and mobility and an enduring hatred of licensing and professional superiority. *Libraries were established in opposition not to censorship but to privilege.*[25]

Nor were public libraries established out of fear of democracy or social revolution, as some historians have argued. It may be true that George Ticknor was a sour, displaced Federalist. But he was also the son of a self-made man and a friend of Thomas Jefferson, and to his European confrères he defined himself as the representative of a country engaged in a democratic experiment. Like Joseph Cogswell (later librarian of the Astor Library), who haunted European courts in stern black republic dress, Ticknor flaunted that republican identification.

Sympathizing with Chateaubriand, he did not share his vision of the future. If he sympathized with Prince John during the 1848 revolutions, he spoke also, in his letters, of the American invulnerability to antimonarchic revolutions—a view shared by the conservative Edward Everett. His distaste was for the Jacksonian revolution, not the French Revolution, and for a blood bath still to come that would test democratic institutions. That test was the Civil War, not the class struggle. One does not distinguish conservatives from liberals in terms of what *united* them against European aristocracies.[26]

Like education, the public library was established within the framework of consensus that united conservatives and liberals, paternalistic elites and workers, unions and philanthropists.[27] Elitism was consonant with its democratic function—even ideal, for it meant the diffusion of elite knowledge to all. Populism, a concession that could win broader user and hence tax support, was not an *alternative* to elitism but a supplement that would extend more, and more humanitarian, services to the public. An experimental policy, it could not be a major goal.

Because populism itself was an undeveloped and controversial ideology, moral censorship, which Ticknor seems to have accepted, was not a significant issue. Moral censorship was assumed and court cases were extremely rare,[28] an indication that publishers met strict standards of propriety. The question was whether mere popular novels could be accepted at all in the public library, as they were not in the school-based libraries. It was on this issue that Ticknor made his notable advance. Without its resolution, immoral books were not likely to come on the agenda.

Nor was the norm of neutrality through exclusion perceived as censorship in a period of fierce partisan political passions, of what might be called mandated advocacy. A battle had only recently been launched in schools and colleges against religious tests to support competency-based criteria of hiring. In 1842, Joseph Quincy's plea for academic freedom was a plea for religious tolerance and freedom from dogmatism.[29]

Like the school, the public library was an agency in the service of secularization, a self-conscious and controversial process of church-state separation in which advocates of secular control contended with dedicated adherents to older values. The norm of neutrality functioned to justify a secular innovation and to protect the library from partisan control.

In an era of personal journalism, moreover, the religious and secular press were both partisan. Religious periodicals existed for every denomination, while many early newspapers were political and depended for support on a party, faction, or individual. Commercial newspapers were equally opinionated. Only later, with mass circulation media geared to politically diverse readers, would the ideal of objectivity become paramount.[30]

The norm of exclusion symbolized a more positive value than the mere official bureaucratic neutrality of the state. It meant a laying down of arms in religious conflict and in political battle in that tense period from the Missouri Compromise and the publication of *Uncle Tom's Cabin* to the outbreak of the Civil War. It represented the library as a place where differences could be forgotten as people met in terms of what they shared. The intent of exclusion was not opinion control but the affirmation of religious and political freedom and, more, of tolerance. In that era, when extreme statements of extreme views circulated in abundance, the library promised noninterference with cherished social identities.

PART I

Missionaries of the Book: 1876–1900

2.

THE CENTENNIAL CONSENSUS: 1876

In 1876, three events occurred that were pivotal to a developing profession. A major historical and contemporary public library survey was published by the U.S. government. At the Philadelphia Centennial Exposition, the American Library Association was formed. And Frederick B. Lleypoldt, publisher of *Publishers Weekly*, launched the first professional publication for librarians, the *American Library Journal* (hereafter *LJ*; the title was changed to *Library Journal* in 1877). These events gave librarians an organizational base and an opportunity to meet and communicate, develop their knowledge and techniques, and act collectively in their interests. Recognizing the special needs of the new popular library, as distinguished from scholarly libraries, the first *LJ* editors promised a "practical, not antiquarian" orientation.[1]

Although public libraries were still few in number and barely institutionalized (only eight large cities could boast a public library), professional pride was defining the library as "not merely a storehouse . . . but . . . an educational institution which shall create wants where they do not exist" and the librarian as no mere custodian but a teacher. The complex technical structure of the field was being built by William F. Poole, Charles Cutter, and Melvil Dewey. And, although no training schools existed, leaders like William Frederick Poole of Chicago had trained recruits and were demanding professional qualifications.[2] Poole, head of the new Chicago Public Library, urged directors to stress training and talent, not local patronage, in hiring. He warned especially against choosing "locals" who had failed in other fields—"broken down ministers, briefless lawyers, . . . physicians without patients." A mere bookworm without the qualities of energy, industry, and tact was "an incubus and a nuisance."[3]

Like other new professions, librarians were engaged in a struggle to define their function and authority, particularly against Spencerian notions that would have limited the state's functions to policing and protecting private property. Josiah Quincy, a trustee, made the library a symbol of social control of private enterprise. "It would be pleasant," he wrote of *laissez-faire* theorists:

to take an evening walk with one of them—Mr. Herbert Spencer, for instance—through the main street of a New England town. . . . He would be
shown the ancient barroom (happily closed) which an unfettered private enterprise once promised as the sole place of evening resort, inviting all male pas-
sers-by. . . .

Our distinguished thinker would learn that this tippling house had been closed
by fiat. . . . This same government [had] audaciously exceeded its proper
functions by opening a spacious library, heated and lighted at the general cost.
Instead of the barkeeper and his satellites, we find modest and pleasing young
women dispensing books over the counter. Here are workingmen, with their
wives and daughters, reading in comfortable seats.

Poole, more cautious, confined himself to defending the public sponsorship of essential utilities, including libraries.[4]

The difference between librarian and trustee was even clearer in their
attitudes toward philanthropy. Where Quincy expressed aloof disdain
for the *nouveau riche* and saw philanthropy as a duty, not a gift, librarians' attitudes ranged from the pragmatic to the obsequious. Poole advised committees to enlist "cultivated and influential citizens" as trustees and to seek "a liberal private subscription and partial endowment."
Samuel Green (Worcester, Mass.) saw factory managers as assistant librarians of factory branch libraries. William I. Fletcher (Watkinson Library, Hartford) was even more deferential. The great men who had
developed the country's "great manufacturing interests" and had received "large wealth as their merited return," had often, to their honor,
spent it liberally for the benefit of the people. What better use of such
wealth

than to employ it in diffusing intelligence among those who have contributed
to its accumulation by honest toil? Such things as these are the most serious
obstacles in the way of those who would array labor against capital as against
a natural enemy.[5]

In these ideal images, the library existed "largely if not mainly for
. . . the uncultivated," serving as " 'the people's college' " for those
who could not attend school.[6] Yet library users did not always share
the tastes of librarians and library sponsors. How could their desires be
meshed with the library's special mission? The answer varied with the
user in question.

Workers were discussed with an eye to their employers' needs. "The
dreariness and dangers of boarding house life," wrote Fletcher, "the
generally unemployed evenings of most of the people, offer conditions
eminently suited to give the public library success." For these artisans
and workers, he suggested useful books that would save employers large

sums. The dilemmas of cultural taste and social distance inherent in a library for workers could be solved with techniques and smiles, with informal architecture and professional friendliness that showed the popular department to be the "object of chief solicitude."[7]

A more serious problem lay in the "shifting population" of factory towns.

> To show how unstable is this population, the fact may be cited that one of our large corporations, employing 4000 hands, reports that it employs and discharges every year a number equal to or even greater than the whole number employed. Such a state of things as this demands of the public library two things: First, the best possible system of keeping account of the books loaned; and second, constant vigilance and promptness in carrying out of the system.

Indifferent to the condition of drifting migrant labor, he recommended deposit requirements to offset losses; mailing notices of overdue books; and messengers who, "put on track of a book," could retrieve it in a few days even if it was borrowed by "persons who have moved out of town."[8]

In discussing youth, Fletcher was more critical. Children under twelve or fourteen could not at the time enroll in the library. Yet by that age, "or even earlier, they are set to work to earn a living" and would have few opportunities for culture. Unless children were admitted sooner, they could hardly be expected to "keep pace intellectually with more favored youth," for their tastes were already fixed on worthless "juvenile literature." To accommodate these youngsters, the library stocked such books in small supply, but it did so at the expense of its educational role.[9]

Adult users, however, were actively defended in terms of a populist ideology invoked against lay trustees. Although trustees urged librarians to distinguish expressed demand from true public need, and the library's functions from those of book clubs, newsstands, and circulating libraries, librarians declined to assert their professional superiority. The popular library had to represent the "real wants of all classes, the mechanic, . . . the sewing-girl, the youth," not the imposed tastes of library directors (i.e. trustees). It was "vain" to buy books that people ought to read then "coax them to read them." The "multitudes," maintained Justin Winsor, the prominent librarian of the Boston Public Library, might lack literary culture, but they were "none the worse citizens" and were indeed "bright thinkers." There was no such thing as a model collection as long as communities differed and individuality survived. Critics who called what was unpalatable to them "trash," forgot that "this much-abused word represents a quality which is not positive, but relative." Poole even argued that taxpayers supported scholars with more than their fair share of public funds:

Fully four fifths of the money appropriated for books is spent in works adapted to the wants of the scholar. It is hardly becoming for scholars, who enjoy the lion's share, to object to the small proportional expenditure for books adapted to the wants of the masses who bear the burden of taxation.[10]

Opposed in principle, both sides compromised in practice. Librarians promised to elevate their readers' tastes by fostering the reading habit, while Quincy lauded Winsor's experiment in popular reading. Nor was the unanimity of sponsors complete. In 1879 Mrs. Kate Gannett Wells, the first female member of the Boston Public Library's examining committee and a prominent minister's daughter, argued that the librarian was a "steward," not an official compelling "proper nutriment." The latter notion was "paternalistic" and "socialistic." It was optional with the public "to select the good or indifferent," eliminating only the "wholly bad."[11]

THE LINE OF EXCLUSION

There is a vast range of ephemeral literature, exciting and fascinating, apologetic of vice, confusing distinctions between plain right and wrong; fostering discontent with the peaceful, homely duties which constitute a large portion of average men's and women's lives; responsible for an immense amount of the mental disease and moral irregularities which are so troublesome an element in modern society—and this is the kind of reading to which multitudes naturally take, which it is not the business of a town library to supply, although for a time it may be expedient to yield to its claims while awaiting the development of a more elevated taste.

—1875 Report, Board of Examiners, Boston Public Library

The populist defense of mass culture embraced bestselling sentimental or "sensational" novels, dime novels (which were often merely cheap pirated reprints of popular foreign works), and juvenile literature that included the innocuous if improbable adventures by Horatio Alger and Oliver Optic. These works were a far cry from the violence-ridden *Police Gazette* and sensational novels of adventure and romance. Alger and Optic wrote largely for slum boys and imbued their works with impeccable moral purpose, in contrast to the British author William Harrison Ainsworth, who was scorned for his glamorization of the outlaw in *Rookwood* (1834), a novel about the robber Dick Turpin, and in *Jack Sheppard* (1839). The bestselling Mrs. E.D.E.N. Southworth, who mixed purity of tone and democratic values with stories of passion, murder, insanity, and vengeance, was less controversial than the British Ouida, author of *Under Two Flags*, who in the process of describing a philanderer's reform wove portraits of bohemians and the demimonde.[12]

Librarians were accommodating toward popular culture. The Boston

Public Library circulated Oliver Optic. Horatio Alger was seen as an alternative to the *Police Gazette*. Silly novels said Samuel Green (Worcester, Mass.), could keep girls out of mischief. Mrs. Southworth and Mrs. Hentz had "a work to do. They mean well and are religious." Ouida was not immoral, yet "she leaves a taint on the pure mind."[13]

Even the most liberal librarians, however, acknowledged a "line of exclusion . . . beyond which readers must not indulge, and up to which they should be." To Poole, "the librarian who should allow an immoral novel in his library for circulation would be as culpable as the manager of a picture gallery who should hang an indecent picture on his walls."[14] Unlike trivial literature, "vicious" literature required neither definition nor debate. Librarians shared a universe of discourse and of common meanings.

American society in 1876 was in the throes of a massive structural change. The depression following the failure of Jay Cooke's bank in 1873 had given the country "its first taste of widespread violence caused by economic hardship as tramps and unemployed factory and farm hands drifted into gangs." The Knights of Labor, formed in 1869, heightened class consciousness and dissent. New technological and bureaucratic inventions, and a national domestic market, linked by a network of railroads, were transforming the nature and organization of work, the structure and perception of opportunity. In rural areas, a writer on libraries observed, "life has so few attractions that the young are anxious to seek the overcrowded cities."[15]

In the cities, in strange and anonymous circumstances, the defenseless of various kinds—women, youth, children, immigrants—were exposed to impersonal, precarious relationships. As the social controls characteristic of small communities—the controls of family, religion, and community—broke down, alarming phenomena erupted—crime and poverty, taverns and pool halls, gambling, prostitution, and cheap literature.

These problems became the subjects of a literature of exposure and of various reform movements. Charles Loring Brace described the slums in *Dangerous Classes of New York*. Mark Twain and Charles Dudley Warner parodied the speculative fever and corruption, masked by a Sunday school rhetoric of success, in *The Gilded Age*. Reform movements coalesced around issues ranging from prison reform, poor relief, and children's aid to temperance, antiprostitution, and the censorship of "licentious literature." Curbs on alcohol, prostitution, and publishing sought to constrain an unbridled commercialism that undermined the family and exploited women.

As one effort to exercise social control over an irresponsible private sector, the Society for the Suppression of Vice was praised for its "social awareness in a hurly burly generation often marked by a heedless disregard for human values," writes Paul Boyer. In 1873, Anthony Comstock, the SSV's leader, lobbied through Congress the Comstock law, which was followed by similar laws in many states. It barred from the mails not only "every obscene, lewd, lascivious, or filthy book" but any literature or object pertaining to abortion or birth control and any matter "tending to incite arson, murder, or assassination." The criterion of obscenity followed the British Cockburn ruling of 1857: "Whether the tendency of the matter is to deprave and corrupt those whose minds are open to such immoral influence and into whose hands a publication of this sort may fall." Comstock also held a special Post Office position to enforce the law, retaining part of the fines he zealously collected.[16]

To avert prosecution and, indeed, maintain their reputations, American publishers carefully censored the language, actions, and heroes and heroines of their publications. Moralists nevertheless lashed out at a commercialist press with much of the old abolitionist zeal. Frederick Beecher Perkins, a lesser light of the family that boasted Harriet Beecher Stowe, and assistant librarian of the Boston Public Library, assailed the Dick Turpins and Jack Sheppards as well as older literary classics:

All such baneful literature should be as inexorably excluded from the public library as arsenic and laudanum and rum should be refused to children. This criterion . . . is demanded by all considerations of Christian civilization. It should exclude such books as Rabelais, the *Decameron*, the *Heptameron* [by Queen Margaret of Navarre], the *Contes drolatiques* of Balzac, . . . all of which are sold in English translations for money by otherwise respectable American publishers. Few, indeed, are those who will object to this exclusion of ribald and immoral books from public circulating libraries.[17]

By the stricter standards of a later age, classics by Fielding, Smollett, Sterne, Richardson (for *Clarissa Harlowe*), and Gautier were also suspect.

Lewis Coser associates moral censorship with elite efforts to "manage" the lower classes once the Industrial Revolution had freed them from religious and traditional restraints. Although mass literacy was required in industrial society, it also exposed workers to novel ideas, especially with the spread of cheap editions and magazines. Unsupervised sexual relations, endangering the family's role in channeling and domesticating sex drives, threatened to hinder the discipline of the work force. Whether obscene literature actually produced such effects, Coser argues, is irrelevant. "The fact is that the powers that be in the Victorian age believed that it did."[18]

Although Coser's thesis is reflected in much thinking of the period, his association of moral censorship with the Industrial Revolution is questionable. Coser argues that censorship did not come to the fore during the Puritan Age. But it did, with the closing of the theaters. He also associates moral censorship with the spread of literacy. This is a common assertion, but *political* censorship was also associated with the spread of literacy (see Chapter 1). And his assertion that "suppression of obscenity and of subversion often go hand in hand" may be true, but there are important counterexamples. Antisedition and antiobscenity laws were passed at different times in both Great Britain and the United States. In America, the Alien and Sedition laws were passed in 1798, the Comstock law in 1873. Great Britain exercised severe political repression in the eighteenth and early nineteenth centuries, but did not pass an obscenity law until 1857. The differences, therefore, may be more significant than the similarities.

Finally, the hypothesis of elite repression does not explain the range of reform groups, supported by a body of academic theorists and professionals, including William Graham Sumner and Elizabeth Blackwell, as well as most publishers themselves, who endorsed censorship, while little collective opposition was mounted against the law.[19] Even if one holds that intellectuals served the elite, the question remains which elite—the old or the new rich—and why attacks were made in the name of anticommercialism by the old rich, a displaced class, if censorship was to manage the work force for the benefit of the *new* rich.

What seems plausible is merely that an orientation to reform through individual rehabilitation, rather than social change, was congenial to the affluent. However, that orientation was a survival of religious attitudes that were waning in a secular age. It was a reflection of, rather than a substitute for, tradition, and was widely diffused through the middle class, not a product of elite manipulation.

Although passing references show that librarians bought books on such subjects as Darwinism and women's rights, discussions of eclecticism were remarkably trivial, merely urging the balance of belletristic and scientific matter and the accommodation of all tastes, from "grave to gay."[20] Despite the rhetoric of democracy and education, the individual as citizen was not a concern. The user was defined in terms of his occupation, age, cultural level, or domesticity, but not as a citizen, member of a class, or part of a dominant or minority group. Given these emphases, political material could be excluded as irrelevant to the library's concerns without raising the issue of censorship.

The few exceptions to these emphases are thus doubly significant. Poole, in defending public support of libraries, referred to early British fears that libraries might be "converted into normal schools of agitation." However,

free libraries have not degenerated into political clubs and schools of agitation. No trouble has arisen in the selection of books, and no censorship of the press was required. It was at first supposed that all books relating to religion and politics—the subjects on which people quarrel most—must be excluded. The experiment of including these books was tried in the Manchester and Liverpool libraries, where the books were purchased by private subscriptions, and no controversy arising therefrom all apprehension of evil from their cause was allayed.[21]

Even more uniquely, Josiah Quincy defined the library in a way that would become common only much later—as an alternative to the journalist and politician, who were "trammelled" with vested interests yet had easy access to the public. He hoped the library would develop "that instructed common sense" on which the nation's founders had relied, to deliver the people from "the wiles of the rhetorician and stump orator," by opening, for the independent thinker, a means of communication with the people.

It will not be the least service rendered by the free library if men of moral force, who may hold unpopular opinions, are able to touch the pores through which the public is receptive.[22]

A similar concern for preserving unconventional thought was apparent in some philanthropic stipulations, even when they dictated policies of exclusion. Dr. James Rush, who in 1860 had focused on banning fiction, "controversial politics," and "those teachers of disjointed thinking, the daily newspapers," specified six years later:

I do not wish that any work should be excluded from the library on account of its difference from the ordinary and conventional opinions on the subject of science, government, medicine, or morals, provided that it contains neither ribaldry nor indecency. Temperate, sincere, and intelligent inquiry and discussion are only to be dreaded by the advocates of error.[23]

Exclusions of sectarian activities or book choices were balanced with recommendations of disinterested scientific inquiry. Charles Merriam, leaving a gift to West Brookfield, Massachusetts, recommended that the library be used only "rarely" for religious meetings and "never for political meetings" or entertainment. It was to be reserved for "purposes as will be unobjectionable to any, such as lectures, scientific exhibitions, and the like." Judge Charles E. Forbes formulated an even more complex policy in his gift to Northampton, Massachusetts. He required that only laymen govern the library, and that the collection be gathered under "democratic" principles, with "strict impartiality" in the choice of literary, scientific, historical, and theological works. The library would provide the means to learn the "marvellous development of modern thought, . . . to judge the destiny of the race on scientific evidence, rather than on metaphysical evidence alone."[24]

These statements are shot through with ambivalence. They seemed to stress activities and selections that the community could agree upon—useful books, scientific material that would foster the advance of knowledge. Yet the donors also demanded unconventional books that might violate the religious or social values of the community's majority. For these works, the criteria for inclusion were scientific evidence and impartiality, not consensus.

The central paradox of these statements, in fact, lies in this simultaneous emphasis on exclusion and inclusion: the exclusion of partisan, hence controversial, material; the inclusion of unconventional, hence controversial, works. That paradox is most obvious in Judge Forbes's prohibition of the clergy as trustees. Seemingly prejudiced against religion, the move resembles the universities' and public schools' efforts to establish lay control. Forbes kept his own denomination (the Congregationalist) from being represented. The norm of exclusion was part of the process of secularization.

This contradiction points to the source of the donors' fears: that dominant political or religious groups might gain control of the library and in turn control—that is, *censor*—its contents. Being majorities, such groups could do so with impunity. The norm of exclusion defended a weak minority group against majority control.

A tension, however, was emerging between the two ways of maintaining impartiality: through exclusion and through the careful balance of opinion. It is expressed vaguely in Judge Forbes's requirement that materials were to be chosen impartially and on clear cognitive grounds; in Rush's emphasis on temperate and reasoned expression of any opinion, however unorthodox; in Poole's assurance that controversial topics had not produced conflict in British libraries. The fear of partisan control sheds light also on Josiah Quincy's wistful hope that nonconformist minority opinion—probably that of his own declining stratum—might be better represented through pamphlets issued by and stored in the library. Thus the library would protect unpopular ideas in an era dominated by a commercial or politically biased majoritarian press.

The criterion of inclusion, finally, was becoming "scientific" authority, a criterion that was itself controversial at a time when scientific criteria of evidence were just coming into dominance and the social sciences, as sciences, had barely been established. Only in 1869 did Fiske, with his heretical Darwinian views, become acceptable to Harvard. Only in the 1870s did the first professionally trained generation of American economists begin to teach in colleges. In 1879 William Graham Sumner, a former minister appointed to Yale over strenuous religious opposition, could be instructed by Noah Porter to remove Herbert Spencer's *Study of Sociology* as a text—in part, interestingly, because of its "pamphleteering" style.[25] In the battle between science and religion, science had not yet won intellectual autonomy.

The prevailing criteria for book choices were reflected in Frederick B. Perkins's *Best Reading*.[26] Popular books were heavily represented—all the controversial juvenile authors, from Horatio Alger to the British Mayne Reid. Mrs. Southworth and Ouida were included, Ouida with a long list of her works, along with Charles Reade, the author of several scandalous exposés. Even Ainsworth, after all of Perkins's railing, was listed with a reference to his "Novels. 16 vols." So, too, were many older classics and current controversial works: Boccaccio and Rabelais; Fielding and Smollett; Eugène Sue's *Mysteries of Paris*; Georges Sand, including her early, rebellious *Indiana*; Emile Gaboriau, whose mysteries would later be excluded from libraries; George Eliot, dealing earnestly with sensational themes; Charles Kingsley's novels of Christian socialism, *Alton Locke* and *Yeast*; and Rebecca Harding Davis's *John Andross*, about life in a factory town.

Certain important omissions symbolize the extent of social tolerance. Balzac was not represented at all, in French or in English, nor was Flaubert's *Madame Bovary*, published in France in 1856. Flaubert and his publisher had been tried in 1857 for publishing a work that offended public morality and religion; the defendants were acquitted but the work censured. Perkins's guide had a section for foreign books, yet *Madame Bovary* was not included even in the original. Among American works, Whitman's *Leaves of Grass* was excluded. Balzac's works and Flaubert's *Madame Bovary* were, however, included in the Boston Athenaeum catalog.[27]

Certain controversies were avoided by the scope of the list, which did not include "polemical theology, law books, Sunday school books," or various technical works. Thus the agnostic Robert Ingersoll was automatically excluded, though a variety of views were represented on evolution and Darwinism. There was nothing by Rousseau, nothing by Voltaire except his *Charles XII*, nothing by Marx or Engels. Since Rousseau, Voltaire, and Marx embodied the most radical attacks on established religion, their exclusion may have been a result of the more general policy of neutrality, avoiding literature polemical in tone. But the application of that criterion indicated the drastic uses to which it could be put. The exclusions also indicate the salience of heresy in a period when religion was still important.

Librarians developed strategies to reconcile the demands of critics, trustees, and users. First was the strategy of limited quantity. The library would include just enough of the "mere confectionary" of literature to entice the "lowest—not depraved—tastes." Readers could then be advised that the "most desired books are all out,' " and be guided to better writers. "If the web of a weird romancer has meshed a curious reader," advised Winsor, "show him the pleasure of disentangling it in the light of history and biography." Or, suggested Fletcher, the fiction and nonfiction catalogs could be combined so that readers, who had to use the catalog to request books, would stumble onto better material.[28]

Another strategy was differential circulation by type of user. All books at that time were delivered by attendants from closed stacks, and certain books were explicitly labeled as not available for circulation or even use, in this manner:

"This book can be CONSULTED only on written permission."	or	"This book can be BORROWED only on written permission."[29]

Although age was generally the criterion for restriction, factors like education were relevant. As Green pointed out:

Such stories as Gautier's *Mlle. de Maupin* I would give out only with discrimination in the *original*. I would place certain restrictions on the use of the novels of Smollett and Fielding, because while in many respects works of the first order, it is best that the young should read only such books as preserve a certain reticence in regard to subjects freely talked and written about in the last century.

English *translations* of French works, however, were excluded because "students of French literature and most other persons who ought to be allowed to read them find them accessible in the original."[30]

A last device was to stock branch libraries, especially in working-class areas, with popular fiction while the main library stocked literature. Boston, following the Manchester pattern, had already adopted a branch system.[31]

These strategies show the same paradox of intent as the philanthropists' stipulations. They emerged at a time when libraries operated under terms of great restrictiveness: age limits, deposits on borrowed books, restricted circulation, and even reference privileges. They were efforts to maintain as free a flow of literature and opinion as current administrative policies and mores permitted. They were an alternative to buying only materials that provoked no objections.

LIBRARIANS: BACKGROUNDS AND ROLE

The early library leaders came from a variety of backgrounds and careers. An analysis of a core sample of early leaders, thirteen signers of the prospectus for the *Library Journal* and the 1876 conference, shows that all were alike in white Anglo-Saxon Protestant origin, often dating back to the Colonial immigrations, and ten had attended college. But otherwise they varied greatly in terms of background and recruitment.

Only four came from distinctly affluent families: Frederick Beecher Perkins, a lawyer's son and kin to the distinguished Beechers; Justin Winsor, a merchant's son; John Fiske; and James Whitney. Three had genteel but modest backgrounds: Ainsworth Spofford, Samuel S. Green, and Charles Cutter. Six stemmed from the rural, artisan, and petit bourgeois classes that were dying out in a transitional society: Reuben Guild, William Frederick Poole, Melvil Dewey, John Shaw Billings, William Fletcher, and Charles Evans. Six went directly into library work from college.[32]

The background and career patterns of this group do not suggest the status anxiety of displaced elites, as some historians have argued in line with Richard Hofstadter's much criticized view of late nineteenth-century reformers and liberals. For most, librarianship was a channel of upward mobility or represented a lateral move, as new professions and opportunities were being created in a new social order.[33] Unlike the self-employed individuals of the old middle class, they were salaried workers in new bureaucracies. The values they expressed did not reflect their own backgrounds so much as their structural locations, their professional interests, and the value conflicts embodied in their roles.

Thus, William Fletcher's peculiar indifference to the plight of the worker was not moderated by his own humble background. The son of a printer, he had never attended college or graduated from high school but was apprenticed at the Boston Athenaeum. His position as an assistant in an endowed library, however, can explain his paternalism to workers and his deference to sponsors.

Justin Winsor's elite background did not make him a snob. On the contrary. A sturdy populism united librarians of such different backgrounds as Winsor, who was a trustee of the Boston Public Library before he became its librarian, and William Frederick Poole, who had struggled to work his way through college.

The emerging professional culture of librarians endorsed populism, accepted moral censorship, and stressed the occupational and cultural needs of library users. Political or religious affiliations were either ignored as irrelevant to the grand designs of cultural elevation, occupational improvement, and advance in scientific knowledge; or they were seen as potential threats to freedom of selection in libraries. So long as these definitions operated, librarians did not have to commit themselves to policies of broad eclecticism and the endorsement of controversial material.

These strategies had not yet been erected into an ideology involving such abstract notions as censorship or the freedom to read. In the next decade, however, the term "censorship" would move into the library literature as an ideological tool in a struggle for control over library policy.

3.

DEBATE AND DIVISION: THE 1880s

I make this appeal to clergymen, teachers, mothers; to all clean-minded people; to the healthy public opinion of San Francisco. . . .

A person in this city is making an obstinate effort to force permission for himself to read a dirty book which was in the library, and which I have removed from circulation and refused to him. Similar applications for other books have been made before, and have always been refused.

—Frederick B. Perkins, 22 November 1885

Over the 1880s, the librarian's role as censor was clarified, most notably in several community conflicts. Few librarians had the urge to censor; but few librarians or trustees could renounce this charge.

Positions of elitism and neutrality were also developed in this decade. Elitism accorded with the library's "missionary purpose," to bring to "the greatest number of people the profitable influences" in books. Elitists, though urging the "selective criticism, or censorship" of "the public opinion of Tom, Dick, and Harry, and the schoolgirls," distinguished it from moral censorship and the officious censorship of thought. Populists, meanwhile, acknowledged that no community would "demand or tolerate immoral fiction."[1]

The value that defined the librarian's position in the community was neutrality, as librarians tried to protect themselves from arbitrary appointments or dismissals. Librarians could be replaced in local political turnovers or dismissed at the whim of the board. Local appointments were common, and librarians came to their positions from journalism, teaching, divinity, sometimes law. Four local appointees in this decade who would become professional leaders—Henry Utley, Herbert Crunden, William Brett, and Frank Carr—replaced librarians who had been fired; three appointments were criticized as arbitrary by *LJ* or the American Library Association.

Perhaps the most important political episode was Justin Winsor's departure from the Boston Public Library to become librarian at Harvard, a position he had initially turned down, in the wake of a city council salary dispute. An *LJ* editorial indignantly linked the city councillors with the 1877 railroad strikers as forces of "demagogic ignorance," finding solace that Winsor, free from politics, could better fight "encroachments" on the library.[2]

As librarians sought freedom from politics and respect for their expertise, some expression of this demand appeared every year from 1883, the year of the Pendleton Civil Service Act, to 1889: an ALA resolution endorsing the civil service principle, contempt for "political hangers-on," a plea that librarians be recognized as a learned profession. One solution was professional training, at a new school established at Columbia University in 1886. Another was the norm of neutrality. In 1882 a librarian in Buffalo affirmed: "There are those who expect of a library that it . . . be exclusive, partisan, one-sided; whereas a public library is the one place above all others that should forever be out of reach of all sectional or partisan control." In 1889 Charles Cutter asserted that the "librarian is of no sect in religion, of no party in politics. He helps all alike, as the physician heals all alike."[3]

The norm of neutrality was no longer a commitment to exclusion— "For the book which will mislead the reader," said Cutter, "there is an antidote on the other side." But it was no ringing endorsement of freedom, either. Librarians, seeking tax and philanthropic support (the latter almost obsessively), were not likely to take a critical posture and rarely looked a gift horse in the mouth. In 1880 the *Library Journal* defended the Astor and Lenox libraries against press attacks on their indifference to public needs; a donor, said *LJ*, had no special duty to do what his critics wanted. Dewey praised Cornelius Vanderbilt for his favors to traveling librarians and his factory library for workers. Cutter complained only mildly about benefactors who left monuments to themselves without providing for library service.[4]

The result was a limited view of the library's mission and clientele. Workers were seen in terms of their contribution to a total enterprise, not as members of a class with its own interests. Thus a library could serve all classes without engendering conflict. By inspiring "latent Lawrences and Arkwrights," it fostered social mobility. Minerva Sanders (Pawtucket, R.I.), a pioneer in children's work, recommended biographies and writings of "working men with honor," books like Carnegie's *Triumphant Democracy* (1886), that would serve as models of enterprise for aspiring young workers; she ended her speech with praise for Ames, Pratt, Carnegie, Newberry, and others.[5]

As various studies have documented, the literature of success legitimates the economic system by encouraging identification with the mobile and affluent and deflecting attention from class consciousness and collective action.[6] These proposals were made when the first national Congressional studies of labor took place, the first Commissioner of Labor was appointed, the rival national unions reached the height of their competition, and anti-laissez-faire movements and literature were growing, albeit largely within and for the middle class. While Carnegie and Spencer and Sumner espoused Social Darwinism, the Social Gospel was being debated in *Robert Elsmere* (1888) and the economic system in *Looking Backward* (1888), Henry Demarest Lloyd's exposé of the Standard Oil monopoly (1891), Richard Ely's *Harper's* article on corporate paternalism in Pullman (1885), *Progress and Poverty* (1889), Marx's *Capital* (translated in 1889), and the new *Forum* and *Arena* magazines. Anarchist publications existed in large cities at least until the Haymarket riots in 1886.

Librarians' distaste for politics was not likely to encourage political consciousness. When the Boston Public Library reported with "surprise" and "pleasure" that women were coming to study current issues in government, political economy, the tariff, and socialism, it assured readers that their interest was of a "wholesome sort, entirely disconnected with female suffrage or any political demands on the part of the sex."[7]

The most poignant testimony to the limited and compromised perspective on clients' needs was Mrs. Sanders's curious blend of humanitarianism and Algerism, her exhortation that libraries "open wide the doors" to young men in "cheap boarding houses" needing attractive reading rooms, to children whose parents could not spare their wages, to "homeless waifs" with no "restraining or guiding influence." Were they to be the charge of charitable institutions and humane societies? "Not so; this is essentially our work, . . . to elevate." Libraries need only to lower their age for admission and take children off the streets.[8]

A notable exception was William F. Poole's sharp endorsement of controversy and insistent references to the user as a political actor. Carefully praising only benefactors of popular libraries ("men of broad views" like the late Peter Cooper), he scored New York City for maintaining a scholarly library but no truly public library. "I have heard since I have been here," he commented in 1885,

that it would be impossible to maintain a public library in the city of New York because it has so many socialists, communists, anarchists, and persons of foreign birth who are not interested in libraries. We have these same classes in Chicago . . . and they give us no trouble. The public library has no better friends than the foreigners, for we give them the books they want to read in their own languages. The socialists and communists are all friends of the library, for we give them the books they want.[9]

Nor did the 1886 disturbances modify his views. He insisted:

New York has no disturbing element which does not exist in Chicago, Cincinnati, or Milwaukee, unless it be the reluctance of wealthy men to be taxed for such an object. . . . The most zealous friends of public libraries in large cities are the middle and poorer classes who carry the vote.

Spoken just two months and three days after the Haymarket riots in his own Chicago, these were bold words indeed, devoid of threatening references to social unrest or conciliatory testimonials to the pacifying influence of public libraries. And in 1887 he repeated the point that controversy did not politicize the library but only increased "the standard of intelligence among the voters."[10]

This liberal populism stemmed no doubt from the local tradition set by the Chicago Public Library trustees themselves when the library was established. At that time, the library board, carefully chosen to represent its geographic, political, ethnic, business, and religious interests to allay a "fear of possible domination of any church interest," had intended to follow the traditional policies of libraries: avoiding controversy and excluding subscriptions to religious and political magazines. But by the time the library opened, the board president stated that it "would be open to, and he hoped would in time receive, representative publications of 'every church, creed, philosophy, profession, or school, nationality, or party.' Even error, he said, might always be tolerated 'whenever truth was absolutely free to combat it.' "[11]

Poole's firm expression of these ideas derived in part from this doctrine. His attitude, however, was not adopted as a guiding principle by other professional leaders or the library press, or defined as part of an occupational identity.

LIBRARIANS AT BAY

The profession's first major censorship controversy arose in the wake of Justin Winsor's departure from the Boston Public Library, as two loyal workers who had resigned with him took issue with the library's subsequent administration. Early in 1880, Frederick B. Perkins complained to Boston's Mayor Prince that the library was "fumbled by a set of committees" while the librarian, Judge Mellen Chamberlain, was "only a head clerk," without the official dignity or authority that his person and office deserved. Later that year, James M. Hubbard, a former minister and cataloger, wrote a series of articles in the *Boston Sunday Herald* charging, rather inconsistently, both that the library bought books exclusively for scholars and that it purchased too much fiction. He asked for "full administrative power" for the librarian and for several other administrative changes.[12]

By 1881 Hubbard found a juicier issue. In the *International Review*, he charged the library with buying "vapid and sensational" books that were read not by the poor but by people in comfortable circumstances and the children of well-to-do parents. Even darker accusations were made in an open letter to the city's school superintendent in the *Boston Evening Transcript*. Disclosing that the library bought "many directly immoral books" that were read by youngsters, Hubbard made four proposals to protect youth: a board of censors to screen material; the labeling of harmless books; a special children's card that would permit "children" (one must remember that they had to be fourteen years or older) to withdraw only harmless books; and a separate children's catalog containing only permissible requests.[13]

The school superintendent was glad to step in. The library's books might not be "directly immoral," but they were certainly trashy, as his own teachers could testify. In fact, Hubbard's proposals were not far-reaching enough. The only effective remedy was to "purge the library at once of all objectionable matter" and involve parents and teachers in choosing books.[14]

As the conflict spread, the *Boston Advertiser* and the *Sunday Herald* came to the aid of the library. The *Advertiser* (March 10, 1884) questioned whether any "special rule of censorship" could work, since the same book affected different readers differently. More pungently, the *Sunday Herald* (March 20) argued that the library was

not a goody-goody Sunday school library. . . . . It is not kept up expressly for the benefit of the Puritan New Englander, [but] is also intended to meet the requirements of the Roman Catholic and Irishman, the atheistic German, the radical Frenchman, all of whom are citizens of Boston. . . . Nobody is forced to read what he does not wish to read.

It also endorsed the trustees' censorship. By their criteria, the works of Zola and Paul de Kock did not circulate.[15]

Unappeased, Hubbard went to the city council with a list of objectionable books and adverse reviews and demanded that the fiction and juvenile departments both be shut down. The library, he charged, was failing in its promise to help in the work of the Society for the Suppression of Vice, for many novels supposedly confined to the "inferno" collection (which held books of dubious morality) were circulating in duplicate.[16]

The trustees now developed an eloquent defense of freedom. Denying that they were "parents, or guardians," to the community, and invoking Milton's protest—humanity was not placed in a world devoid of temptation—they held that a standard of censorship excluding *Jane Eyre*, *Adam Bede*, and *The Scarlet Letter* could not "satisfy the just demands of the community." Fielding, Smollett, Swift, and Richardson were necessary to a public library so long as their use was limited to the mature. No work could depict life fairly that presented only fair weather and blue skies, without sickness or suffering, vice or crime. However, where the immoral work made vice appear attractive, fiction that painted "the fatal consequences of error and wickedness, with the concomitant suffering and distress," though painful to read, left "no moral stain on the mind of either youth or age."[17]

The examining committee endorsed the trustees' policies. No foreign fiction was received unless the trustees ordered it, and domestic fiction was sent only upon examination. It also affirmed a policy of freedom:

The literature of every age and land and language embraces works classed as products of genius, in which the literary, historical, biographical, moral, or imaginative elements, that are of the highest interest and value to us, are wrought in with coarse, impure, indelicate material. . . . A censorship for discriminating and pronouncing upon these objectionable qualities would follow tests and standards of a most variable, vague, and inconsistent character.

Even the Old Testament and Shakespeare were expurgated for households, while historical societies, with their goals of fidelity and accuracy, printed what was unfit for school and home.[18]

That bold posture did not last. Hubbard soon published a pamphlet appealing to the "parents, clergymen, and teachers" of Boston, quoting a number of damaging reviews. The library retreated. It quietly removed objectionable material from its shelves. The next trustees' report praised the librarian and his assistants for their care in removing all possibly offensive books, though an adamant minority urged stricter screening of works that encouraged "irreverence" toward religion and virtue. By 1885 the library had met Hubbard's demands: separate cards for younger users, separate fiction and juvenile collections, limits on the board president's selection powers, and more authority to the librarian and his staff in "suppressing all works discovered to be vicious."[19]

Several years later, Frederick B. Perkins, transplanted to San Francisco, used a similar ploy, trying to win community support for his censorship policies (see quote at the beginning of this chapter). But he faced a different situation. The trustees were lax, and the community mounted more opposition to censorship. When Perkins had arrived in San Francisco, he explained, the trustees had allowed him to lock away books like the Pinkerton crime novels, *Jack Sheppard*, and Zola's works. But his strictures aroused opposition in the press and from the "Odd Fellows" Library Association (a benevolent society in California), which protested his weeding of the collection as "a species of censorship." Nor did his trustees always support him. Once they had ordered him to return to the shelf a book "full of fornication and filth," only to have it fall into the hands of a boy whose mother very properly sent it to the Society for the Suppression of Vice. Since some "amateur of vulgarity" had already marked the worst passages, it was easy for the Society to have the book removed. Perkins now feared that a journalist might succeed in obtaining Fielding's "brutally gross" *History of Jonathan the Wild* by appealing to the library trustees. Accordingly, he carefully spelled out his criteria of privileged access or, as he called them, "immunities."[20]

Perkins's defensiveness shows how far an ideology of freedom had been developed in San Francisco, for he took pains to answer each objection. The arguments were: that any book should be lent any adult; that even immoral classics should circulate, since the Bible itself could be withheld by similar criteria; that "to the pure all things are pure"; and that, at the least, immunities should be more liberally granted. Perkins answered in terms of his concept of the public interest. The journalist, who had wanted the book merely for his amusement, had no special claim. Immunities were granted only to noncommercial agencies, whose motives were divorced from profit and geared to the public good, or whose profits from using the works would accrue to the public good. Newspapers, however, were private property managed for private gain—journalists were no different from grocers.

Whenever they can prove that they are better, wiser, more disinterested than other people, and that they can devote to public uses the money which they gain by exercising the immunities of public institutions—that is, when they do really become true missionaries of civilization . . . the case will be different.[21]

Librarians as a group were not avid censors. Justin Winsor, in fact, scored his old employee Hubbard: "Mischief, and enough of it, may lurk in books. It will do its work in spite of us; but if we would keep it to its minimum, we do not wisely make this mischief prominent." And he criticized the "narrow visionaries, who magnify an evil the better to eradicate it." *LJ* was circumspect throughout. It tactfully defined the difference between Hubbard and the trustees as "a matter of degree" and called for research and "statistics" to determine whether reading Ouida really led readers to better things, or if the library would lose these clients if it denied them books "suited to a strong taste."[22]

Yet the utility of Hubbard's proposals was apparent. In May 1881, the Indianapolis Public Library announced that it would prepare a catalog of novels and juvenile books for children under sixteen and permit no other books to be issued to youngsters. Eventually, separate children's collections and cards became the standard apparatus of public libraries.[23]

At the end of the decade, Hubbard renewed his attacks on trustees and the spreading inferno collections, calling for state boards of censors to review books that circulated from libraries in order to assess the extent of the evil influence. He was not challenged in the name of freedom. William Fletcher argued that inferno collections contained only immoral works "with a recognized place in literature" and did not lend themselves to prurient interest. William Howard Brett, admitting that inferno collections raised the most difficult problems in book selection, felt that libraries were trying to provide the very moral guidance that Hubbard sought from state censors.[24]

Nor was *LJ* more courageous. Although the idea evoked "heretics burned at the stake," the editor accepted the efficiency of censorship, since it would centralize book selection and eliminate duplication. The "occasional exclusion of a harmless book" would not seriously injure any public library. The attitude was more a publisher's than a librarian's, for a censorship plan that would assure predictability of the market was approved, while Hubbard's proposals for the free distribution of certain books (which would destroy such a market) was severely criticized.[25]

Yet parallels between *LJ* and its cousin *Publishers Weekly* (hereafter *PW*), issued by the same publisher, stemmed less from *LJ*'s following the industry than from publishers' self-censorship. *PW* promised to warn readers of cheap imitations of the "fleshly" school by appending "not recommended" to its descriptive notices of such books. (Considering the much-discussed spur that censure gave to sales, the warning was a dubious threat.) Neither journal did more than criticize the vice societies mildly. *PW*, in 1890 felt that they were condemning coarse but morally innocuous books while allowing more "subtly vicious" literature to slip by. And *LJ* feared that public opinion might react against the societies and prevent them from excluding books that warranted exclusion or at least restricted circulation.[26]

The nature of these literary controversies is suggested by an 1881 ALA survey of questionable authors and by Hubbard's list of adverse reviews. The ALA questionnaire listed thirteen writers of juvenile and "sensational" novels—including Horatio Alger and Mrs. Southworth—plus fifteen British authors (eight male, seven female) who were more controversial. The males included writers who glorified criminals—for example, William Ainsworth, Bulwer-Lytton for his *Falkland* (1827), Wilkie Collins, originator of the detective story, and society gossips like Edmund Yates, a skillful writer about adulterers, scoundrels, dissipated noblemen, and gamblers. The female novelists wrote romantic, sometimes criminal, adventures and glamorous if critical portraits of high society, centering on adultery or bigamy.[27]

The Hubbard pamphlet confined itself to British authors and works (except for Henry Adams's anonymous *Democracy*), and to females (except for Yates). It concentrated on a "base herd" of female writers who had been adversely reviewed in the (English) *Saturday Review*, London *Atheneum*, and *Spectator*. This severely biased collection of excerpts thus provides a rich clue to the nature of the literary and moral standards that the writers violated.[28]

Obviously, the critics were concerned with themes of crime and sex, especially adultery. Yet the adulterous woman had a long literary tradition ranging from Clytemnestra, Francesca da Rimini, Iseult, the ladies of chivalric poetry, and Gertrude of Denmark, down to Hester Prynne. Apparently, more than the subject was alarming.

A consistent theme in their complaints was disdain for the "fine writing," the "caricatures of high life," and the "class of readers" for whom the novels were presumably written. The works (e.g., *Viva*) seemed to be compensatory fantasies for working girls—"ladies' maids and milliners' apprentices." Yet critics were even more concerned that middle-class young ladies might stumble on them. "It is too bad," wrote a *London Examiner* critic (12 February 1870) of Rhoda Broughton's *Red as a Rose Is She*,

that our daughters should be taught to consider the speeches, and conduct, and behavior . . . as possible to any English lady. . . . Indeed we seriously deprecate the effect of such books as this upon the girlhood of England, and our best wish is that the innocent eyes which may scan these pages may be blind to their real meaning.

Critics called on authors, publishers, and librarians to protect the public from poor literature and models of behavior. For one, the remedy lay "in the hand of the librarians, who, if they never sent out an unwholesome book *that was not asked for* [italics in original] would effect a great and salutary change."

Curiously, it was no help that the books were immoral by suggestion only—"too prudish for the really prurient," too oblique for the innocent, hypocritical because temptation "just escapes real crime." Even in *Theodora* ("a book against marriage"), complained the critic, "not a single married couple remains true, except in the most conventional [sic] sense." In *The Loves of Arden*, Miss Braddon's "nastiest" novel, after the reader had been led on, "there is not even any actual adultery; . . . virtue triumphs in the end."

The highly personal responses suggest that adultery acquired new meaning in these novels as the emblem of woman's status and her demand for freedom, in tacit or explicit ways. Tacit legitimations of adultery did not challenge the social code, but they exposed the constraints of marriage in the dilemmas of idealized, innocent victims. Explicit legitimations of adultery criticized marriage or stressed male domination. The former works evoked charges of hypocrisy, the latter of immorality. Critics protested the treatment of husbands as "fiends" and "the hostility entertained by average lady novelists like Mrs. Forrester against husbands." Miss Braddon in *Dead-Sea Fruit* was chastised for her "left-handed blows at legal provisions that are a hindrance to gentlemen who wish to marry their friends' wives." In other words, what the novelists attacked and the critics defended were sometimes merely existing divorce laws.[29]

Research on these minor novelists supports the idea that adultery was linked to new ideologies of protest.

The sensational novels that came late in the nineteenth century—almost unknown to most modern readers—reveal feminine protest in astoundingly open forms: heroines who murder, or try to murder their husbands, abandon their children, act out their suppressed desires; punished, perhaps, at the novel's end, but nonetheless revealing a lurid aspect of female sensibility. Feminist fiction developed soon afterwards.[30]

In a single society, writes Bernard Barber, different ideological forms for the same values may coexist in different social strata. "There may be high-brow, middle-brow, and low-brow versions of the supporting ideologies." In theme, these second-rate novels were popularized versions of oppositional ideologies that combined disenchanted social commentary with sexual themes: Zola's *Nana*, published in America in 1880, Flaubert's *Mme. Bovary*, published here in 1881, Tolstoi's *Anna Karenina* in 1885, all best-sellers. Less overwhelmingly popular authors would add to this stream. Mme. Collet in Norway carried a feminist message. In 1883 Strindberg published *Giftad* (*Marriage*), a collection of outspokenly realistic short stories that was prosecuted for blasphemy. Ibsen followed *A Doll's House* (1879) with the heroines of *Rosmersholm* (1886), *The Lady from the Sea* (1888), and *Hedda Gabler* (1890).[31]

Isolated American works were also controversial. In 1881 (about the time of the Hubbard episode) the Boston Society for the Suppression of Vice had *Leaves of Grass* suppressed, but the book was soon published in Philadelphia. In 1884 the Concord, Massachusetts, library trustees banned *Huckleberry Finn*, to elicit Mark Twain's bitter attack on these "moral icebergs" and his promise that the ban would double his sales. Their move paralleled Louisa May Alcott's oft-quoted comment: "If Mr. Clemens cannot think of something better to tell our pure-minded lads and lasses, he had best stop writing for them."[32]

American authors, however, had not yet raised the controversy that European authors did, and even liberal critics were cautious. William Dean Howells admired *Anna Karenina*, but it was a book to be kept locked away from children. When *LJ* and *PW* coped with Zola, they were careful to distinguish truly high culture, the " 'freshly' school of undoubted literary ability and with a moral to tell," from imitations without moral purpose, and to limit their defense to "healthy-minded" or "cultivated" readers, not the "unwary." Their argument, assuming the differential effects of reading, had its parallel in the censorship laws.[33]

Librarians also operated within a framework of values and literary standards in which censorship was expected. The same was true of trustees. In both Boston and Los Angeles, they were tolerant until vigilance was forced upon them.

It is significant that librarians who did challenge authority asserted their autonomy in the name of censorship. They used that value to demonstrate their professionalism on intellectual and ethical grounds—their superior judgment, or expertise, on harmful literature, and their greater commitment to the public good. Although both Hubbard and Perkins invoked the value of censorship to advance their own causes, the same activities and goals masked different kinds of motivation. There was opportunism in Hubbard's strategies—in his shifting charges and the fact that, as an ex-employee, he had nothing to lose. Perkins, on the other hand, displayed commitment, or he would not have made life so difficult for himself. He sought a voice in library policy, not its mere technical management.

Leaders of the profession, by contrast, were more moderate—both more tolerant and more discreet. They had private and public reservations about the degree of censorship to exercise, but arguments defending freedom did not win widespread support. A variety of motivations underlay the presumed value consensus, largely because the goals of the vice societies were too respectable to oppose.

Even at a much later date, antipornography movements have been classified as respectable and "nonfactional"—that is, generally unopposed, and meeting with, at most, indifference and token support rather than outright opposition. Since late nineteenth-century movements had far stronger religious and intellectual support, the Society for the Suppression of Vice, buttressed by the law, was accepted as an organization representing the public interest.

The main concern of librarians was still the elitist-populist dilemma. They were gradually shifting their attention, in fact, from the needs of the worker, and working youth, to younger children and children in schools, where that dilemma was less acute. Although Samuel Green complained that library schools were becoming elitist, stressing language, literature, and history rather than the technical information needed by workingmen, the shift in attention was largely unacknowledged and its ideological implications unrecognized.

The 1890s, however, would witness an increasing self-consciousness on all aspects of the librarians' culture: elitism and the library's educational role; censorship and the new literature; neutrality and political debate. The literature of naturalism was growing abroad and in the

United States. The escalation of protest and its culmination in the election of 1896 would force a new political consciousness on the country and on the attention of librarians. In that context, they would be forced to consider more carefully what their neutrality meant in terms of receptivity to new and deviant ideas.

4.

PIVOT OF CHANGE: 1890–1900

I can remember a state of things in which it was difficult for a man in common life to join himself with other men much beyond his neighborhood in any effectual way, except . . . on the lines of an old political party or in an older church. But today, leagues, unions, federations, associations, orders, rings, form themselves among the restless, unstable elements of the time as easily as clouds. . . . Any boldly ignorant inventor of a new economical theory or a new political doctrine, or a new cornerstone for the fabric of society, can set on foot a movement from Maine to California. . . . This is what invests popular ignorance with terror which never appeared in it before.
—Josephus Larned, ALA President, 1894

Has it not often come sharply home to every one of you—the hopelessness of the task we assume to set ourselves? the triviality of the great mass of the free public library's educational work? the discouraging nature of the field: the pettiness, the awful pettiness, of results?
—John Cotton Dana, ALA president, 1896

In retrospect, it was a decade of spectacular achievement. Services spread to new groups: schools, children, settlement houses, women's clubs. Career librarians were chosen for two illustrious posts, to head the Library of Congress and the New York Public Library. The innovation of open shelves meant new freedom for the user. Above all, Carnegie's millions, increasing over the decade, augured a new era in philanthropy.[1]

Yet librarians who lived through these years suffered turmoil, disillusion, bewilderment. With the abysmal depression of 1893–1897, class schisms, movements, third parties were set into motion—Grangers and Greenbackers, single-taxers and Kellogists, Socialists and Populists, labor groups and labor parties. The Pullman and Homestead strikes, the march of Coxey's army, the black antiutopia of the Populist novelist Ignatius Donnelly's *Caesar's Column*, lent an apocalyptic intensity to these conflicts. A nation of island communities had become a national society, linked by a national communications network—people "whisper in each other's ears across the continent," said Larned.[2] The old local identities of sect and party were replaced by the national-cosmopolitan polarities of class, region, or movement.

The idea of freedom took on new meanings, shaped by responses to the new social order and the literatures it produced, the themes of social protest, the movements it spawned, the ideas that served as its heralds. With this collision of viewpoints attention focused on the processes themselves by which opinions were formed. As they surveyed the changing social order and its intellectual productions, some librarians produced new interpretations of their role. In that historical situation, freedom came to mean the freedom to accept new ideas.

NORMAL AND CRISIS IDEOLOGY

Until 1894, professional debates centered on the old elitist-populist theme. In an ALA survey, Ellen Coe, head of the New York Free Circulating Library, asked such leading questions as "Do you deprecate the reading of Fiction to the extent now practiced?" And, to an 1894 panel: "Is a free public library justified in supplying . . . books which are neither for instruction nor for the cultivation of taste . . . such, for example, as the ruck of common novels?"[3]

Librarians of tax-supported libraries (as hers was not), however, were less zealous to instruct than to provide workers in crowded cities with entertainment that would help them forget the "petty matters of their everyday lives." They criticized imperious middle-class readers and librarians with their heads "so high in the clouds as to forget . . . the vast majority."[4]

Paul Leicester Ford, then an editor of *LJ*, also deplored the elitism of librarians like William Fletcher. If libraries drew a man from "the saloon, the street corner, or even the foul-aired tenement, we have done the best part of it, without much regard to what he reads." A YWCA library worker, describing the "less exacting of the newly formed classes," the women in New York shops and factories, and their "weary struggle for their daily bread," despaired, "They must have amusement. If they drift to our doors we *must* attract their interest, . . . arouse and educate their mental forces. We must at least try to give them something to think about."[5]

As the depression deepened, bringing large numbers of unemployed into the reading rooms for long hours ("boarders," they were called), the discrepancy between intent and reality became sharper. Josephus Larned, ALA president in 1894, put these questions to a panel:

Do the people who are attracted to a library by the current daily newspapers . . . ever read anything else?

Are they not, for the most part, a vagrant and mal-odorous class, whose presence in the reading room repels many who would receive more benefit from it?

If the greater part of the contents of the daily newspapers most in demand was put between book covers, would any library think of buying it, to place it in circulation?

Considering the functions of the public library as an educational institution, are there good and sufficient reasons for making it a purveyor of daily newspaper reading?

So far as concerns the business need in a community for some collection of current newspapers . . . should not that [need] be met by a Board of Trade, or other commercial organization?

Again, public librarians resisted, though with some discomfiture. They termed the questions "conjectures," usually indicating that their libraries did accommodate tramps. "Entice them away," James Bain (Toronto) answered airily, to a congenial game room where they would not feel embarrassed. James Whelpley (Cincinnati) indignantly defended both newspapers and the library's responsibility to both "classes and masses." Did tramps repel others? Possibly.

But if the masses (sometimes, in political language called "the great unwashed"), mal-odorous though they be, take the advantages provided in the newspaper reading rooms, and are contented, nay, eager to read, it shows there is hope for them, and that they may still rise to heights of cleanliness. . . . I take it as a fundamentally wrong idea that a public library should be the aristocratic institution of the community. . . . It is in the broadest sense an institution for the betterment and education of that class which contains so many who come under the term malodorous.[6]

Even more passionately, Tessa Kelso (Los Angeles Public Library), in the liberal magazine *Arena*, assailed a profession barely a generation old for its inordinate administrative expenses, obsession with catalogs and indexes, endless debates on flabby fiction, and idealization of service to the student to the exclusion of other functions. Libraries had crippled themselves by trying to turn everyone into a student—"the one person who, by virtue of his title, is least to be considered; since to the student books are his working materials." The highest promise of libraries lay, rather, in their recreational function for the poor, in their "power to add to the fast diminishing store of human pleasure, to be a means of overcoming the intemperance of work." That end was challenged on the grounds that the library would become a loafing place for the city's idlers. "But if the library did no more than become the recognized loafing centre of a city, its existence on that basis would be warranted." What was to be done with a boy in a crowded city if books were taken from him because they were "only amusing"? If the library provided not only books, but the "baseballs, indoor games, magic lanterns, and the whole paraphernalia of healthy wholesome amusement" that the average child could not afford any more than books, there would be an increase in library membership and a corresponding decrease in " 'petty offenders.' "[7]

So unorthodox was this view that the *LJ* editor took issue, in a footnote, with Kelso's criticism of student priorities. For service to youth was to be the salvation of public libraries.

Where tramps represented the limitations of the present, youth were symbols of the future. With limited resources, librarians were placing their money on the best bet. Thus the shift from working-class to middle-class youth, which had gained little notice in the 1880s, now became part of the ideology of service. Pressure increased for lowering age limits from twelve or thirteen years to as soon as the child was old enough to read.

Librarians were conscious of this issue in client selection. In fact, John Cotton Dana, a young lawyer and surveyor turned Denver librarian, transformed the entire discussion of the library's responsibility to "tramps" into one of budget priorities: Funds diverted to reading rooms could not be used for work in schools, or "for purposes that we consider more serious and of more importance than the reading of the daily paper." His thoughts were quickly accepted. Frederick Crunden (St. Louis) assented that "no appreciable portion" of the public used reading rooms, none "that counts for anything." Those whose opinions amounted to anything got the newspapers elsewhere. Better to spend the $1,000 on a woman who looked after children's reading

where there is some hope. There is very little hope in men who drift around the public reading rooms. The best thing that I can say of it is that it keeps those men out of the saloons. That is in itself a good thing. They go, perhaps, some of them, to the saloon because they have nowhere else to go. . . . Is not the money spent for Miss [Lutie] Stearns's salary much better employed?

And Larned, immediately, "I would rather pay $1000 for Miss Stearns than . . . for all the newspapers published on the American continent."[8]

IDEOLOGIES OF CRISIS, 1894–1896

Between 1894 and 1896 a shift took place in professional concerns as they were affected by external change and dislocation. Normal ideology defined the profession's relationship to society in its stable aspects, including poverty as a persistent aspect of social structure; it accepted conditions that would later be defined as inhumane, such as eleven-hour working days for children.[9] The issue was simply how to adapt to these conditions.

The ideologies of crisis were responses not to these objective conditions but to the consciousness that they produced: the bitter strikes, new political parties, organs of expression, and modes of analysis; to the new literature and mass media. The ideologies of crisis were not uniform, but they shared a cognition of passage from a simpler time into an unknown future, a sensitivity to the problems of intellectual authority and of deviant ideas, to opinion and civic education. Proposing to shape public opinion, Josephus Larned and William Howard Brett (Cleveland) claimed that they were taking libraries in a new direction.[10] John Cotton Dana, rejecting all notions of guidance, sought simple utilities in a world in which notions of authority were themselves under fire.

Josephus Larned, full of gloom and nostalgia, reflected on the loss of community and the breakdown of old identities through the spread of new movements with new ideas. Democracy was ill equipped to deal with change of these dimensions. Schools were inadequate to the task of forming public opinion. And the press, an educating power that might have transformed culture, was "a mere business, . . . pandering to popular ignorance," "skimming . . . the rich daily news of the world for the scum and the froth of it," feeding on "public sores and private drains," exploiting a "latent, undeveloped taste for such ferments."

The great hope of the library lay precisely in this test of democracy, for it might serve as antidote to the fusion of the ignorant in the public and the unscrupulous in the press. Untainted by commercialism or vested interest, it could carry out the mission of good books. But that charge would impose on the library the "delicate, difficult, very grave duty" of discrimination in the choice of ideas:

To judge books with an adequate knowledge and sufficient hospitality of mind; to exercise a just choice among them without offensive censorship; to defend his shelves against the endless siege of vulgar literature, and yet not waste his strength in the resistance—these are really the crucial demands made on every librarian.[11]

William Howard Brett saw an even more direct civic function for the library, arguing that libraries, like schools, existed not for individual development but to promote good citizenship. In fact, "the larger enforced contribution of the rich man" was justified only by his "larger interest in the prosperity of the country, the stability of its institutions, and the maintenance of order." Reviewing decades of hardship for workers, class antagonisms, evangelism, skepticism, "visionary political projects and earnest advocacy of various social panaceas," he urged libraries to join other agencies—colleges, religious organizations, clubs, journals—that were heightening civic consciousness. Although some were diverted to propaganda, they were at least sensitive to important issues, and many avoided partisanship.

Given that objective, the library's main task was to choose material for the citizen in his capacity as voter, especially in the growing field of sociology. "In no other department is the possibility greater of doing evil as well as good." The head of this department would need the qualifications of a college instructor and would have to know the most important writers with different views on even the "most keenly controverted" subjects in order to guide readers. "All of this is quite consistent with an entire lack of partisanship or any attempt at propaganda." Other departments could nurture patriotism with "the same discriminating care in the selection or exclusion of books."[12]

Although Brett was not endorsing censorship, his concern with scholarly authority and his structured, almost didactic, approach raised questions. William Fletcher protested his "utilitarianism," preferring the "different and higher plea" of individual enrichment. John Cotton Dana objected to both Brett's and Larned's pessimistic views of social unrest as "omens of greater ills" rather than sources of comfort. Nor could he see the library as an engine for creating citizens or an extension of university education when it should be the opposite. It was not an institution teaching accepted canons or any set system of instruction. It was the extension "into every man's home of the possibility of knowledge" and wisdom, the extension to the humblest of the chance to learn the "latest thing that is being taught and being said." The library contributed to the general unrest because of its openness to new doctrines and fads, because it educated for the one thing most essential to the progress of the human race—

that there shall be a multitude of differing opinions. . . . Let us bear in mind the remark that a good man will not obey the laws too well. We should rejoice that we have in our hands an instrument by means of which we may create, perhaps, not the man who fits exactly into the social order today, but possibly here and there the man who does not fit into the social order today, but may, none the less, prove to be the man who will give the world a fillip on its way.[13]

Crunden seconded that defense of nonconformity: he welcomed all opinions, even some that seemed ridiculous. "They may be the opinions that fifty years from now will be accepted." Brett grumbled; he had not opposed new ideas at all. He had wanted merely to discuss the functions of the state. At a symposium the next year, Brett interjected the same advocacy of dissent: the radical idea of today would be the conservative idea of tomorrow.[14]

In 1896, during the prolonged depression, Dana again assailed the missionary role with a bitterness and utter candor that members would remember for years. Clearly, libraries were "not altogether halls of learning." Their habitués were rejects—"largely men who either have failed in a career, or never had a career, or do not wish a career. We all know our own indolents, our own idlers, our own 'Boarders.' " One could find little that was inspiring about the men who gathered in newspaper reading rooms, or in the readers of cheap fiction. Worse, the library, as a state agency, stunted initiative by preventing the idle and incompetent and indifferent from working in order to earn funds for their reading matter. He adjured librarians to stop forcing "on others our views of their duty" and instead seek out willing supporters, move into the community, advertise their services, work with bookmen and newspapers and book lovers and women's clubs, and gain the good will of the press, the clergy, the businessmen:

Do the businessmen and businesswomen, the active people, those who feed us and clothe us and transport us, those who have brought about in the last few decades the great increase in creature comforts for every one, do these business people take an active interest in your library? . . . If not, is it their fault?

In contrast to Larned's visionary promise, Dana appealed to pragmatism and publicity (he was the originator of library promotion) and immediate interest. "Your modern librarian is . . . no disputatious economist, idly wavering, like the fabled donkey, between the loose hay of a crass individualism and the chopped feed of a perfectionist socialism. He is a worker."[15]

Professional responses to Dana's candor were ambivalent, while encomia for Josephus Larned's hopeful vision, expressed again at that conference,[16] persisted through the year. Yet Dana's view would be more influential. The humanitarian mission had imposed an impossible charge made absurd in depression. Dana offered, instead, an end to ideology.

The defeat of Western Populism with McKinley's election left a smoldering resentment at appeals to unity. "We are willing to put our grade of 'national pride' up against the world, Wall Street included," wrote an anonymous Nebraska librarian.[17] Frederick Crunden spoke in compensatory certainty that in the long run conservatism could not win and made the library the harbor of new ideas, voices not of protest but of change.

In a bitter chronicle of freedom suppressed, Crunden reviewed witchcraft trials and Quaker persecutions, the murder of Elijah Lovejoy, "a martyr in the cause of free speech," the failure of the recently won tolerance of religious and scientific ideas to extend to "live topics." In economics and sociology, the advocate of new ideas found vested interests alert to "resist inquiry." Social and business ostracism were still effective, while tar-buckets or bullets were sometimes suggested.

For the most part, however, we content ourselves with denouncing the proposer of any marked departure from existing political or sociological conditions as a "socialist," a "communist," or "anarchist.". . . There is always a certain meanness in the argument of conservatism, joined with a certain superiority in its fact. It affirms because it holds.

History was a struggle of the weak and ignorant to win rights against the "superior strength and cunning of the few." The continued progress of that cause required careful attention to new and radical ideas, to critiques of a patently unjust social system in which poverty was explained by "the absurdity of 'overproduction' of the very things for which millions are suffering." But to effect social change one would have to "revolutionize men's minds" through the unbiased study of social problems and the cultivation of open-mindedness. To that end, the library might exert "incalculable influence in the solution of the social problems of today." The wisdom for that task could not be attained in school or college, for it required "the higher education of mature minds— the masses"—which the library alone could give. "It is better to trust the well-informed common sense of the people than the learning of the schoolmen." [18]

The new views of the library's function that emerged in the 1890s and the new concepts of freedom were not necessarily linked. For Brett and Larned, the function of molding public opinion or civic consciousness *could* have been compatible with either censorship as much as freedom—an ambiguity that Dana was quick to pick up—although it happened not to be. Seated at the base of Rockefeller's empire, Brett may have been sensitive to the relationship between taxation of the rich and the public functions of the state, but his major concern was to maintain an open-minded neutrality on even the most controversial issues. That posture was hardly consonant with censorship. Similarly, Larned sought to mold public opinion through "just choice . . . without offensive censorship" (see p. 45), through responsible information, not indoctrination. The trouble was that, in their concern with education and with authoritative opinion, they left open the possibility of a dogmatism verging on censorship.

With Dana, by contrast, the idea of freedom was linked to a militant individualism and the rejection of any formal or directive—much less civic—role for the library. He endorsed self-education at most, with no missionary overtones. An Easterner transplanted to Denver, he had created a controversy in 1894 for circulating material "on both sides" of the "goldbug" issue in a community that fought the gold standard. [19] He was well aware of the problems of unorthodoxy. Dana's position, a negative liberalism embracing idiosyncrasy along with unorthodoxy, was consistent with his lack of sympathy with the worker, his opposition to state agencies, his conservative indifference to bimetallism. He geared the library to cultural elites—hardly the groups to put radical ideas to radical use.

Only with Crunden was responsiveness to new ideas associated with the educational function of libraries, and this was because he linked that educational role to social reform. Both Dana's and Crunden's concern with freedom was linked, if only indirectly, to the desire for the freer diffusion of their own ideas.

The upheavals of the 1890s had an enduring impact. Civic education entered the repertoire of library functions. Libraries were praised for having met the demand for information on "both sides" of election issues, and ex-governor Altgeld's suggestion of "economic circulating libraries" won cautious approval: the information might be partisan, but one could rely on the opposing party to provide competing propaganda.[20]

As philanthropic sponsorship increased, the issue of "tainted money" had to be confronted. Labor dismissed Carnegie's gospel of wealth as so much "flapdoodle and slush," claiming that the "almighty Andrew Philanthropist Library Carnegie" endowed the "public at the expense of your slaves." A liberal church review charged "owners of capital" with trying to subjugate the masses by controlling "the organs of intelligence"—the city press and "the reins of public information." It was shrewd of millionaires to spend a trifle of the gains they had made off the people by giving them public libraries. "Why libraries? Because he who selects the libraries, as he who makes the songs of the people, may be expected to frame its laws."[21]

Indignantly, Samuel Ranck (Enoch Pratt Free Library, Baltimore) retorted that philanthropists might not have the purest motives, but they were still to be judged by their acts. He knew of no provision or restriction that justified the charge that they tried to control information or that libraries kept the masses in submission.[22]

It was a naive denial. True, Carnegie rarely interfered with library administration and endorsed exposure to all sides of economic questions—being sure the result would be sympathy with the problems of capitalists. Moreover, he saw libraries as the workers' property, supported by them as an "agency which helps only those who help themselves, which attacks pauperism and want at the root, about which no taint of demoralizing charity hovers." Yet that ideology, undermined by depression, was being further diluted. High schools absorbed an increasing segment of working-class youth. For a growing unskilled labor force, vocational education, in libraries or out, was irrelevant. And skilled labor was finding its salvation in collective action by unions. In 1898, Herbert Putnam (Boston) reported that workers seldom used the Boston Public Library, though their children did.[23]

Moreover, in a period of sharp polarities, a commitment to class harmony itself suggested partisanship. Libraries were called agents in relieving social tension and preventing strikes. In Gloversville, New York, a librarian, A. L. Peck, launched a program to teach workers their true interests as against the goals propounded by labor leaders. The workers used the course to set up a cooperative, then established their own lecture series.[24]

At the same time, librarians shifted their missionary function from workers to the immigrant, to whom the goal of individual cultural improvement was relevant. Librarians pleaded for cultural tolerance and defended foreign-language books as aids to Americanization. Books would reduce crime and insanity among immigrants, said Gratia Countryman in 1898 (she would be ALA president in 1934), prevent rebellion and disloyalty and defection to the "ranks of the anarchists."[25]

With this orientation, the goals of libraries meshed fully with the most sincere advocacy of clients' interests and the dominant ideology of tolerance, equal opportunity, cultural elevation, and assimilation. For countless immigrant children the outcome matched that professed intent. "I lived half my childhood in the library," reminisced Abram Kardiner. "It kept me off the streets." With the school it nourished dreams of mobility. "Education for the licensed professions. They were your ticket to the middle class."[26]

5.

FREEDOM OF ACCESS: 1890–1900

Freedom was the slogan of the decade, freedom to use open-shelves, freedom to take out more than one book. Symbolically appealing and economically sound (it reduced the need for attendants), the open-shelf system was adopted by most American libraries by the end of the decade.

Yet this freedom was highly limited. The "two-book" system was really a way to cut fiction circulation, since the second book could not be a novel. Nor did all readers have access to all shelves, especially in large libraries.[1] It was the open-shelf system that literally exposed existing censorship policies, for where all books had once been concealed, closed shelves now remained only for restricted books.

These policies were made even more conspicuous with the surge of new literature. Abroad and at home, old values were challenged by serious and popular writers, by aesthetes and by naturalists. "There is no such thing as a moral or immoral book," announced Oscar Wilde in the preface to *The Picture of Dorian Gray* (1891). "Books are well written, or badly written. That is all." George Moore, whose works had been censored by British circulating libraries since the mid–1880s, was engaged in a constant attack on Victorian morality; his most shocking novel, *Esther Waters*, appeared in 1894. In Britain, Sarah Grand, a leading women's rights novelist, had to publish privately her novel dealing with syphillis, *The Heavenly Twins*. In America, Hamlin Garland's first works were turned down as too coarse, and Stephen Crane had to publish privately the Zolasque *Maggie: a Girl of the Streets* (1893). In 1896, Appleton published an expurgated version.[2]

In the decade of the Pullman and Homestead strikes, the march of Coxey's army, and the growth of the Populist party, the literature of social criticism took a darker turn. The romantic utopian vision of *Looking Backward* (1888) became the morbid fantasy of the Populist *Caesar's Column* (1891). William Dean Howells's remarkable novel, *A Hazard of New Fortunes* (1890), ended with the New York City streetcar strike of 1888.

The realism that William Dean Howells had fostered among young writers was reinforced by Zola's influence and the journalistic trends that brought newsmen into the slums. The growth of journalism launched the careers of a number of novelists whose work would be stamped by their early experience—Stephen Crane, Frank Norris, Theodore Dreiser. Zola's naturalism created a genre of slum fiction and other "problem" novels. They were criticized not for their eroticism but for their unrelenting and morbid pessimism. This critique of the literature of exposure would echo through several decades of muckraking novels. Among European novels, Tolstoi's *Kreutzer Sonata* was barred by a customs office in 1890 (Theodore Roosevelt called Tolstoi a "sexual and moral pervert"), Zola's *La Terre* in 1894.[3]

Libraries were also embroiled in literary controversies. In Philadelphia, *Trilby*, by George du Maurier, was debated, and works by the popular Rudyard Kipling were removed from library shelves. In Los Angeles, a daily newspaper attacked the library trustees for having purchased *Le Cadet* by Jean Richepin, in French, two years earlier. A local minister, capitalizing on the publicity, prayed for the soul of the librarian, Tessa Kelso—who promptly sued him, since she was neither a member of his church nor "empowered to exercise any censorship as to what French books shall be admitted to the library," that choice belonging to a book committee. In Indianapolis, the press supported the library against a minister's attack, calling it one of the carefully guarded in the country, whose few pernicious works were all specially listed and available only on special permission. The minister backed down, and a concerned *LJ* implored the clergy to work with libraries, which needed the help of all good citizens in their common cause.[4]

Only once was censorship questioned by *LJ*, on the ground that works not in themselves immoral should not be censored just because of an author's reputation. Such a policy could produce gaps in the ranks of the classics, it argued, and prompt an artificial demand stemming from morbid curiosity. The author in question was Oscar Wilde, whose arrest for homosexuality had spurred the press in St. Louis to condemn his writings. Reporters had asked the librarian, Herbert Crunden, his intentions, and it was his removal of the book (along with Frank Hill's similar move in Newark) that prompted the *LJ* editorial. Crunden explained that he had removed the book, "untouched for years," merely for examination. Then, concurring that unobjectionable works should not be condemned for their author's reputation, he had returned them to the shelves—without notifying the press.[5]

THE PARADOX OF ACCOUNTABILITY

Librarians were extremely vulnerable—fashionable targets for ministers and for an unreliable press that inflated any controversy. Understandably, they did not seek autonomy from trustees; generally, they chose books to be approved by book committees.[6] Autonomy from the public meant deference to trustees.

On the other hand, trustees themselves stressed responsiveness to public demand. In fact, Charles Francis Adams, Jr., made responsiveness the central feature, the duty, of the small popular library, as distinct from the large research library.[7] Yet that responsiveness was also restrictive as the large research library became a haven for books that were held to be unsuitable for the general public.

The rationale for this division of library publics was implicit in the 1894 Worthington decision, which turned down Anthony Comstock's suit to keep a publisher from selling expensive editions of several classics, among them Rousseau's *Confessions*, Fielding's *Tom Jones*, the *Decameron*, and the *Arabian Nights*. Maintaining that they were not the kinds of books that the Society for the Suppression of Vice sought to ban, the court used the important whole-book criterion for determining obscenity: One could not condemn a work "because of a few episodes," for most English-language authors would be barred from circulation on those grounds. But it also expressed a subtle class bias. "No evil" need be feared "from the sale of these rare and costly books," since they "would not be bought or appreciated by the class of people from whom unclean publications should be withheld." Nor would they corrupt the young, "for they are unlikely to reach them."[8]

Price, however, was no deterrent in libraries that circulated books free to the public. The Astor library in 1894 removed the works of Fielding and Smollett to its reference collection.[9]

These distinctions gave a special role to research and university libraries. In 1892 the trustees of the John Crerar bequest began to act on his stipulation that works be chosen to create "a healthy moral and Christian sentiment," with "all nastiness and immorality" excluded.

I do not mean by this that there shall not be anything but hymn books and sermons, but I mean that dirty French novels and all skeptical trash and works of questionable moral tone shall never be found in this library. I want its atmosphere that of Christian refinement, and its aim and object the building up of character.

The trustees announced themselves "in no way embarrassed or limited" by these provisions, and in a few months the reason was clear. They had decided to design the Crerar as a library of "exceedingly wide" scope, embracing "the entire domain of pure and applied science"— engineering, architecture, astronomy, and "sociology in all its ramifications."[10]

The *Chicago Tribune* affirmed piously that the trustees were fulfilling the "unspoken wishes" of the founder. More candidly, the *LJ* editor conjectured that Crerar would probably have termed skeptical trash "many books that will find a rightful place in the Crerar library of science." And Mary Ahern, editor of the new journal *Public Libraries* (hereafter *PL*) declared that the wants of Chicago's citizens would now be divided among three libraries: the Newberry for belles-lettres, the Crerar for science, and the public library for "all the good, wholesome, entertaining books which people who are not special students desire."[11]

The same criterion was used at an 1895 panel on "precautions exercised to avoid the selection of undesirable books" and the "treatment of those found objectionable after purchase." Books proper for a large university library might be "essentially improper for the general mass of the people," said Theresa West, Milwaukee public librarian. A public library could buy outspoken books "which speak truth concerning normal, wholesome conditions." But books dealing with "morbid, diseased conditions of the individual man, or of society," were for "students of special subjects." They were bought only after due consideration of the just relation of the comparative rights of students and general readers and were lent only on request. "This taboo question, however, is treated quietly."[12]

The compatibility of populism and censorship, and of elitism and freedom, was shown in Josephus Larned's strictures *against* censorship at this meeting. "It is that challenge [arbitrary censorship]—even the appearance of it—and that assumption—even the suspicion of it—that I would have every library avoid as far as it may be possible to do so." If a book offended many readers, a library with a small budget could exercise "a certain legitimate and proper censorship." It would not be challenging any strong convictions or arbitrarily deciding a dispute in morals or literary taste. Coarser classics would not circulate but could be kept on the shelves. One had best let demand build up for controversial books before buying them, then warn the reader, and, finally, "cast responsibility on the public" to read at its own risk.[13]

Larned's elitism explains his desire to avoid censorship. Improper books were gaining literary acceptance, hence legitimacy. It was a controversial legitimacy, but controversy was an advance over disapproval. By *virtue* of his disregard for popular taste (in a library that was not yet a public library), Larned was involved in the literary disputes of high culture. It was with respect to those debates that he declined to serve as censor.

BOOKS FOR THE SMALL LIBRARY

In 1893 ALA proudly offered its first, 5,000-title, book guide for small popular libraries and branches, as a collection that one could "recommend to any trustees." Prepared by a committee under Josephus Larned, it broke down into 16 percent fiction (809 titles), 15 percent history, 8 percent sociology, and 4 percent religion.

The work seems elitist at first glance. It gave short shrift to older popular writers. Horatio Alger and Oliver Optic, E. P. Roe, Ouida, and Mrs. Southworth were all omitted. It compensated, however, by including newer popular writers like Alfred George Henty, Hall Caine, F. Marion Crawford, and the controversial mystery writer Arthur Conan Doyle. Indeed, John Townsend Trowbridge was listed with five novels and Mark Twain with only two. Twain's *Tom Sawyer* and *The Prince and the Pauper* were cited, but *Huckleberry Finn* and the best-selling *Life on the Mississippi* were excluded.

In the case of controversial classics, some were listed but others, of equal reputation, excluded. Fielding and Lawrence Sterne were included, but Samuel Richardson and Tobias Smollett were not. A controversial author might be represented, but with a less controversial and less important work. Anatole France, Flaubert, and Gautier were each represented with one lesser work while *Thaïs, Mme. Bovary,* and *Mlle. de Maupin*—all thrusts at the family and church—were excluded. Other authors—for example, Rabelais and Boccaccio—were excluded altogether. Balzac was represented with four novels, a skimpy selection compared with Henty's eight titles. Oscar Wilde, author by then of *Poems, The Happy Prince,* and *The Picture of Dorian Gray,* was excluded— even before his celebrated arrest. George Moore was excluded. However, Thomas Hardy's *Tess of the d'Urbervilles* was listed; it would be removed in the 1904 edition of the catalog, after a trustee spoke against it in 1896.

Perhaps the most surprising exclusions were of Voltaire and Rousseau. Nothing by Rousseau was included, though a biography *about* him was listed. This discrepancy between a writer's reputation and the acceptance of his work is a good indicator of censorship: exclusion on grounds other than insignificance.

Contemporary social fiction was reflected in William Morris's *News from Nowhere,* Bellamy's *Looking Backward,* and Helen Hunt Jackson's *Century of Dishonour.* Omitted, however, were Ignatius Donnelly's *Caesar's Column,* Hamlin Garland's four social-political novels (including *Jason Edwards, A Spoil of Office,* and *A Member of the Third House*), and Hans Halmar Boyessen's novels of social criticism. Thomas B. Aldrich's *Stillwater Tragedy* was listed. However, the conservative labor novel, *The Breadwinners* by John Hay, and the radical *The Moneymakers* by John Keenan were both omitted.

The collection did not eschew unpleasant subjects as such. George Eliot, Tolstoi, William Dean Howells dealt with illegitimacy, adultery, and divorce. But attitudes toward institutions were another matter. Temperate social novels and criticism were acceptable, but not exposés of political immorality or attacks on organized religion, the family, or society. Indeed, in nonfiction, atheism seems to have been more controversial than socialism. Marx and Gronlund were included (though not *The Communist Manifesto*) but not the widely read atheist Robert Ingersoll.

Among popular and academic writers, Jacob Riis, Josiah Strong, and Richard Ely were included, but not Altgeld, George Herron, or Henry Demarest Lloyd's *A Strike of Millionaires Against Miners* (*Wealth Against Commonwealth* was not yet published). The thirty-two journals included twelve British publications and a number of journals of social criticism, but no labor publications—not surprisingly, in view of strictures against partisan materials.[14]

THE NEW CRITICISM: CONFLICT AND CONSENSUS

The conflict and compromise underlying professional agreement are usually hidden in resolutions, reports, and lists. An exception was the open meeting of 1896 on a supplement to the ALA catalog. Although the compilers hoped for a broader list geared to a "larger" library, the meeting turned out to be a "critical inquest" at which, the *LJ* editor reported, "the admissibility of George Meredith's novels" had to be submitted to "a hasty show of hands."[15]

Josephus Larned, chairman of the fiction section, lamented that a "theory of purposelessness" had combined with a "theory of realism" to produce a literature of dubious purpose.

The spirit in which that kind of literature is dealt out to us . . . is a spirit which would bring toadstools and toads and old bones into our parlors, and would send us to the garbage dumps for our picknicking. . . . Those are the ugly things which we have and have got, I say, to deal with; but it is not necessary that we would undertake to make them any part of the decorative outline of life.

The first work on the agenda was *A Lady of Quality* by Mrs. Frances Hodgson Burnett, author of *Little Lord Fauntleroy*. It was about a woman, grumbled Samuel Green (Worcester), whose life was "very wrong" but who reformed and married into great wealth. "She ought to have gone into obscurity instead." Demurring, James Hosmer (Minneapolis) found it powerful and uncompromising: "No veil is thrown over . . . matters that are commonly concealed." Mrs. Zelia Dixon suggested classifying it as a work for professors of criminology and students of sociology only; but several librarians objected, and Crunden moved that the committee respect its colleagues' judgment and omit it.

The Red Badge of Courage was charged as unrealistically profane. Tessa Kelso (with Scribner's by then) protested that it was a contribution to the literature of arbitration, "the finest thing in the world to put into the hands of people to make them converts to the abolition of war." But Caroline Hewins (New Haven) objected: there was a better war book, Suttner's *Ground Arms*. Gardner M. Jones (Salem) felt that the book's critical acclaim showed only the weakness of the literary press; the critics were too young to judge the realism they praised. Like Crane's two other books on New York life, this was "vulgar, and nothing but vulgar."

Larned had thought it a "wonderful piece of writing." But if, as his colleagues said, Crane had not imagined the Civil War correctly, it had best be omitted. Crunden agreed that, as in other cases of doubt, it should be removed.

The attitudes of the better-known librarians suggest some tentative observations. First, older librarians were not more restrictive. The conservative Samuel Green and Caroline Hewins were part of the older generation, but the more tolerant Larned and James Hosmer were also over sixty. Second, gender did not differentiate attitudes. Tessa Kelso was more tolerant than most of her male colleagues, and Mrs. Dixon was a mediator. The participants in the discussion that follows support these inferences. The prissy Hiller Wellman (head of branches, Boston), a Harvard graduate, was barely twenty-five. The more liberal Linda Eastman was twenty-nine, and just moving up as vice-librarian to William Howard Brett in Cleveland. Both Wellman and Miss Eastman would be presidents of ALA. Wellman, thirty years later, would lead a librarians' anticensorship campaign.[16]

Harold Frederic's *Damnation of Theron Ware*, the story of a minister's moral degeneration, met with sharp disagreement. Attacked as "a slur on religion," it was defended by Gardner Jones as "a great book," true to life, with an important moral question. Dr. Whelpley (Cincinnati) also voted not to throw it out. But Hiller Wellman raised a new argument: Did the association want "to recommend a book which has made a large number of our members who have read it feel worse off for reading it. I do not think we ought to recommend it." Although Green proposed a compromise, "the intermediate department, not for circulation," another librarian, who had no intention of reading the work, objected that it could "produce very much evil. . . . It is all right for the librarians to read it, but they are not the persons who will be harmed by it." A third refused to approve "any book that two librarians will stand up here and declare to be a bad book." A majority voted to "expunge" it. Exasperated, Miss Kelso requested: "We may discuss it as much as we like, but we should exclude Fiction . . . from the printed list bearing the imprint of the ALA."

Arthur Morrison's *Tales of Mean Streets*, a British Zolaesque novel, was dismissed with a few puns, and when Hamlin Garland's *Rose of Dutch-*

er's Coolly came up, William Fletcher (Amherst) and Bernard Steiner (Baltimore) both advised against it. Linda Eastman read a letter from Garland explaining his purpose in writing the book. When she finished, a majority voted without discussion to exclude it.

Henry Utley (Detroit), objecting on principle to detective stories, would have liked a discussion of Arthur Conan Doyle and Émile Gaboriau. Mr. Larned asked for an opinion on George Meredith's novels, whereupon A. L. Peck (Gloversville, N.Y.), who two years earlier had boasted of his censorship excursions and entrapments in bookstores, offered: "I believe it would be advisable to exclude at least *Lord Ormont and His Aminta* and *The Amazing Marriage.*"[17]

In the end, the outcome of the meeting subverted its intent, which had been to compile a more liberal list than the 1893 collection. But group solidarity militated against the leaders' judgment, favoring the less important members—a form of *noblesse oblige,* perhaps, but one in which professional leaders compromised their loyalty to professional standards for the sake of loyalty to peers. The outcome was a set of prescriptions that deviated from the thinking of professional leaders.[18]

The distinction between loyalty to norms and loyalty to peers is obscured by the fact that all were interpreting shared norms and accepted some degree of censorship. And when Hiller Wellman claimed that a book made him feel "worse" after reading it, he was invoking Josephus Larned's own principle of literary criticism. Yet Larned's keen appreciation of Stephen Crane, after he had condemned the new literature, shows how hard it is to impute specific judgments on the basis of general standards. The interpretation and application of these principles permitted varying degrees of tolerance that underlay the disputes.[19]

In the history and sociology sections, the heat of contemporary conflict brought nonprofessional concerns into the discussion. Where, for battles of the past, like the Civil War, opposed perceptions were carefully sought, agreement was harder to reach on contemporary conflicts. Crunden, chairman of the sociology section, confessed that

Whatever may be the right thing, the best thing, it is not that which we have now. . . . I can clasp hands with anybody except the rock-ribbed conservative. Therefore my votes have been in this matter of sociology in favor of the books that propose new theories. They may not be sound, but at any rate they are worth considering.

He praised John R. Commons's *Proportional Representation* lavishly.

William Fletcher, an Easterner, called "attention to this Call's *Coming Revolution*. . . . I do not know who this Call is," he said suspiciously.

Crunden defended it ardently. He had read it with "great interest" and, when the committee had expressed doubt, had double-starred it. It was an "awakener of thought."

At which point Fletcher, more candidly, indicated that he knew the work, if not the author.

I am a little in doubt, with all respect to friend Crunden's views, about our recommending books whose chief recommendations are that they set people to thinking. I do not know what is best to do about this, but knowing a little about the character of the book, and not knowing who the author is, I should question the advisability of the Association recommending it. We have a long list on Political Economy, and it seems to me that we might cut it down a little.[20]

In the next edition of the *ALA Catalog* in 1904 (see Chapter 7), none of these disputed works appeared—not Call, nor *A Lady of Quality*, nor *A Summer in Arcady* (which Larned had also defended), nor Meredith's *Lord Ormont* or *The Amazing Marriage*, *The Damnation of Theron Ware*, *The Red Badge of Courage*, *A Summer in Arcady*, nor *Rose of Dutcher's Coolly*. Not even Hall Caine's *The Manxman*, which, though challenged, had been approved, was listed.

A developing professional consciousness made librarians more decisive as guardians of the public taste. For a while yellow journalism seemed the "most serious problem that confronts us," and early in 1897, at the height of the Pulitzer-Hearst debate, the Newark Public Library cancelled its subscriptions to the rival *New York World* and *Herald*, to be followed by several libraries and elicit praise from the *Nation*. In Allegheny, William Stevenson impatiently weeded the library of a mass of second-rate fiction, from Alger, Southworth and E. P. Roe to the newer "Marion Harland" (Mrs. Terhune), inspiring praise and blame.[21]

The new realism that Larned deplored became a special target of criticism. Unlike erotic fiction, it was held offensive because of its "morbid and unsavory pessimism," its depictions of "diseased souls and distorted lives," of "the Maggies, Arties, and other children of the Jago," who revealed the vice and squalor of all large cities with the "hard clearness of the camera, unsoftened by the tints of art." These conditions might be real, said Helen Haines, a young *LJ* editor and ALA reviewer, who would be one of the profession's most important literary critics. "But we do not choose treatises on psychomania for family reading, nor do we send our sons and daughters to stalebeer dives or opium joints that they may learn what life is." When a novelist exploited the vulgar and repulsive, it became the right and duty of those in charge of those novels "to exercise a censorship in their selection"— censorship of the strictest sort, in fact, since these works were not recommended even for restricted circulation.[22] Despite the acknowledged literary excellence of some of the authors, a young person was considered far better off with the old-fashioned trashy novel than with Fletcher's *God's Failures*, with the "inbruted vulgarity of [Stephen Crane's] *Maggie, a Girl of the Streets*, the perverted hysteria of *A Superfluous Woman*, or the morbid unpleasantness of [George Moore's] *Celibates*." Behind this critique was a developing ideology of conservative populism, whereby William Stevenson, who had weeded his collection of popular drivel, was attacked as a censor for *excluding* works that were "not hurtful" and *including* sensational but excellent fiction.[23]

These reviews, however, were not as fastidious or class-biased as they seem. Helen Haines, who would later be extremely liberal, showed clarity, sensitivity, and scrupulous fairness at this time. She strongly endorsed *The Damnation of Theron Ware*, which the ALA had rejected, as essential reading. Unlike keynote fiction, "it does not make moral weakness attractive or pitiful." It was about a man whose heart was "rotten at the core, but surrounded by a crust of conventionality and seeming fairness" that broke with the first breath of temptation. She recommended *Quo Vadis*, despite its "torture and slaughter," as a restricted book for all fair-sized libraries.

She did not comment on the conservatism of the popular F. Hopkinson Smith's labor novel *Tom Grogan*, but criticized it as "sensational rather than dramatic, strained in effect, and often false to life." Robert Barr's *The Mutable Many*, an important labor novel, gave both sides of a long strike with "common-sense fairness":

The central idea seems to be that, no matter what the right of the cause of labor, and though the cause of capital may have injustice on its side, labor will generally lose in the struggle on account of qualities inherent in itself. The "mutable many"—the mob—lose on account of their very mutability; because they have not the coherence and the organization to carry through their work and gain their ends. The story is crude and has the trail of the journalist, . . . but it is forcible, gives both sides, and I thought it good.[24]

Similarly, Mrs. (Evelyn) Steel's *On the Face of the Waters*, about the Indian Mutiny, was impartial, "too impartial," and true to fact, a bit too sympathetic, but "in implication only," to the natives. Was it suitable for circulation? someone asked. "I do not see," said Miss Haines, "how that question can be raised. . . . It is not written for children. . . . It is about men and women in a time of fierce conflict and unnatural conditions; but I do not see how it can hurt any one, or how its stern teaching can be misinterpreted." Olive Schreiner's *Trooper Peter Halket*, another arraignment of British cruelties in South Africa, was a "politico-religious" tract, with "harrowing" incidents, but she could not see it hurting anyone. The young Ellen Glasgow's *The Descendant*, about an outcast impelled by ambition "to ruthless disregard of all laws," was "very strong, unpleasant in parts," but possessing a "wonderful force in its teaching."[25]

Thus, harsh portrayal, by contemporary standards, was acceptable, and a moral could be subtle. However, these critical standards required not only that sin be punished, but also that it not be made attractive. They ruled out even pathos, or compassion for the morally weak, since they suggested that such traits were excusable. Fairness and balance were seen as important qualities *within a single novel*; thus the distortion in slum fiction was an aesthetic flaw.

The reviewing of nonfiction was also marked by a painstaking concern for fairness. Where an academic reviewer like Franklyn Giddings stressed depth, adequacy of treatment, and degree of duplication of existing works, rather than approach, Josephus Larned focused more on the writer's perspective. Marx's *Revolution and Counterrevolution; or Germany in 1848* showed "with how sane and sound a judgment Marx looked at the revolutionary movements of 1848 in his own country, from which he had already been in exile for several years." John Burgess's *Middle Period, 1817–1958* was poor in style, good in substance, but open to the criticism of leaning backward to be impartial, "almost to the prejudice of the antislavery view sometimes; but it is an honest attempt to deal fairly with those great questions; and . . . it deals with them more fairly, more thoughtfully, more fully and instructively than any other work I know."[26]

"THE OTHER SIDE"

Despite a few outsiders' objections to library "surveillance" (Thomas Wentworth Higginson complained that most books in Boston's Inferno could go into any home), little dissent was expressed within the profession until two librarians at the Boston Public Library exploded in protest. The fact that they expressed their views publicly is itself remarkable, and may be explained by the hiatus in the library's administration between Herbert Putnam's resignation on April 3, 1899, to become Librarian of Congress, and the appointment of his successor, James Whitney, on December 22. The authors in question were Lindsay Swift, author of *Brook Farm* (1900), who worked as an editor, and Worthington C. Ford, a historian and friend of Bowker, the publisher of *LJ*.[27]

Almost apologetically, the *LJ* editor introducing Swift invoked *LJ* as a "parliament" of opinion. Swift's thesis, that even the "highest missionary impulse" could lead to "narrowness of faith and act," represented "the other side." It expressed the "criticism, not hitherto fully voiced or generally recognized in the line of a reaction, perhaps not altogether unwholesome, against a principle which in some cases is carried too far."[28]

Swift's diatribe, delivered to the Massachusetts Library Club, was a wholesale critique of much that was modern in libraries—paternalism, the tendency to decide for others, and a general "managing spirit in library work" that was rooted in "an essential mediocrity." This officiousness underlay such new trends as library work with schools, with their "research" assignments and "deliberate indoctrination" of patriotism, and the new children's rooms, with their narrow fastidiousness and expurgated editions of Shakespeare, the Bible, and Jonathan Swift.

Swift was outraged above all by the book selection committees, "a group mostly of one sex, let us admit, and of a rather narrow social range," that excluded H. G. Wells (*Wheels of Change*) and Rudyard Kipling (*Guns of the Fore and Aft*). All had to be pleased, the clergyman, the lady from the Purity League. "What with one warped mind or another, a book has to be very good or pretty colorless . . . to run the gauntlet."

It was true that the small library with limited funds had to choose carefully. "But the manner of the choice is what disturbs me." The fiction choices of the Massachusetts Library Club (the group he was addressing) reflected either commonplace minds or the harmlessness of the books. Harmlessness generally meant mediocrity, since any "new note in morals or society" immediately suggested "a possible injuriousness."

He found paternalism most evident in three types of literature: vulgar books, books treating sex, and books thought menacing to the social structure (as when a "very earnest and effective library woman" told him that imaginative works would cause workers to be dissatisfied). Vulgarity was the reason for excluding many works, among them the entire genre of slum fiction typified in *Chimmie Fadden*. But Dickens, too, had been attacked for exposing the "horrible substratum of British respectability." *Wheels of Change* was "gloriously" vulgar. And the new slum literature was honest and vital.

Is it to be wondered at that people blessed with the paternal impulse should be the very ones who fail to grasp the great significance of a dawning literature which is to bring forward the life, thoughts, ideals, and actions of the East End of London, the Third Avenue of New York, and the South End of Boston—all teeming with human interest and containing some of the possibilities of the future? If we want intelligent opinions on these books they must be sought not from the tidy inhabitants of Fifth Avenue or Ward Eleven, but from the men and women who are in . . . the main current, newspaper people, college settlement girls, and some—only some, alas!—ministers and priests. These are the people whom I would trust not to turn down a book as vulgar which is dealing with the human tragedy in its humblest phases.

As for books dealing with sex, those most concerned with improper books were "not those whom I would implicitly trust in the wider realm of morals." He did not mean to defend the "deliberately salacious . . .

buzzards . . . always smelling about in our public libraries." But he did object to library restrictions on Émile Zola, Thomas Hardy, and George Meredith.[29]

What he called "paternalism" was obviously the developing professional consciousness of librarians, which linked the missionary spirit— the professional impulse to lead and educate—with censorship. He did defend the librarian's professional autonomy, or prerogative to choose, against laymen, lay book committees, and specialized experts. But he did so in the name of freedom. Against laymen he urged that a library granting one sect a place in the library could not refuse a competing view. Against lay book committees he levelled the charge of paternalism. It was a charge, however, that he raised against librarians, too. For he was not defending professional prerogatives per se, but one view of professionalism that was linked to his view of the library's *uniqueness* as a *non*pedagogic institution.

Hence his objection to experts. Swift held that reliance on *outside* experts (i.e., outside authority) was itself atypical of professions and was useful for libraries only in terms of a broader scheme. Second, the library's criteria for selection differed from specialists' criteria of authority. Scholars had no taste for popular books and were trained to focus on a narrow problem and reject extraneous knowledge. They could not appreciate the broader problem of storing the deviant offshoots that marked the growth of new knowledge. To them the insanities of theosophy, psychic phenomena, osteopathy, and Christian Science were menacing now, as vaccination, transcendentalism, and antislavery opinion once had been. Libraries by contrast had no disciplinary bias; their approach paralleled the successful battle for freedom from theological restriction. Now that freedom from religious interference had been won, the library could not concede any other "interference with intellectual freedom." To try to please all was impossible and demeaning to librarians. Rather than sponsoring "each new fad and excitement," libraries would do well to stand aloof, remaining, like "great secular cathedrals, sanctuaries of learning and freedom," open to all, "strong and vital in themselves."[30]

Swift received an immediate and warm endorsement from John Cotton Dana. Dana had felt "lonesome" in his views on state-supported libraries. But where one was "nobody, not daring to speak," two were a crowd. The library could balance the "inevitable harm of its fundamental paternalism," he held, only by eclecticism. Schools, "born of the rank and file," had to serve the typical and could not encourage genius, but the library could be all things to all men. It might someday be ruled, not by forty copies of *Janice Meredith* and a careful exclusion of all "questionable books" but by inclusion of "all wholesome records of human thought and action."

Yet he could not condemn Boston's book selection committee, and he also defended children's rooms, though they might be too closely "picked over." He even regretted that Swift had confined himself to the "smaller evils of the paternal method" and neglected to mention the "greater danger from the general state-socialism method of the free library." Indeed, Swift's special points were not of great concern; but then, social philosophy was not considered appropriate to *LJ*.[31]

Dana's letter reflected much more than an economic conservative to whom socialism was worse than censorship. His position was that of a man with a stake in a profession. Swift was not professionally active, and he cut ruthlessly to the heart of professional activity and its *internal* censorship. Dana played down that thrust yet perceived it shrewdly enough to try to rescue the system, dismissing restrictive policies as a trivial issue. The reasons are obvious. Swift had parodied what Dana saw as the wave of the future and professional expansion: schools, children's rooms, women's clubs.

The contrast shows again the paradox of peer control. Dana, an iconoclast, had, as a professional leader, to excuse the flaws of his colleagues. Swift, more peripheral, could make a less compromised appeal to the value of freedom—which Dana invoked yet chose not to *perceive* as violated by library policy. His negation, not of the facts, but of their interpretation, shows why the ideology of freedom did not become dominant. It was not central to the profession's key interests.

Where Swift defended freedom in terms of the "democratic principle of least [state] interference," Worthington C. Ford made freedom in libraries a corollary of the functions of the state. The values he expressed—anti-imperialism, concern with class legislation and business and labor monopoly, increasing stratification and the narrowing of opportunity—suggest Eastern Progressivism on the verge of acceptance of state intrusion, in part to save capitalism. In that context Ford defined the function of the state: to permit but not mandate, to provide the opportunity for university education but not require it, to maintain libraries but not intrude beyond this enabling activity.

Thus censorship, the imposition of uniformity in libraries, violated the limits of state action. No one could dictate what good literature was or expect it to transform people. "No city was ever reformed by Sunday-school books . . . any more than our associated charities have abolished poverty." Good work they had done, but it would be "Chimmie Fadden and his speech who will reach those who stand in need of modification, for reformation is out of the question."

Yet if the library could not reform, it could not ignore the world of *Chimmie Fadden, Tales of Mean Streets,* or *Child of the Jago*. "The West End cannot be obliterated by sprinkling rose water over it, nor can an anarchist be changed (however much improved) by giving him a bath and clean linen." No battle was won by running from the enemy. The

Chartists had been quieted by concession; German socialism had been reduced through compromise to "a harmless and rather wholesome activity." Similarly, social agitation in America—the Negro issue, silver agitation, labor strikes—could not be passed over without an effort to understand "their motives and extent, or neglected with eyes shut and scented handkerchief to the nose." Nor could one "hold up one's hands in holy horror at what seems to us social heresy and political madness. These phases must be studied, and the conditions upon which they are being based questioned and put on trial."

The criminal and pauper were as valid objects of study as captains of industry. The people might speak in a strange voice or fail to express their needs, but they suggested reforms or awaited the men who could express their inarticulate wants.

It is in the public library that the record of its pleas and complaints should be accumulated and find as ready a hearing as a history of the past and the policies of factions and parties long since dead. Herr Most, Eugene Debs, John Altgeld, and George Francis Train, suspects and nondescripts, should take their place with Jacob Riis, Josiah Flynt, and Wyckoff, who have lived in slums and served as tramps; with Lloyd, Ely, Gunton, Herron and Mayo Smith, who have sought to express in more careful or scientific terms the social problems of the day. The radical of yesterday is the conservative of today. In a great library there is room for all, and in the extended use of a great library lies one of the best correctives for ills afflicting the body social, for it is equally suggestive as to cause and remedy. Catholicity is its only safe rule, for no man is cursed with omniscience, or with omnipotence to give it effect. . . . One of the features of the Roman Catholic church is that its doors are always open, and spiritual comfort may be had at any time and for every occasion. Does not the Library offer as timely a privilege, though more worldly, and give an opportunity for amusement, instruction, assistance, and improvement?[32]

The language that Swift and Ford used intimates that women were responsible for the suppression of slum stories and other vulgar books. The norms of censorship, however, were strongly advocated by men, by Josephus Larned, by male members of the Massachusetts Library Club who were vocal at the 1896 conference, by William Howard Brett, who restricted the works of Fielding and affirmed, democratically enough, that he would prefer "not . . . to buy anything which cannot be placed in general circulation unless it has extraordinary merit or value." He preferred to ban a book rather than have a large collection that was not available to all.[33]

Herbert Putnam at Boston, though close to Ford in background and personal ties, lived very well with censorship. As Massachusetts Library Club president in 1897, he feared that the librarian had "a more difficult problem . . . in this age of free thought, free speech, and unlicensed publication." The library had to be "progressive in many things, but conservative where it concerns a question of morals and social order"; librarians were urged to "use their influence in counteracting the revolutionary tendency of the age." A few months later, reporters queried the library on Putnam's edict refusing unrestricted access to writings of French and German socialists. As Lindsay Swift described it, Putnam felt that "rabid" anarchistic publications could remain in the library, "but Mr. Putnam and his assistants reserve to themselves the right to choose the readers, and most commonsense people will agree. . . . The average man of anarchistic or socialistic tendencies is not qualified by education or judgment to read the works." But Putnam quickly denied such an avowal, insisting that the only restricted books were the salacious works in the Inferno that had been there when he arrived and that could be withdrawn by adults upon special application.[34]

The conflicts of the 1890s also clarified the norm of impartiality—the "growing feeling," as one *LJ* writer put it, that the library, more than other agencies of civilization, had to "know and recognize no distinctions" if it was to "occupy its ideal position toward the entire community." At a library dedication in 1900 in Providence, Rhode Island, where an important academic freedom controversy on bimetallism, involving the president of Brown University, had recently taken place, that norm of impartiality was expressed by a trustee and a librarian, "independently," as the *LJ* writer admiringly noted, "with no knowledge on the part of either of what the other had to say." Trustees, said one library trustee, had

no opinion. Theology, sociology, politics, economics are to us abstract ideas. . . . Our business is to furnish, so far as we are able, the means for acquiring information, and then to say, *come, study, think and decide*. [All italics in original.]

The librarian, William Foster, also defined the library's commitment to the "entire public" as one recognizing "absolutely no class distinctions, whether of *religion*, of *politics*, or of *school of thought*." [Italics in original.][35]

That principle could have been an argument for freedom in collections, but in fact it was not, as is clear from a symposium on "what classes, if any, should have access to the shelves in large libraries?" Purd Wright advised that "collections of so-called 'Inferno' nature should be behind dark doors"—that is, opaque doors, as against glass doors or wire screens, so that the unsuspecting would never know their contents while the serious student would know how to get what he wanted through the card catalog. William Foster explained why his experimental "Standard Library" in Providence, an open-shelf collection, had no works of nonfiction but only works of imagination. The reason was that the problem of selection, which was crucial in a library in which only some shelves were open, was easier to solve. The literature of inspiration, or imagination, could involve only authors whose reputations were secure, without question, and not likely to change in the future.

Time, with its long unerring finger, has long ere this decided the rank of nearly every author admitted into this select company. . . . In the literature of information, on the other hand, the best books of today are by no means the best books of tomorrow. . . . Such a collection would be in a constant state of flux and reflux. Nor would it be possible to make the entries of the best books under certain headings without awakening serious challenge.

To take an instance which I have already cited—political economy—the ideal treatment of a subject like this varies very much according as it is the work of Henry C. Carey, William G. Sumner, or Henry George, and the adherents of one of the three would be likely to consider the work of the other two as merely rubbish.[36]

Thus the paradox of accountability, of populism combined with censorship, defined the choices for open shelves. The criteria were the test of time and unchallengeable reputation, or consensus, which defined quality in fiction and nonfiction. Of course, both the criterion and the example ruled out controversy, on which by definition there is no consensus. Moreover, criteria of literary quality and intellectual authority were conflated. Because disputed opinions were considered rubbish by some, their quality declined. If the Providence library excluded William Graham Sumner and Henry George for lack of consensus, there was little chance for Eugene Debs. The impartial or "colorless" library was indeed without dogma; it was governed by neutrality through exclusion.

Thus the goal of quality, defined in that particular way, ruled out controversy or the legitimacy of dissent. That intellectual terrain had so recently been reviewed by Worthington Ford, but with little effect. Freedom of access meant open shelves and dark doors.

6.

CENSORSHIP, FREEDOM, AND PROFESSIONAL AUTONOMY: A THEORETICAL REVIEW

By 1900, a full-blown defense of freedom had emerged in response to the new literature, even as censorship also emerged. The defense of freedom had several versions, the antistatist (Dana, Swift), the form that accepted limited state intervention (Ford), and the version that endorsed state activism in social reform (Crunden). These versions differed along the dimensions of what Seymour Martin Lipset calls economic and noneconomic liberalism. Economic liberalism involves issues of state intervention and the distribution of property. Noneconomic liberalism is relevant to such issues as civil rights, civil liberties, and tolerance.[1] Nineteenth-century liberals endorsed noneconomic liberalism but were conservative, by twentieth-century standards, on economic issues. Twentieth-century liberals are liberal on both counts. Dana and Swift reflected nineteenth-century, Ford and Crunden twentieth-century, liberalism.

This study suggests a further refinement of noneconomic liberalism. Most advocates of freedom accepted moral censorship in public statements, though they were not fanatic about it. Poole, Crunden, and Tessa Kelso are examples. Attitudes toward free speech, then and now (as the positions of some lawyers and feminists make clear today), will differ for freedom of political expression and freedom to publish morally or sexually offensive literature.

Because they were united on the issues of noneconomic liberalism, men with such different political positions as Dana and Crunden shared a commitment to freedom. Because of their different political positions, they differed in defining the function of the library adhering to that freedom. Dana limited the library's educational role to the permissive one of self-direction; implicit in its promise was a commitment to the ascending middle class. It did not necessarily oppose reform; it was indifferent to it. Crunden gave the library an active educational role in publicizing unconventional utopian or reformist ideas. It retained a missionary function, and its promise lay in an unknown future.

These were all minority views and the views of men who were dissenters, whose minority positions or *non*professional (i.e., nonlibrary) commitments were reflected in their views. Dana was an Eastern conservative in a Western state. References in Crunden's 1897 speech indicate that he was a Western populist and a Christian Socialist, concerned with social change and reform. Worthington Ford reflects both Eastern Progressivism and a scholarly concern with untrammeled intellectual inquiry, while Swift showed the same concern with freedom of ideas coupled with antistatism.

By contrast, most professional leaders supported censorship, differing only on the degree of censorship required. Professional elites may have believed in freedom, but they did not affirm it publicly, and even John Cotton Dana compromised his position when it came to criticizing a particular library. The dominant constellation of values was populism, neutrality, and censorship; the subordinate constellation of values was elitism, neutrality, and censorship.

Professional hagiography has not made heroes out of these early advocates of freedom. Only Dana is remembered—but largely for his utilitarian, careerist, and potentially conservative achievements: originating library public relations and launching services to business. By contrast, the academic casualties and victors in the academic freedom disputes of the 1890s are part of an inspiring history of freedom for university professors. They involve such figures as Richard Ely, John R. Commons, Edward Bemis, J. Allen Smith, the minister-teacher George Herron, E. A. Ross, and others. All but Ely lost their positions because of their ideas.[2]

Among librarians, at least two seem to have lost their positions because they had the wrong ideas for their communities; Frederick Crunden claimed such victims obliquely in 1897. But the contemporary reader of his references can only guess at their identities. One was apparently John Cotton Dana, who moved back north shortly after the 1896 election. The other may have been Tessa Kelso, who resigned from the Los Angeles Public Library in 1895.[3]

Although a comparison of librarianship and academic teaching can only be preliminary and exploratory, it has a bearing on the structural approach, adopted here, to the analysis of motivation, in contrast to psychological (or sexist) interpretations of the timidity and conservatism of the library profession as a whole, and of the failure of leaders to take risks to carry out professional values. A comparison of the two professions also sheds light on the reason why different defenses of professional autonomy emerged in the two professions at different times.

Libraries and universities had different structural locations in their communities, and librarians and university professors had different functions and role relationships. Faculty served a select student clientele and, despite governance by businessmen trustees, were at one remove from their communities. Public libraries served their entire communities and depended on their local communities for economic support. Their chief administrators were involved with community influentials. Thus their position was more like that of university presidents, who were more cautious and conservative than their faculties. At the University of Chicago, President Harper fired Edward Bemis. Albion Small, head of its sociology department and eager to advance its reputation, concurred in public criticism of Bemis despite sympathy with Bemis's views. At Stanford University, President David Starr Jordan eventually yielded to Mrs. Leland Stanford in dismissing two professors, one of them E. A. Ross.[4]

Nor was a code of academic freedom adopted. It would not be until 1915. Richard Ely never invoked academic freedom as an ideological defense when he was put on trial. In fact, he carefully maintained that *if the charges against him were true*, he should be dismissed. Nor did the academic community intervene formally in any controversy until 1897, when Benjamin Andrews, Brown university president, was dismissed on the issue of bimetallism, an issue well within the framework of conventional debate. These early controversies helped determine which battles the profession would choose to fight. Academic economists adopted a more technical, less critical, concept of their role and undertook problems (e.g., theories of marginal utility) that did not challenge the economic framework, as did the institutional economics of Richard Ely's radical school. This shift in focus is true for Ely himself.[5]

Thus was the tension between advocacy and objectivity resolved. Judicious problem selection made it possible collectively to *avoid* issues in which academic freedom would have to be invoked. It set limits to permissible debate and hence the arenas of discussion—a process that allowed individual careerism and collective ambition to coincide. It pinpointed issues on which the association could take a stand, in which competence was more clearly demonstrated, and in which the advocate did not compromise the scientist.

Librarians also chose the more rewarding paths, in terms of esteem and potential success, that did not present impossible goals and insuperable dilemmas. In their careful interpretations, the dominant role was the occupational role; like members of other new professions (as Wiebe describes them), they were interested in social reform insofar as it met their professional needs. Moving from a focus on workers, they did not have to become their advocates. Adopting a position of neutrality, they protected themselves from controversy. Confining themselves largely to the elitist-populist issue, they did not have to cope with the thornier problems of the intellectual authority of new ideas. Adopting the norm of censorship at a time when books were held to have potentially harmful effects, they adhered to a popular definition of the public interest. Their professional code had the function of reducing conflict with members of the community by stipulating the professionally approved behavior.[6]

In fact, their posture was uniquely professional as definitions of professionalism go. The librarian has since been criticized for having little power over his clientele, for being a "gatekeeper who can exclude no one." According to this view of professionalism:

> Intellectually, the librarian must work within the client's limitations, instead of imposing his professional categories, conceptions and authority on the client. In other professions, too, the practitioner must understand the client's notions, but only enough to elicit adequate information and cooperation from him. The practitioner can solve the problem even if the client never understands what the professional is doing.
>
> Thus serving the reader means "helping" him, learning his wishes and satisfying them. This comes dangerously close to the position taken by a minority of librarians, that their duty is to give the people what they want. In such a conception not only must the librarian—a clerk serving his customers—compete with commercial entertainment, but he yields a central meaning of service, the commitment to run personal risks in order to fulfil a high obligation to society, to *educate* [italics in original] the reader and the public. This strain between the wishes and the real needs of a clientele is perhaps to be found in all professions, but in established professions more often it is resolved by the professional's decision.[7]

These words have a familiar ring. They are the words that early librarians used to define their function and establish their professionalism. Librarians of the late nineteenth century did perceive themselves as superior to laymen. Moreover, however solicitous they were of clients, they saw their social obligation as precisely to educate; it was the focus of their missionary zeal. The value of censorship established both their expertise and their ethical obligation. It provided one basis of the librarian's professional autonomy of the client (though not of the trustee, as did the value of academic freedom). Have librarians, then, become less professional?

That question may not be answerable within the framework of this study, which does not trace the development of an aspiring profession, along a continuum, toward a closer approximation to an ideal type. Rather the task is to seek out the ways in which a profession, as a group with material and ideal interests, seeks to advance both sets of interests and to establish a place in the sun—not a claim to unequal rewards. That pursuit takes place in an environment bristling at once with potential conflict and rich alternatives for work and professional enhancement, for pursuing, and choosing among, several goals. These goals, and the values that support them, will vary with the historical situation.

On the basis of the findings in the preceding chapters, the following generalizations are offered:

1. A profession, like other groups, has several goals and alternative ways of reaching them. Pursuing its mission with a combination of idealism and pragmatism, a profession will develop norms and controls that mesh individual motives with institutional goals,[8] defining goals that enhance professional prestige and individual careers.

It follows that an element of rational calculation will enter into the formulation of those goals themselves. Such a process of "rationalizing" the professional domain is not a denial of dedication. It eliminates the confusion of individual experimentation with priorities and solutions.

2. Since choices must be made among competing, and sometimes conflicting, goals, these choices will not eliminate conflict, for unfulfilled goals are still a source of "strain" or potential conflict. One aspect of rationalization involves choosing goals and priorities, and distributing energy, to minimize such conflict.

3. Thus, role-set conflicts become sources of individual autonomy[9] and, it is hypothesized in this study, professional autonomy. That autonomy is limited, but the limits do not dictate choices; they determine the range of alternatives from which choices are made. In science, research grants direct and limit the choice of problems without compromising the intellectual integrity of the research. For librarians, service to children and schools helped them to expand and ensure their usefulness.

Autonomy is also limited by the remaining conflict in the role-set, since no choice among alternatives meets all needs.

4. Just as role-set conflicts can be seen as sources of autonomy, or professional freedom, so can the different strategies for coping with conflict, for the librarian can choose among them. He may invoke professional values. But he can also favor the most interested role partners (Dana), restrict the role-set to exclude undesirables (Larned), pit clients against trustees (Dewey), defer to the most powerful member, segregate role activities (children's cards, Inferno collections), conceal some activities (dark doors). Thus, inconsistent values can coexist in one social system if they are distributed among different statuses.[10] Professionals can also engage in role negotiation, in issue, client, and status selection.

5. Invoking professional values is not always the best way to handle conflict. Their usefulness depends on several factors. One is the degree to which they are accepted in the community. The notion of censorship

or freedom requires a community mandate, acceptance of the librarian's values and authority.[11] If the norm is not seriously challenged, it is effective in the everyday operation of the library. Another factor is the possibility of backing up the simple assertion of values with other mechanisms, like the mobilization of community support. The support of colleagues alone may give the librarian courage to act upon his principles, but it will not ensure the outcome.

If professional norms are seen as ethical, rather than functional, norms—that is, if they are treated in terms of the Weberian ethic of ultimate ends, without regard for consequences, rather than the ethic of responsibility, which recognizes political and practical limitations, they raise the problem of "the imperious immediacy of interests." A profession is never totally autonomous and wins its prerogatives largely on the basis of its legitimacy to laymen. If scientists ignore the social consequences of the disinterested pursuit of truth, their efforts deprive them of social support. If librarians pursue innovative ideas single-mindedly, their efforts will boomerang. Neither science nor other professions can safely challenge the ruling values of society. Thus, the single-minded pursuit of a single value may produce its opposite as opponents react and resist the principle. Instead of reducing conflict in the role-set, the invocation of a norm can *increase* conflict.[12]

6. Professional leaders do not prefer to invoke values, certainly not as an ethic of ultimate ends. They may believe in and act upon these values, but they prefer not to use them as ideological tools. The invocation of norms hinders flexibility. It fails to acknowledge *inherent* conflict—*sociological* ambivalence—in the situation. It ignores the varying interpretations and applications that can be given to these norms. It neglects the possibility of opposition in the community. So librarians were warned *not* to announce their book bans in order not to spark demand. In contrast to the claims of some sociologists[13] that professional norms are invoked but violated, norms were adhered to but not invoked so as to minimize conflict.

7. If the codes of ethics of new professions are vague, it is not because their knowledge base is undeveloped, as Barber maintains, but because of inherent conflict in the situation. Professions adopt codes of particular kinds for various reasons. Aspiring professions adopt codes by imitation and some established professions do not have codes. Ministers and scientists do not; nor did academicians in the 1890s, despite the need for a code of academic freedom.[14]

8. Professional leaders, stressing the pragmatic function of the code, are likely to avoid defining it too precisely, and to invoke it only when other mechanisms can also be used, with a view to its instrumental value. They are likely to prefer other strategies than invoking the code in order to reduce conflict.

Figure 6.1
LIBRARIANS' POSITIONS ON CENSORSHIP AND FREEDOM, IDEALISTIC
AND PRAGMATIC VERSIONS, 1876–1900

	CENSORSHIP		FREEDOM	
ETHIC OF RESPONSIBILITY	Winsor	1881	Boston Public Library	1881
	LJ	1881		
	Brett	1889		
	Fletcher	1889	Dana	1899
	LJ	1888		
	LJ	1889		
	PW	1889		
	PW	1890		
	Larned (fiction meeting)	1896		
	PL	1897		
	Putnam	1897		
	Haines	1897		
	Brett	1900		
	Foster	1900		
	Purdy	1900		
ETHIC OF ULTIMATE ENDS	Hubbard	1881	Poole	1876
	Perkins	1885	Poole	1886
	Hubbard	1889	Crunden	1897
	Pennock	1900	Swift	1899
			Ford	1900

It follows that elites not only define and affirm their associations' values, as Barber states, but that they may also compromise their code and overlook its violation, even define that violation as acceptable for the sake of group cohesion. This conclusion is suggested by the structural vulnerability of leaders and the fact that professions protect their inept, conceal their mistakes, and adopt attitudes of *noblesse oblige* toward their colleagues.[15]

Elites are therefore also likely to avoid defining a situation as warranting the assertion of the professional code. Everett Hughes has described the inconvenience of such overzealous idealism:

The ardor of a person with a peculiar mission may become an insufferable reproach to his colleagues and contain a trace of insubordination to his superiors. The neophyte who is too exalted can be borne, but a certain relaxation of ardor is demanded in course of time. In a well-established institution, ardor must be kept within the limits demanded by authority and decorum.[16]

9. Idealists or fanatics are not likely to be leaders, and are likely to invoke norms in a struggle for power. These are strategies, not indications of insincerity, and they may connote idealism.

The points in the preceding propositions are illustrated in the distribution of opinions in Figure 6.1. They indicate that, for varying motives, professional leaders adhered to or tolerated censorship policies but did not erect them into absolutes. Idealistic proponents of censorship or freedom were generally not leaders and used their weapons to attack authority. Poole and Crunden may seem to be exceptions in the "freedom" column, but both had supporting climates of opinion in their communities. They did not influence their association on these issues. The most interesting cases are those of Hubbard and Perkins, Swift and Ford, all of whom challenged authority in their local communities—a practice inconsistent with ALA leaders' policies of coopting influentials.

These generalizations derive from one profession in one time period. Whether they can be extended is the subject of the remaining chapters.

PART II

Structures of Ambivalence: 1900–1922

7.

THE LIBRARIAN AS A CENSOR: 1900–1908

"Some are born great; some achieve greatness; some have greatness thrust upon them." It is in this last way that the librarian has become a censor of literature. Originally the custodian of volumes placed in his care by others, he has ended by becoming in these latter days much else, including a selector and distributor. . . . As the library's audience becomes larger, as its educational functions spread and are brought to bear on more and more of the young and immature, the duty of sifting its material becomes more imperative.
—Arthur E. Bostwick, ALA President, 1908

The years from 1900 through World War I saw the rise and fall of the Progressive "movement"—a constellation of shifting coalitions and issue publics that was marked by a curious blend of political liberalism and moral conservatism, civil service and business reform, blue laws and temperance crusades, antiprostitution campaigns and the persistence of censorship norms in the new century.[1] This combination of political liberalism and moral conservatism was reflected in library service. The idea of freedom was barely mentioned until the end of that period, and censorship crystallized as a symbol of the librarian's role, autonomy, and guiding function.

The dimensions of tolerance of the Progressive "era" can be symbolized by several key events. The Socialist party, formed in 1901, grew in legitimacy and influence, especially at the state and local levels, culminating in the 1912 election in which Eugene Debs won 6 percent of the vote. On the other hand, deportation laws for alien radicals and anarchists, passed in 1903, permitted summary executive decision to eliminate the dissident actor, as an alternative to suppressing his speech. The International Workers of the World, formed in 1905, was persecuted with vicious vigilante action in the Northwest and with sabotage frameups, while anarchists like Emma Goldman were cruelly mistreated, in large cities and small, with little protest from labor unions or from most Socialists, who sought respectability.[2]

A rich and varied literature on social problems was being produced by the radicals of the 1890s—Ely, Bemis, Commons, and Ross—who were now assimilated into the new order; by government and foundations; by the new mass magazines, *McClure's*, *Munsey's*, *Cosmopolitan*, which carried muckraking to a vast public. Some of this literature was resisted. In 1899 R. R. Bowker (publisher of *LJ* and *PW*) helped Gustavus Myers publish his *History of Tammany Hall*, which eight publishers, including Putnam, had turned down for fear of its political consequences. Myers's later *History of the Great American Fortunes* was issued by the Socialist publisher Charles Kerr. Labor magazines were supplemented with three Socialist journals, including *Appeal to Reason*, which first published Upton Sinclair's *The Jungle*. Other works and authors included Josiah Flynt's studies of tramps, Owen Kildare on city life, Socialist Algie M. Simons's *Packingtown*, Robert Hunter's *Poverty*, William English Walling, and John Spargo.[3]

In literature, naturalism was stunted with the early deaths of Stephen Crane and Frank Norris and the 1900 suppression of Theodore Dreiser's *Sister Carrie* by its own publisher, Doubleday, a blow that resulted in Dreiser's gloomy ten-year silence. The great novels of these years were Henry James's masterpieces exploring the themes of adultery and extramarital sex—*The Ambassadors*, *The Golden Bowl*, *The Wings of the Dove*, *What Maisie Knew*. Revolution was brewing in England, however. George Bernard Shaw made the constraints of Victorian morality the subject of his plays, which were suppressed. H. G. Wells and May Sinclair (a follower of Shaw and Wells) wrote and advocated controversial problem novels, studies of the lower middle class, and espousals of socialism and feminism. The first popular novel to be banned in America, in 1908, was the British novelist Eleanor Glyn's best-selling *Three Weeks*.[4]

The new problem novel ranged in theme from Progressive Winston Churchill's treatment of political corruption and David Graham Phillips's exposés of political and economic corruption and studies of marriage and women's status to the labor and Socialist novels of Vida Scudder, Isaac K. Friedman, Upton Sinclair, and occasionally Jack London. Between 1900 and 1909, twenty-one radical novels were published. At the University of Chicago, Robert Herrick followed his older colleague Henry Fuller with critiques of American commercialism.[5]

THE CARNEGIE ERA

From 1899 to 1917 libraries expanded enormously as Carnegie gifts spread a network of small libraries and branches across the country.

His sponsorship did not go unchallenged. It was opposed by labor groups, in portions of the South, by taxpayers reluctant to supplement his support, by ethnic groups objecting to a new public agency. In New York, Carnegie was charged with having taken workers' earnings to give libraries to men living in hovels. Frank Hill (Brooklyn) admitted that librarians could not judge whether the funds might have been better spent, but only whether "we as trustees have made the best possible use" of them.[6]

Librarians also had to respond to complaints that reading could be frivolous or even harmful. William Dean Howells warned about "reading to stupidity," and the distant Lord Rosebery fretted that reading would destroy independent thinking, that "stagnant literature" would produce "intellectual malaria." John Shaw Billings, head of the newly established New York Public Library, apologized that he could not prove, statistically, that the "library experiment" reduced crime, increased happiness, or helped inventors and captains of industry. But it did reduce the power of the demagogue, and it relaxed tired readers without the aftereffects of soporifics. Arthur Bostwick (NYPL) also disclaimed warnings of "fiction drunkenness" with the dubious assurance that "harmful literature is excluded, but we cannot be expected to see that books which in themselves are not injurious are not sometimes used to excess."[7]

The populist case for recreational reading was strengthened, however, as competition from new forms of leisure increased. From 1910 on, librarians defended large fiction collections as antidotes to commercial fiction, cheap theater, and the film, to which workers' starved imaginations impelled them.[8]

As cities became preponderantly centers of foreign-born populations, the worker was increasingly the immigrant, and Americanization became a dominant goal of the library. As an instrument of social cohesion based on value consensus, it would create citizens out of a heterogeneous population. Henry Legler, an immigrant himself, defended both melting-pot and cultural pluralist theories in library work.[9]

Though these efforts seem to imply indoctrination, librarians were at the liberal end of a spectrum of opinion whose conservative extreme was expressed in warnings of race suicide. They were aligned with cultural liberals who pleaded tolerance, with citizens who remembered their immigrant roots, with businessmen who wanted a large and cheap labor market. And they were opposed to other strata: to intellectuals like E. A. Ross and John R. Commons, who objected to immigration on both racial and economic grounds; to labor and its "strange alliance" with patricians against immigrants.[10]

Librarians' focus on the nonwork role of the client allowed them to ignore the divisions between labor and immigrant and address both at once. They sympathized with labor's struggle and could see what shorter work hours would mean for library service. But they did little to forge class consciousness in a period of continuing conflict marked by strikes at Coeur d'Aléne, Cripple Creek, and Danbury, by the Triangle fire, the Paterson strike, the Ludlow massacre. In Cripple Creek a few years before the famous strike, Big Bill Haywood remembered, the miners had had

8000 volumes in their library, housed in a new union building. This fact was typical. The Western Federation of Miners had increased from 12,000 members in 1896 to 25,000 in 1901 and all over the Rocky Mountains they were building new union halls, conducting classes, holding debates and lectures on everything from the possibility of a nationwide industrial union to the drama and English literature. It was this sudden predilection for thinking on the part of men who felt they were as capable as any Americans living that frightened the mine owners more than the miners' determination to defend their homes and jobs.[11]

Librarians' legends focused rather on individual mobility, on Edison in Detroit, Jack London in San Francisco, Wilbur Wright in Dayton, all reading in the library. But the neglect of labor advocacy does not signify repressiveness. Crunden saw no conflict between requesting Carnegie funds and opening his library to all users. In one week at the St. Louis Public Library Crunden branch in 1911 (soon after Crunden's death), an array of groups including Socialists, labor groups, and the IWW met in the library. Marilla Freeman sought Socialist party endorsement of her socialism booklist. Even a union leader whose views were solicited by Lutie Stearns (then with the Wisconsin Library Commission) did not ask for an activist library program. It was one thing to host groups, another to engage in partisan campaigns.[12]

What "partisan" meant, however, varied from community to community. Where St. Louis hosted an array of political groups, the New York Public Library denied its meeting rooms to political groups, the women's movement, or a mass meeting to oppose tenement legislation. Although the New York policy suggests a less secure library in a polarized community, the distinction between civic and political activity was itself characteristic of the Progressive era, in which centers of political power moved away from the local unit, and the notion of a public interest transcending and reconciling political and class divisions was entrenched.[13]

The dominant ideology stressed the "transpolitical" state in arbitration and maintenance of social cohesion. In the 1902 anthracite strike, Theodore Roosevelt established that image by acting as arbiter, not protector of property. Government and research agencies sought neutral scientific information, and Justice Brandeis used objective social science data in his briefs. Business professed interest in social reform: Rockefeller and Schiff served on a committee studying the condition of tenements. A National Civic Federation linked Samuel Gompers with J. P. Morgan and Mark Hanna, even while the National Association of Manufacturers launched its campaign for an open shop. In 1913 Henry Legler praised the responsible businessmen who had become socially aware.[14]

The emphasis on individual mobility, recreation, and the library as a cultural center made it unlikely that the choice of goals would occasion controversy; so did the emphasis on civic, as distinct from political, concerns. Yet the appeal to the values of the dominant class did not necessarily compromise the library. With the expanding economy of the early twentieth century, reform could be effected with the social surplus. "The fear of Bolshevism had not yet taken hold; a change in attitude toward the working class and the urban poor was possible."[15] More than that, one cannot impute to reformers omniscience about the dynamics of social stability and change. They were limited by their own perspectives.

Censorship was still a familiar term in the elitist-populist debate because of its association with professional guidance. Elitists like William Foster (Providence) and Horace Wadlin (Boston), who restricted fiction purchases, defended their standards against charges of censorship, with only an occasional protest that a novel was called "wholesome" as if it were some kind of cheese. Populists like James Hosmer (Minneapolis) opposed paternalism, "overofficious guidance," and any effort to assume "to any great extent the character of the censor." Anna Rockwell (New Britain, Conn.) saw most would-be censorship as personal, variable, a matter of taste. She insisted that the tastes of working girls were purer than those who wanted to blacklist E. P. Roe, and she defended the "plain people" whom the politicians heeded against the elitism of the Albany school, Putnam, Dana, and Stevenson, expert scholars in London or Washington, and all ALA committees.[16]

Censorship also operated as a form of responsiveness to community demand, reflecting the library's neutrality in factional disputes. The new New York Public Library's position on partisan material recalls that of the first public library, a half-century earlier, in Boston. Like Boston, which had faced both opposition to secular encroachment and efforts at partisan control, New York City in 1901 faced Catholic and other sects that opposed Carnegie libraries for the same reasons that they objected to free schools. These groups also sought to censor books in both agencies. Such demands, said John Shaw Billings, the library's director, would doubtless increase if it were thought they would succeed. The question would "usually be decided for each locality by political party requirements, which vary much at short intervals." There was no immediate danger to libraries from this form of opposition, "except for a short time in some limited locality."[17]

He was more concerned that public opinion was less tolerant in matters of morals and manners than on religious issues, and he advised that such opinion be respected. His solution was to keep the materials out of branches but keep them in the central reference library. There, selection had to be broader, since "even the most ardent propagandist" would want to know what his opponents were saying in order to specify their errors and would not object to finding their publications in the reference library—"provided they are carefully put away for the use of experts like himself and are not placed on open shelves consulted by the general public."[18]

Arthur Bostwick, his assistant, also mentioned the idea of representing both sides as a suggestion, not an assumption: "An impartial book is hard to find; . . . I am not sure that two partisan books, one on each side, with the reader as judge, do not constitute a winning combination." Violent and personal polemics, however, were out of bounds. As the library supplied all creeds, classes, and schools with their own literature, while each complained about attacks on its own tenets, the library could use such protests, though they were often unjustified, to weed out its collection.[19]

DILEMMAS OF CHOICE

As library collections developed, and knowledge changed over time, the dilemmas of accepting new and not yet authoritative knowledge, and of retaining or discarding obsolete knowledge, became more acute. The problem stems from the simple economic fact of scarcity. Libraries cannot buy everything and must choose the most authoritative literature without closing themselves off from new knowledge. As knowledge changes, moreover, they must put aside dated materials without falling victim to intellectual fads and destroying the structure of intellectual development.

The problem resembles the dilemma science confronts between the requirement that it be open to new ideas yet critical of any new claim to knowledge. Hence Michael Polanyi, the physicist whose own theory of adsorption waited decades before it was accepted, defends scientific dogmatism, despite the hindrance it presents to innovation, on the grounds that otherwise scientific advance—the cumulation of knowledge—is impossible.[20]

Broached in the 1890s, the issue surfaced again in 1902 when Richard Ely, director of the University of Wisconsin school of economics, assailed a proposal to the ALA for a comprehensive system of expert reviews in all fields that would systematize thinking and discourage the "crank" literature in economics and sociology that was, according to its proponent, "attempting to force society into false channels." For Ely, the system was a menace to scientific progress. The proposed authorities did not exist. Journals were partisan and sometimes vindictive, reviewers young and inexperienced, "zealous for some sect." Should such reviews be "crystallized" into a permanent library apparatus? Social sciences, especially, lacked objective standards, and codifying such knowledge could produce what Bagehot had called a "crust," hindering scientific development.

We have been laboring for years to obtain scientific freedom, freedom in teaching, freedom in learning, freedom in expression. . . . Indeed, every new movement has to struggle to make itself felt, and to struggle precisely against those who control the most respectable avenues of publication; against the very ones who would be selected to give expert opinions and to make evaluations of literature.

To maintain a fluid current of opinion and the opportunity for change, libraries had a duty to watch impartially the struggles among schools of thought and above all to keep open a "free way for truth."[21]

Ironically, Ely imposed on libraries a stricter standard for freedom—receptivity to new ideas—than science itself demanded, while librarians sought an authority no less strict and no less responsible than that of science. Libraries faced the dilemma, as Ernest Richardson (Princeton) described it, "always a double one," of serving in the discovery of new knowledge and in the diffusion of common knowledge.[22] It was the latter function that public libraries would carry out. In effect, then, ideas had to stand the test of time. (The same solution, in fact, was proposed for fiction, too, so that libraries would not be filled with the unwanted best sellers of yesteryear.)

Obsolete knowledge was an equally complex problem. In 1902 Harvard president Charles W. Eliot charged that libraries would have to discard "dead" books, a demand so disturbing to the professional conscience that four ALA presidents (among others) addressed themselves to it. In 1911 Lord Rosebery gave the issue new form when, dedicating a British library, he ungraciously worried that vapid novels, "forgotten science, superseded history," would be the staple of the new public libraries. Sir Edmund Gosse, House of Lords librarian, echoed that the Carnegie libraries in England were producing an absolute nightmare. He had long favored an "enormous destruction of books," preferring select libraries like those in London drawing rooms.[23]

Newspapers took up the debate. Who would choose the books to burn, complained a writer in the *London Mail*, Betty Barnes the cook? In America John Thomson (Philadelphia Free Library), interviewed for the Philadelphia *Public Ledger*, called a dead book a "vile phrase." One might store old editions, but "beware of burning them," for students needed them to trace a theory that might be branching into wholly unexpected lines of work. How would Rosebery and Gosse look to posterity were they allowed through the great libraries of St. Petersburg, Paris, and London?[24]

Carnegie, however, voiced only airy accord with his critics. Thousands of books could be "reverently entombed in the basement" for the "curious pedant," to make room for new and indispensable books.

"You do not agree then," said the reporter, "with the policy of our great libraries not to exclude any books on moral grounds, but merely to supervise their reading?"

"I hesitate to differ with my good friends, the librarians," answered Carnegie, "but I would err on the safe side. Certain books I would consign to flames and think I was doing God's service thereby, books in the category of pornography."[25]

For the small library, then, said the *LJ* editor, the problem of censorship was solved. If only one book could be bought, it would likely be the one of equal literary rank that was also unobjectionable to the critic of morals, though the problem was compounded if a leading and popular novelist discussed matters unsuitable for fiction.[26]

The censor's role was clearest in children's work. An extreme, though happily rare, case of professional zeal was the 1903 censorship crusade conducted by Electra Doren, librarian of the Dayton Public Library, to combat the great number of "pernicious and immoral books . . . outside of those usually tabooed," that were available to "all classes of children and youth." She had seen that if libraries had aggressively to instill a love of books, they had to fight bad ones as aggressively. Once inquiry began "there seemed no end to the evidence." Miss Doren was invited to speak at PTAs, women's clubs, men's clubs—twenty-three groups in five months. A mass meeting of citizens was held to "inform public sentiment"; pulpits took up the cause; the board of education cooperated; and plans were made to set up neighborhood libraries in schools. A committee of seven men and two women was formed "to receive and report for prosecution, violations of the law in respect to vile literature, improper billboards, and sensational plays."[27]

Children's rooms were often severely restricted. *Huckleberry Finn* was widely censored. In Brooklyn, it was kept off the shelves of children's rooms on the grounds that "Huck not only itched but scratched, and that he said sweat when he should have said perspiration." When a branch librarian, Asa Don Dickinson, trying to remove the ban, appealed to Mark Twain, he received Twain's famous letter:

It always distresses me when I find that boys and girls have been allowed access to . . . [*Tom Sawyer* and *Huckleberry Finn*]. The mind that became soiled in youth can never again be washed clean. . . . To this day I cherish an unappeasable bitterness against the unfaithful guardians of my young life, who not only permitted but compelled me to read an unexpurgated Bible through before I was 15.[28]

Two years later, Edmund Pearson, a librarian and writer, blasted children's librarians for excluding *Huck* and *Tom Sawyer* on the grounds of irreligion and mischief. Arthur Bostwick offered purely aesthetic criteria for choosing boys' books. And Pearson in 1911 claimed that the notions of the influence of books taught in library schools had been widely exaggerated. "We used to estimate the 'social effect' and 'present value' of books on a numerical scale," and entertain grandiose ideas of the quick effect of books.[29]

Female squeamishness was often blamed for this kind of censorship, but these views were common. In Britain, a debate raged over whether *Westward Ho*! should be excluded from libraries because it might encourage some little boy to smoke. As late as 1910, William Dean Howells was tempted to expurgate the violence and beer-drinking from *Tom Brown's School Days* but decided to leave them in, "like the warts on Cromwell's nose." Nor were female librarians uniformly squeamish. As far back as 1882, Caroline Hewins had listed *Huckleberry Finn* and *Tom Sawyer* in her books for the young, and in 1907 Alice Miller Jordan defended the controversial new genre, the western, as harmless adventure.[30]

Bostwick himself created a minor furor when he decided in 1905 to exclude George Bernard Shaw's *Man and Superman* from the New York Public Library open shelves, feeling that books "calculated to make light of dishonesty and criminality were worse than books merely indecent in statement." How would "a little eastsider" react to a book that said "judges in general (not bad ones)" were quite as bad as the criminals on whom they pronounced judgment? The *New York Times* joked at his restricting a book that youngsters were not likely to read, suggested he have his "bumps felt," and wondered if Brooklyn, where the book was not restricted, might suffer an epidemic of youth crimes. In London, Shaw gleefully joined in with cablegrams deriding American Comstockery. (Comstock, who had not known anything of Shaw, promised to get on his track and tried unsuccessfully in New York to have *Mrs. Warren's Profession* banned.)[31]

John Cotton Dana, delighted with Shaw's attacks, commended them to his friends: "They apply to no particular librarian but to the whole Sweet Branch of Very Pure Librarians." The library director, John Shaw Billings, used bureaucratic ploys, blaming budget restrictions and explaining that the book was always obtainable through interlibrary loan. But *LJ*, distressed at several "irresponsible" press outbursts against library censorship, quoted a *New York Evening Post* endorsement of the librarian's role as censor. When a *Times* reporter later asked a library official if the ban on the books was lifted, he was told to "go to the counter and ask for them; you can find out what you want to know by that method." Obtaining the books, the reporter was satisfied that the ban had been lifted. That conclusion is not so obvious. The books were among many not on open shelves but available to adults on request, and the reporter was, after all, in that privileged category.[32]

As muckraking and problem novels became a popular genre, the issue of subjects suitable for treatment in fiction became paramount. Anna Rockwell—who protested the exclusions of *Tess of the d'Urbervilles* and *The Eternal City,* who argued that young people did not need protection from books and had access to them anyway, who was amused at the way novels once considered morbid became required reading in schools—distinguished legitimate and arbitrary censorship. One was a "personal equation," reflecting the objections of an individual or group. However, the library could justifiably censor slum and problem novels that presented problems without solution or that undermined the social and moral order. The library was founded and maintained by persons who believed in an ordered universe, in law and government, and its agents had no authority to buy fiction "whose avowed aim or real effect is to teach atheism, revolutionary anarchy, or free love."[33]

For Arthur Bostwick—singed, perhaps, by the Shaw episode—censorship took on a symbolic value that transcended pragmatic considerations. That can be seen in the peculiar integrity of his presidential address (see quote at the beginning of this chapter), for he disdained the common excuse of budgetary restriction, which for him hardly involved censorship at all. True censorship focused on the one objectionable feature that might mar an otherwise inoffensive work—an inaccuracy, undesirable moral teaching or effect, or some impropriety or indecency.[34]

Bostwick took pains to distinguish immorality, which confused vice with virtue, from indecency—a distinction he said women tended to confuse. No immoral book, however decent in expression, belonged on the open shelf. *Raffles,* for example (a novel about a gentleman rogue), though not indecent, was immoral. By contrast, the Bible, the works of Shakespeare, and the *Decameron* might be indecent but they were never immoral; they never confused vice with virtue. Whether to censor an indecent book depended on the degree and kind of impropriety and the likely, as well as intended, audience.

Bostwick tried bravely to cope with the problem novel. Though immorality and candor were not the same ("surely we have outlived the idea that innocence and ignorance are the same thing"), he saw no need to seek out descriptions that dwelt so much upon "evil phases of life" that they distorted the truth. Moreover, the narrative was often the sugar coating for content that belonged to the study of medicine and law. Finally, "lurid tints" implied that the evil depicted was a matter of indifference, and that violations were common and were overlooked. On the other hand, exposing immorality did not constitute harmful exposure for youth. It was better than conveying a false cheerfulness that was certain to end in disillusionment.[35]

The strength of Bostwick's position is shown in the strong editorial support he received and the *LJ* survey he inspired on the question "What Shall Libraries Do About Bad Books?"[36] Representatives of thirteen leading libraries showed great similarities in policy. More striking, however, are the differences in attitude and the broad range of motives and application that underlay similar rules.

Five respondents were clearly conservative. They felt "overwhelmed" by objectionable books and carefully scrutinized even well-written books for a few objectionable parts, taking Bostwick's comments too seriously. They removed European fiction from the shelves when it seemed too popular with young people. They felt that their policies reflected majority wishes and urged resistance to outside influence, even from heavy taxpayers (Frank Hill, Brooklyn). They blamed publishers and the press for publicizing salacious books. Lutie Stearns (Wisconsin Library Commission) felt that most recent fiction was not wholesome enough for traveling libraries in rural areas, where people, "praise be," would not tolerate modern degenerate authors or "the sort of thing read by many city borrowers." In the Brooklyn Public Library, undesirable books were kept by, and circulated only with the permission of, the reference librarian; they were loaned to branches very rarely and then through the branch librarian's application. A few books could not circulate at all.

Two moderates had no strict rules. Bostwick handled books individually. William Howard Brett (Cleveland) excluded books of low moral tone unless they had distinct merits, "literary or other," that warranted keeping a single copy as a restricted book at the main library, available to mature readers in branches at the request of the branch librarian.

Six librarians, who might be called latent liberals, were humorous or confessed to being lax (William Yust, Louisville, Ky.), or questioned the standards (Sara Vann de Carr, Newark), or even asked for "rules of inclusion" (Samuel P. Ranck, Grand Rapids). They willingly bought many questionable or "many suggestive books" (Mary Frances Isom, Portland Library Association; Isabel Ely Lord, Pratt Institute Free Library, Brooklyn). Miss Lord marked one book "Read all, or not at all"— the opposite of the New Bedford librarian who scoured a good book for one offensive page. For Miss Isom, if a novel was a real contribution to literature—"which, alas, seldom happens"—it was "quickly purchased, immoral in tendency or not." Miss Vann de Carr had on open shelves many books "that most people would not consider wholesome for the young," and held that many librarians' problems with determined young people stemmed from too much restraint. William Yust doubted that rules for exclusion could be applied "with a written guarantee under the pure food law." If some watchful guardian complained about a book, he put it on closed shelves or in locked cases, "where such treasures are kept." If a book required a librarian's permission, some were deterred. Others spoke to him, and after being told why they should not read it went away "satisfied—perhaps to use some older person as a tool to get the book." Miss Isom was concerned that slushy books were worse than immoral books: "Librarians could well take a stand against publishers and booksellers to save the brains of the country as well as the morals." Samuel Ranck complained that some libraries excluded all books on socialism—and even, until lately, all of William Jennings Bryan's works, or works criticizing the social order, as likely to awaken or engender class strife, and hence inappropriate to the library. He urged that indecent books with great moral, literary, or scientific value, like those by Tolstoi and Havelock Ellis, be adopted for restricted shelves and asked for rules of inclusion of all views.

THE PROGRESSIVE SYNTHESIS

The common Progressive conjunction of moral conservatism with political liberalism and even radicalism shows up clearly in Samuel Ranck's qualified endorsement of moral censorship, coupled with advocacy of political dissent, and even more sharply in Lutie Stearns's combination of prudishness (she was one of the female "conservatives") with political radicalism. In 1911 Miss Stearns, attacking the new mass circulation magazines, especially *Cosmopolitan*, for their "outspoken and daring sensualism," complained that few magazines reflected labor interests, and that special interests controlled various journals. A magazine for libraries had to be useful or oriented to reform, providing an unbiased account of events "untinctured by editorial statements in the interests of the real owners of the magazines." She urged librarians to watch the way editorial policies were controlled by advertisements and changed as ownership changed.[37]

These separable dimensions, which indicate that moral and political censorship do not go hand in hand, have implications for the sociological analysis of mass culture critiques. Herbert Gans, describing the "homegrown American version of the mass culture critique," writes that it:

took the form of a crusade against liquor, sex, and later vaudeville and movies, with elite WASP Americans condemning the poor, particularly those coming from Europe, for not living up to their Puritan standards. This critique was never fully developed intellectually, but appeared in reform and anti-immigrant political writing of the late nineteenth and early twentieth century.[38]

Most attitudes in this study were elitist critiques or popular defenses of mass culture. Yet, as Lutie Stearns's attack on the "interests" shows, a liberal-radical version of the mass culture critique existed in Wisconsin, in a period of Socialist strength, under the Lafollette administration. At the opposite pole of this radical elitism was the conservative *defense* of the mass media, the coupling of populism with censorship.

It is also clear that a number of librarians were tacit supporters of freedom, though they lacked the language and ideology to express it. The conservative and moderate categories included more major leaders (three ALA presidents) and fewer women (two out of seven) than the liberal category, which included four women and two men. These responses suggest that the attribution of prudishness to females as a *distinguishing* sex trait was often a projection, a case of "ingroup virtues, outgroup vices." This was a period in which the profession was feminized (in 1910, females made up 78.5 percent of the profession, compared to 57 percent in social work), and they tended to be blamed for its faults, from prudishness to a fussy love of detail. However, only in children's work (in which clients had no voice) was there feminine-based censorship. As Edmund Pearson noted even while criticizing the female sex, "old-maidenism" was "bisexual."[39] The acceptance of censorship united librarians of such diverse backgrounds as Nathaniel Hodges (Cincinnati), Harvard-educated and a member of the American Association for the Advancement of Science; and Henry Legler, an immigrant with little formal education, an advocate of workers, minorities, and immigrants, who in 1911 launched a vigorous campaign of fiction censorship in the Chicago Public Library.[40] It united elitist males, like Arthur Bostwick, with populist females, like Anna Rockwell.

These writings also suggest that the professionalization of library education did not encourage censorship. It may have stressed moral uplift and an elitist perspective, an intense seriousness about "the almost holy mission of librarians." But these were positive impulses. Pearson humorously recalled the annual field trip by library school students to the public library.

Some male members of the library staff, dressed in blue overalls and provided with dinner pails, placed here and there about the library reading Tacitus and Baudelaire, may gain the library a reputation for "reaching the people," which will endure forever.

And, describing the aplomb of a library assistant answering students' questions "like a Chinese diplomat": "What kind of book support do you use?' asked one student, and 'Moral' came his ready answer, and 'Moral' was jotted down in all the notebooks."[41]

Self-conscious censorship, however, was more conspicuous among library leaders who were not library school graduates (e.g., Frank B. Hill, Arthur Bostwick). Library school graduates figure among the comparative liberals—Edmund Pearson, Asa Don Dickinson, Isabel Lord, and Mary Isom.

The combination of moral mission and censor's role did lead to a preoccupation with what really *made* a novel moral or immoral. Was it subject or treatment? This question, which kept recurring, was addressed in detail by Corinne Bacon, an Albany library school graduate and faculty member who in 1914 would become editor of the H. W. Wilson *Fiction Catalog*. Developing Bostwick's approach to literature—but without his dread of a rising tide of ignorance and vulgarity to be resisted in the name of censorship—she distinguished immorality (the teaching of sin) from coarseness. *Tom Jones* was coarse, David Graham Phillips's *Old Wives for New* was superficial and vulgar, Balzac, Flaubert, and Tolstoi had unpleasant details, but they "never confused our moral sense." However, Meredith's *Lord Ormont*, and perhaps Robert Herrick's *Together*, did. Henry James's and Guy de Maupassant's treatments of illicit love demoralized. Daudet's *Sappho*, however, did not, since the sin worked itself out to its natural and tragic end, the ruin of character.

Another fallacy of treatment was lack of balance in depiction. Zola, *The Kreutzer Sonata*, *Rose of Dutcher's Coolly* were true up to a point, but their one-sidedness lacked a horizon, while Hardy's morbid *Jude the Obscure* depicted a "life so common and so diseased as to find its proper place and treatment in medicine than in fiction." On the other hand, Maxim Gorky's *Mother* was far more acceptable than his early stories.

More strongly than Bostwick, Miss Bacon took an anticensorship position in maintaining that the young were overprotected. The voting of *Les Miserables* out of a library by a Philadelphia school committee (with the single dissent of one woman) because it mentioned a *grisette* was an example of such mistaken concern. More subtly, Miss Bacon was defending her own sex. Her references to literary critics show *their* continuing preoccupation with protecting women. By contrast, she held it better for a girl to read Fielding than many modern female novelists. She criticized *Pamela*, who held out for a "higher price" (marriage), as more immoral than Hester Prynne of *The Scarlet Letter*.[42]

Her judgments again indicate that prudishness was imputed to women more than it characterized them. Her references to the demoralizing novels by James and the imbalance of Zola and Hardy reflect astonishing limitations in perspective. Yet her analysis was exceptionally well received. And, despite these limitations and what seem to a modern reader to be rationalizations for excluding literary classics, especially the works of Henry James, Miss Bacon defended many authors—Flaubert, Tolstoi, Daudet, Phillips—who were being censored in the American Library Association catalogs.

THE NEW CATALOGS: 1904 AND 1908

The 1904 *ALA Catalog* reflected the stricter standards of this period.[43] A blacklist continued of Ovid, Rabelais, Boccaccio, Smollett, Richardson, George Moore, Oscar Wilde, Stephen Crane, and Flaubert. The *Arabian Nights* was listed—but in Andrew Lang's edition recommended for children. Voltaire was still represented only with *Charles XII*, Rousseau only by his *Confessions*. The exclusion of books by Ovid, Rabelais, Merimée, and Voltaire while books *about* these writers were listed is again an indication of censorship—a discrepancy between an author's significance and his inclusion. Tolstoi's *Gospel Stories* were added but not his extremely influential *Confessions*. Shaw was listed only with *Fabian Essays in Socialism*, though two volumes of his plays had been published. And H. G. Wells was included with only two novels, not including the debated bicycle novel of 1896, or *War of the Worlds*, or *The Time Machine*. Muckraking literature had barely begun, but the volume had no works by Robert Herrick, Henry Fuller, or David Graham Phillips. Henry James's great novels, *The Wings of the Dove* and *The Ambassadors*, dealing with adultery and nonmarital sex, were left out.

In nonfiction, the ALA guide included a wide range of works on social issues, emphasizing academic work and reputable social criticism. W.E.B. Du Bois was promptly recognized with two works. Shaw's *Fabian Essays* and Beatrice and Sidney Webb's work on socialism were included. But the atheist Robert Ingersoll, dead by then, was still omitted. Richard Ely was well represented with eight titles, including *Socialism* (1894), John R. Commons with two works; Thorstein Veblen with *Theory of the Leisure Class*; the radical John Jay Chapman with two titles. Religious and other social critics included Josiah Strong and Washington Gladden, but not the prolific Socialist writer George Herron. William J. Ghent's *Benevolent Feudalism* (1902) was included, but his *Masses and Classes* (1904), hailed by the Socialist publisher Charles Kerr as the first Socialist work to be issued by a commercial publisher, was not; it may have appeared too late for listing. Also left out were Algie Martin Simons, the Socialist author of *Packingtown*, and Gustavus Myers, author of *History of Tammany Hall*. None of the radicals and advocates whom Worthington Ford had cited was listed—not Altgeld, Debs, or Johann Most; nor was William Jennings Bryan. Perhaps not all works were

Table 7.1

ALA CATALOG, 1904, AND FICTION CATALOG, 1908: CONVERGENCES IN EXCLUSION OF NOVELS

	ALA Catalog 1904	Fiction Catalog 1908
CONTINENTAL		
Flaubert. Mme. Bovary	X	X
Zola. Nana	x	x
Germinal	x	x
La Terre	x	x
Anatole France. Thaïs	x	x
Alphonse Daudet. Sappho	x	x
D'Annunzio. Triumph of Death	x	x
Theophile Gautier. Mlle. de Maupin	x	x
Tolstoi. Kreutzer Sonata	x	x
Maxim Gorky.	X	X
Dostoievski*	X	X
BRITISH		
Thomas Hardy. Tess	x	x
Jude	x	x
George Meredith. Lord Ormont	x	x
Amazing Marriage	x	x
Oscar Wilde. Dorian Grey	X	X
George Moore. Esther Waters	X	x
Celibates	X	x
Arnold Bennett. Anna of the Five Towns*	x	x
Earnest Hornung. Raffles	x	x
Arthur Morrison. Tales of Mean St.	X	x
AMERICAN		
Herman Melville. Moby Dick	x	X
Henry James.		
Princess Cassamassima	x	x
What Maisie Knew (1897)	x	x
The Turn of the Screw (1898)	x	x
The Awkward Age	x	x
The Sacred Fount	x	x
The Wings of the Dove	x	x
The Ambassadors	x	x

Table 7.1 (continued)

	ALA Catalog 1904	Fiction Catalog 1908
AMERICAN (cont.)		
William D. Howells.		
Traveler from Altruria*	x	x
Hamlin Garland.		
Rose of Dutcher's Coolly	x	x
Stephen Crane. Maggie	x	x
Frank Norris. Mcteague	x	x
Vandever and the Brute	x	x
Ambrose Bierce.	X	X
Horatio Alger, Oliver Optic.*	X	X (NR)

X = author excluded   x = title excluded
NR= not relevant
*The exclusions of Dostoievski and Melville suggest literary neglect rather than explicit censorship. Nevertheless, comments accompanying Dostoievski's later acceptance indicate that he was considered sordid. A similar criticism of Gorky was more explicit.

    The exclusion of Horatio Alger and Oliver Optic from the Fiction Catalog of 1908 is explained by the fact that the Fiction Catalog did not include works for children.

available in book form. Those of Altgeld and Bryan were. Missing, too, was Jack London's *People of the Abyss*, his work on the London slums.

In 1908, the H. W. Wilson Company issued its first *Fiction Catalog*, a two thousand-title list compiled from several sources, including ALA guides, Pittsburgh Public Library choices, and the Newark list of one hundred best novels. It was announced as a model but not definitive list for small libraries and circulating—that is, unrestricted—collections in large libraries.[44] Thus, it provides a useful comparison of the degree to which the profession agreed on what was worthy of free public access.

Throughout, the *Fiction Catalog* was more liberal than the ALA list. It listed four titles by Zola, including *Truth*, a "deliberate arraignment of the Roman Catholic priesthood," dealing with the Dreyfuss affair; two novels by Shaw; a work by the novelist Arthur Morrison (author of *Tales of Mean Streets*); and works (though not the most controversial works) by George Moore. Included also were *A Lady of Quality*, *The Damnation*

Table 7.2
ALA CATALOG, 1904, AND FICTION CATALOG, 1908: VARIATIONS IN
EXCLUSION OF NOVELS

	ALA Catalog 1904	Fiction Catalog 1908
PRE-NINETEENTH CENTURY		
Samuel Richardson	X	✓
Tobias Smollett	X	✓
CONTINENTAL		
Zola. Truth	x	✓
Eugene Sue. Mysteries of Paris	x	✓
Dumas fils. La Dame aux Camélias	x	✓
Prosper Merimée. Carmen	x	✓
Tolstoi. Resurrection*	x	✓
Master and Man	x	✓
BRITISH		
George Moore. Evelyn Innes	X	✓
Sister Theresa	X	✓
George Bernard Shaw. An Unsocial Socialist	x	✓
H. G. Wells. War of the Worlds	x	✓
The Time Machine	x	✓
George Gissing. House of Cobwebs	X	✓
Our Friend the Charlatan	X	✓
Whirlpool	X	✓
Hall Caine. The Christian	x	✓
Arthur Morrison. Hole in the Wall	x	✓
Marie Corelli.	X	✓
Ouida. Under Two Flags	x	✓
AMERICAN		
Henry James. The Golden Bowl (1904)*	(x)	✓
Harold Frederic. Damnation of Theron Ware	x	✓
Stephen Crane. The Red Badge of Courage	x	✓
Frank Norris. Moran and the Lady Letty	✓	x
Henry Fuller. The Cliff-Dwellers	x	✓
With the Procession (1895)	x	✓
Robert Herrick. The Web of Life (1900)	x	✓
The Real World (1901)	x	✓
David Graham Phillips. The Great God Success (1901)	x	✓
Upton Sinclair. Manassas	x	✓
Gertrude Atherton. The Conqueror (1902)	X	✓

✓ = included   x = work excluded   ·X = author excluded

*Tolstoi is an indication that some differences may have
been differences in taste. In the case of Henry James' The
Golden Bowl, publication may have come too late for the 1904 ALA
Catalog.   But since the work was left out of the 1911 supplement
as well, it does demonstrate variations in tolerance between the
two catalogs.

of Theron Ware, and *The Red Badge of Courage*. Of James's later novels, *The Golden Bowl* (1904), a study of adultery, was listed.

The *Fiction Catalog* also showed a finer political sensitivity, including *The White Terror and the Red* by Abraham Cahan, editor of the Jewish Socialist *Daily Forward*; works by Henry Fuller and Robert Herrick; and six muckraking novels by David Graham Phillips, including *The Plum Tree*, about "the evolution of a young country lawyer into a national political boss." Upton Sinclair's *The Jungle* (1906) had appeared too late for listing in the ALA catalog. It was included here along with Sinclair's earlier *Manassas*.

The two catalogs converged, however, in certain important omissions: The common exclusions in the two booklists define the framework of moral consensus, transcending community differences, that determined the boundaries of permissible choice (see Table 7.1). Some works had been involved in litigation: Zola, *The Kreutzer Sonata*, *The Triumph of Death*. Others reflected social values upheld by librarians' professional standards.

Within that framework of consensus lay a gray area of tolerance that defined the bounds of controversy. It is reflected in the *differences* between the catalogs (Table 7.2), controlled for their dates of publication. These differences involved not only the new classics but problem novels, Socialist novels, novels (e.g. by Jack London) that raised charges of brutality. The *Fiction Catalog* showed greater receptivity to these trends; but in 1904, the year of the ALA catalog, these forces were too new to be measured.

8.

EROSION: 1908–1917

The tenuous Progressive "synthesis" broke down before the first decade of the twentieth century was up. New publishers appeared with new criteria of selection. Flourishing literary circles combined political with artistic radicalism—in Chicago, in Provincetown, in New York's Greenwich Village and Mabel Luhan's salon. The issues of private sin and public morality were separated. As reformers themselves called for candid discussions of sex issues as part of their "social hygiene" programs, they split the coalition of Progressive reformers and the vice societies.[1]

The change occurred on the frontiers of both literary and political radicalism. In the political sphere, court decisions from 1909 to 1914 upheld the free speech rights of the IWW, while from 1910 on Emma Goldman became increasingly acceptable to more prestigious audiences. On the literary front, an exuberant union of literary and political radicalism was symbolized in the establishment of *Masses* in 1911. Its editors and writers included Max Eastman, Floyd Dell, John Reed.[2]

The radical novel also saw its height, not so much in increased quality—twenty-one "radical" novels were published between 1900 and 1909 and twenty-five between 1910 to 1919—as in their popularity and acceptance by established publishers. Leroy Scott's *Walking Delegate* and Sinclair's *The Jungle* were published by Doubleday; Isaac K. Friedman's *The Radical* and Charlotte Teller's *The Cage* by Appleton; Susan Glaspell's *The Visioning* (1911) by Stokes; Arthur Bullard's *Comrade Yetta* (1913) and Jack London's *The Iron Heel*—the only Socialist novel of violent revolution—by Macmillan. The peak of success was probably reached with Ernest Poole's *The Harbor* (Macmillan, 1915), a bestseller, and Abraham Cahan's *The Rise of David Levinsky* (Harper, 1917). An anthology of protest literature edited by Upton Sinclair appeared in 1915.

Socialism also found its literary critic in Van Wyck Brooks, who in *America Comes of Age* (1915) urged the American writer to resist American materialism without fleeing it. His models were Ruskin, William Morris, Tolstoi, and Nietzsche, three of them Socialists.[3]

Increasing boldness among problem novelists troubled literary communities and social groups. In England H. G. Wells spoke for women's sexual liberation in the controversial *Ann Veronica* (1909). May Sinclair put Freud to the service of the women's movement in *Three Sisters* (1914). Joseph Conrad explored the father complex and lesbianism in *Change* (1914). D. H. Lawrence made his reputation with *Sons and Lovers* (1913). In 1915 *The Rainbow* was banned as obscene and an entire print run destroyed.[4]

In America, David Graham Phillips's *Susan Lenox: Her Fall and Rise* (1911) was hailed into court in 1917. Nevertheless, writers could now publish work that would not have been accepted ten years earlier. Dreiser's *Sister Carrie* was reissued in 1910, to be followed by *Jennie Gerhardt* (1911), *The Financier* (1912), and *The Titan* (1914), the latter two carefully censored by their publisher. Kreymbourg's "Edna, a Girl of the Street," about a conversation between a prostitute and a young sociologist, was published in 1914 in *Bruno's Magazine*, ten years after it was written.[5]

Soon American novelists joined their European confreres in collisions with the law. In 1913 the first obscenity suit involving an American novel took place over Daniel Goodman's *Hagar Revelly*, a cautionary but not overly judgmental account of a girl gone wrong. It was followed by Kreymbourg's "Edna" in 1915, Dreiser's *The Genius* in 1916, Phillips's *Susan Lenox* in 1917. In the meantime the cause of free speech was taken up by Theodore Schroeder, a lawyer and admirer of Robert Ingersoll, who for years had been defending both "obscene" literature and the rights of anarchist expression. He formed the Free Speech League in 1914, and was joined in its direction by Hutchins Hapgood, Brand Whitlock, and Lincoln Steffens.[6]

From early in the century, a trickle of protest had been mounting against library censorship from the press, writers, and the public. In 1905, censorship in Denver was criticized in the press. In 1906, Owen Wister, in a declaration of freedom for the writer, told librarians that any subject was fit for fiction—given the appropriate treatment. Willard Huntington Wright, literary editor of the *Los Angeles Times* (he would later write mysteries as S. S. Van Dine) criticized the "subterranean" censorship of library boards in 1911, sanctioning only the limited legal censorship of "wildly hortatory tracts advocating lawlessness." He found informal censorship more dangerous than legal censorship because the latter was impartial, limited, and geared to the public interest, not individual opinion. It was baffling that Dumas fils, Pinero and Suderman were stamped immoral while the equally immoral rascals of Hawthorne, Conrad, and Conan Doyle passed muster. Since morality was merely majority custom, any progress not sanctioned by the majority was immoral. Only in leniency toward immorality was progress possible.[7]

Robert Herrick, too, criticized library censorship in answering a questionnaire sent out by ALA president Henry Legler in 1913. Herrick's *Together* was being restricted by libraries—an assessment shared by the dean of literary critics, William Dean Howells, who had written to Herrick that he was disturbed by its "several potential or actual adulteries." Herrick felt that since libraries already bought and circulated almost any serious book on any subject under certain restrictions, the issue was whether all kinds of books might circulate. Though he hesitated to advocate dropping all restrictions, he felt that intelligent librarians would hesitate to ban a book from a reputable publisher, since such a work had already passed a severe prepublication censorship. Moreover, a bestselling novel like *The Rosary* was "infinitely more pernicious" than *The Kreutzer Sonata, La Terre,* or *Germinale.* Presumably, the librarian was at least equal to his community in culture and idealism. As communities improved, librarians too would gain in intelligence and culture and "exercise their censorial powers with more real discrimination."[8]

Librarians advocating censorship were increasingly defensive. Herbert Putnam, Librarian of Congress, insisted that

The library is no censor. It does not dictate to the individual, he is still free to read what he fancies—at his own expense. Its responsibility is merely to see to the right expenditure of public funds. . . . Against the bad books it opposes an array of the good books. It does not denounce the one nor champion the other. It champions only that sound preference in the community itself which really wants the best and looks to its public authorities to provide this. Against the new books . . . it may wisely oppose the book tried by time, a steadying influence, much needed in a democracy. . . . It ignores the current fashion and trusts itself to those which in the judgment of time have become "standard." We do not call it old-fashioned.[9]

As "his bovine majesty," the irate taxpayer, became the terror of the desk assistant, librarians were cautioned that they had no right to refuse a book to adults, but should advise them of the contents to spare them the shock of finding out for themselves. Horace Wadlin (Boston) used populist arguments to answer an attack in the *Boston Evening Transcript* after a journalist checked the library's holdings of eighty-four recent books that had been reviewed in *The Nation.* Of twenty-two works of "permanent literary significance," the library had only three; of forty-four "distinguished" works, the library had thirteen; and of eighteen "colorless" but "innocent" works, the library had ten. The writer also listed ten novels that a cultivated person should read and found that where the New York Public Library had all, the Boston Public Library had none. They included works by Arnold Bennett, Joseph Conrad, John Masefield, H. G. Wells, Hugh Walpole, and Oliver Onions.[10]

Wadlin, incredibly, contested neither the findings nor the interpretation, but appealed instead to populist ideology. The library did not practice censorship, but it had to consider factors other than literary merit, for example, "adaptability to uncultivated readers, human interest, unquestionable moral tone, and fitness for circulation from open shelves to readers of all ages." In a 1916 *Boston Transcript* article, Edmund Pearson, that champion of boys' books, stoutly defended Wadlin's censorship policies.[11]

Although leading librarians were more vocal in resisting the new literature, and though liberal librarians were not especially vocal, and did not organize to defend freedom, the less articulate librarians sometimes exercised a subterranean influence. Charles Lummis, the colorful librarian of the Los Angeles Public Library, 1905–1910, put Rider Haggard on the open shelves and organized the "Bibliosmiles" at a "rally of librarians who are nevertheless human." Among the Bibliosmiles were John Cotton Dana, Edmund Pearson, Tessa Kelso and her erstwhile assistant Adelaide Hasse, Purd Wright, and Samuel Green. A number of fortuitous but interesting professional propinquities also suggest liberal associations: William F. Yust employed Marilla Freeman and Jennie Flexner (niece of Abraham Flexner) who would be professional leaders. Miss Freeman and Corinne Bacon, as well as Miss Vann de Carr, all worked briefly at Dana's Newark Public Library.[12]

Miss Bacon had moved by 1913 to a stronger affirmation of freedom and to broader issues of public morality, sex education, and race hatred. She attacked the racist Thomas Dixon, Jr., author of *The Clansman*, and defended sex education books in the library. Above all, she praised Reginald Kauffman's *House of Bondage*, an exposé of prostitution. It was "horrible, like a surgical operation," but had the "restraint of art" and never confused moral issues. A political tract rather than a novel, it was not for young people leading sheltered lives, but it was "for young people exposed to the dangers of which it treats, and for all adults. . . . No one can read it and doubt that the wages of sin is death."[13]

This was a bold affirmation, for Kauffman's remorseless exposé was not only a sensational muckraking topic and an important issue in Progressive reform. It was a treatment by a Socialist writer who placed prostitution as a social institution within the framework of capitalist society, depicting it as a channel of exploitation and universal political corruption.[14]

Miss Bacon counselled librarians not to shut out novels for treating disagreeable subjects and not to exclude books to which some would object—though not to buy "a novel that the majority of the community would think ethically rotten." With respect to nonfiction she adjured,

Avoid all bias, religious, political, or economic. Have books on both sides of a question. If you put in what Spargo and Walling have to say of socialism, don't refuse to put in what Ming says against it. Be as hospitable to Ida Tarbell as to Olive Schreiner when you come to the woman question.[15]

These injunctions reflect in part the liberalism of the day, for her warning was to include the conservatives, Ming and Tarbell. Socialism belonged within the framework of permissible discussion, while racism was no longer a subject of legitimate controversy.

Though the community, for Miss Bacon, was still defined in terms of majoritarian considerations, the assumptions of that consensus were being revised. Thomas Dixon's popularity would have dictated including his racist work; yet racism was held to undermine that consensus. Moreover, the burden of proof was now on the outside censor to show that he represented such a consensus. This was the opposite interpretation to that of Hill (1908), to whom the few demanding freedom in libraries were seen as a minority.

No outright defense of freedom was formulated until the close of the Progressive era. A quite different issue, the library's neutrality in the face of political interference, was defended by James Wyer, ALA president in 1911. In 1916, Mary Wright Plummer, head of the Pratt library school in New York, delivered, as ALA president, the first sustained defense of library autonomy in the pursuit of truth. Europe was at war by then, and at home the country was divided over pacifism, the taxing of the poor and middle class to finance war preparedness, the corruption exposed by journalists, novelists, and Congressional committees. D. H. Lawrence, Somerset Maugham (*Of Human Bondage* was published in 1915), and Theodore Dreiser were generating controversy. Charles Beard's *Economic Interpretation of the Constitution* (1913) had horrified conservatives, while socialism was pervading literature, literary criticism, and scholarship.[16]

Miss Plummer blamed the atmosphere of moral uncertainty and challenge to authority on the efforts of leaders, from parents to rulers, to direct others' thoughts and protect truth from the challenge of dangerous ideas. The churches had failed so long to trust the truth and the people that they were now mistrusted themselves. The schools of learning were on trial and people were asking "if and why plain truths or facts cannot be spoken in some of them." The press vacillated between suppression and exaggeration; governments professed basic truths but denied them in action. Social classes, "buttressed by distrust," and refusing to let truth penetrate, might some day see their defenses destroyed as suppressed ideas burst through. "If but one way is left open, the catastrophe may be avoided. Shall the public library be that way?"

So far, the public trusted libraries to provide all materials for decisions, yet few librarians were really free to choose books. Trustees were often either active censors or fearful of communities, withdrawing books as a sop to prejudice. The result could only be mistrust of an institution that feared a book, since no book could permanently damage truth: it evoked objections and thus produced a forum. Even more damaging than open attacks on books was "the interpenetration of a library's policy by insidious and gradual changes in its personnel, or in its rules, or in its guiding factors." Those seeking a fair field for argument would have to be everlastingly vigilant. "Nothing is lost that has not been yielded up."

She found hope in the fact that this generation was the first to "face facts however disconcerting, however disappointing, however shocking." Terrible things were coming to light through the new drama, the novels, "the new contact between class and class, even through the falling out of thieves. We can no longer turn our backs on these in the Victorian manner; . . . too much has been shown of all conditions." With the spirit of truth abroad in the world, was it not a wonderful grace that the library could be "truth's handmaid"?[17]

Miss Plummer reflected a mood of ambivalence and rebellion that was shared by writers, publishers, and academicians. Publishers like Scribner's proudly adhered to censorship policies while others as proudly flouted them. Shortly after Miss Plummer spoke, Dreiser was embroiled in a dispute over the censorship of *The Genius*, but a divided Authors' League declined to come to his rescue. That year, *PW*, reprinting the major arguments for and against censorship, asked for clearer legal definition of borderline cases but voiced support of both censorship and the vice societies.[18]

In academia, a broader mood of dissent and professional self-consciousness was making itself felt. Just after Christmas 1914, the American Sociological Society held its annual conference on the subject of freedom in communications. In January 1915 the American Association of University Professors (AAUP) was organized, its priorities set with the immediate establishment of an Academic Freedom and Tenure committee. Its defense of faculty against superiors was reflected in the initial exclusion of college deans and presidents from its membership. Early in 1916 the AAUP reported on Scott Nearing's dismissal from the University of Pennsylvania's Wharton school.[19]

In none of these sectors was the idea of freedom a common assumption or claim. The AAUP aroused suspicion in the profession it served and hostility in the general public. A main effort in its first years was to win respectability, and it could not afford a bellicose attitude toward trustees, a militant stand on freedom, or any postures of the trade union.[20] Even less were librarians prepared to mobilize in defense of freedom.

The old assumptions of value consensus, however, were eroded. These tendencies had always coexisted with the more conservative values of the Progressive era. But in the later years, an undertow of dissent became a discernible current, if not the mainstream, of opinion.

THE 1904–1911 ALA SUPPLEMENT AND THE 1914 FICTION CATALOG

The 1904–1911 *ALA Supplement* showed the same strict policies as the 1904 catalog.[21] Excluded was George Moore's *Memoirs of a Dead Life* (1906), which had been well reviewed but criticized by *Dial* as not entirely free of "unwholesomeness." So were Anatole France's later works, including *Penguin Island* (1908). Oscar Wilde was still blacklisted, despite excellent reviews of *De Profundis*, and only one novel by H. G. Wells was added. Even Galsworthy's *A Man of Property* (Putnam, 1906 ed.) was given this annotation from the *Spectator*: "A novel at once so able that it cannot be overlooked, and so ugly in places that it cannot be recommended without a serious caution." However, Gorky's *Mother* (1907) was enthusiastically described as "a socialistic novel depicting present day life in Russia without exaggeration or morbidity." This oblique contrast with Gorky's grim depictions of his impoverished background in *Creatures That Once Were Men* and *The Lower Depths* suggests that fastidiousness, rather than doctrinal aversion, lay behind some exclusions.

Among American novels, Howells's second Socialist novel, *The Eye of the Needle* (1907), was added. For Henry James three volumes of essays and criticism were included, but none of the great novels of this decade. Completely omitted were Ambrose Bierce and Theodore Dreiser, as well as the prolific David Graham Phillips. Robert Herrick was represented with two novels but not his important *Memoirs of an American Citizen* (Macmillan, 1905), his controversial *Together*, or his labor novel *An Eye for An Eye*. Four of Jack London's works were included, but none had a political theme. No Socialist novel was listed. Even Upton Sinclair's *The Jungle*, incredibly, was omitted.

The *Fiction Catalog*[22] was again far broader. It included more of H. G. Wells, added four novels by Dostoievski, four by Anatole France, and Gertrude Atherton's novel on the British suffragette movement. (Miss Atherton, a novelist of some literary distinction, never appeared in any ALA catalog in the time span of this study.) The *Fiction Catalog* went further to the left and right of the ALA supplement, by including W.E.B. Du Bois' *Quest of the Silver Fleece* and Thomas Dixon's *The Southerner*. Dreiser's *Financier* was listed—a bold inclusion—with the explanation: "Possessing financial genius but no conscience, the central character represents a discreditable type in American life." Problem novelists were well received: David Graham Phillips was updated and Robert Herrick represented more broadly. Socialist novels included Sinclair's *The Jun-*

gle, Arthur Bullard's *Comrade Yetta* (Macmillan, 1913), and Susan Glaspell's *The Visioning* (Stokes, 1911), the latter with the exhortation from the *North American Review:* "It is a book to give to the young without hesitation. It will interest and it will not hurt." Kauffman's work on prostitution was excluded, but Jack London's *The Iron Heel*, to whose violence even Socialists objected, was listed.

The addition of older works in the *Fiction Catalog* is more significant, because it reflects changing values rather than responses to current literature: Added in this edition were *Tess of the d'Urbervilles*, Meredith's *The Amazing Marriage*, and Henry James's *The Awkward Age* and *What Maisie Knew*—the latter dealing with multiple adulteries seen through the eyes of a ten-year-old child.

By definition, the ALA supplement cannot be systematically compared with the *Fiction Catalog* for older works. Yet despite that avowed policy, the ALA list did cite new editions of Shaw's *Three Plays for Puritans* and *Plays Pleasant and Unpleasant*, both of which had been omitted in 1904.

Despite professional injunctions to resist popular demand, the ALA supplement adopted *all* the bestselling writers published between 1904 and 1911, excepting only Eleanor Glyn, whose *Three Weeks* had been banned as obscene, Kathleen Norris, Rex Beach, and Upton Sinclair. Those "prophets of commercialism," as one librarian had called them, Harold Bell Wright and Gene Stratton Porter, were amply represented.[23] Herbert Gans has pointed out that librarians like to advocate supplier-oriented service (analogous to elitism) as part of their faith; it plays a symbolic and cohesive role in professional conferences and publications. But in the libraries' actual choices, a user-oriented approach (analogous to populism) is adopted, "if only . . . to get the library budget approved by the city fathers."[24]

The selection of nonfiction in the ALA supplement was surprisingly liberal. Of the seven titles on socialism, no less than six were sympathetic treatments. The religion section included the prominent Christian Socialist Walter Rauschenbusch. John Spargo was represented with three titles, Scott Nearing with *Solution of the Child Labor Problem*, William Jennings Bryan with his collected speeches. There was nothing on prostitution, but three works on "physiology," analogous to today's sex education, were listed, some intended for youth.

On the other hand, quite apart from certain expected omissions—e.g., of anarchists, books by Daniel DeLeon, publications of Emma Goldman's Mother Earth Press—there are some surprising gaps. Eugene Debs was excluded, although he had already run for the presidency several times. Astonishingly, muckraking literature was excluded. None of the major muckraking books were listed: Lincoln Steffens, Ida Tarbell, whose works were still in print, Charles Edward Russell, William English

Figure 8.1
ELITISM AND POPULISM: CONSERVATIVE AND LIBERAL VERSIONS, 1900–1914

| | | POPULAR CULTURE | |
		Critique ("Elitism")	Defense ("Populism")
	Conservative	William Foster (1904) Horace Wadlin (1904) Arthur Bostwick (1908) Herbert Putnam (1903) (Electra Doren, 1903) (Brooklyn Public Library, Children's Room policy, 1905) (Julia Rankin, 1908)	William Brett Frank Hill (1908) Henry Legler (1911) Horace Wadlin (1914)
CENSORSHIP	Liberal	John C. Dana Mary Isom (1908) Corinne Bacon (1912)	Mary Rollins (1904) James Hosmer (1903) Marilla Freeman (1908) Anna Rockwell (1903) Corinne Bacon (1913)
	Radical	Lutie E. Stearns (1908)	

Walling, Hutchins Hapgood, Frederick C. Howe, the posthumous works of Henry Demarest Lloyd. No titles were listed under Dewey number 323—civil liberties and free speech—though Theodore Schroeder's collected essays were available through the Free Speech League.

The liberal but conventional spectrum of opinion in the ALA catalog appealed to the lowest common denominator on proper literature and adopted a narrow range for "both" sides of an issue, leaving much decision making to local discretion. In literature it restricted both moral and social themes, while its inclusion of bestsellers exhibits the by now familiar pattern of conservative populism. It ignored muckraking and despite its Socialist titles ignored some of the richest Socialist analyses, as distinct from analyses *of* socialism.

As in the preceding decade, liberal sentiment was as commonly expressed by women as by men, and library school faculty, exemplified by Corinne Bacon and Mary Plummer (Miss Plummer was head of the Pratt library school) were liberal, in contrast to the leader of a large city library, like Horace Wadlin, and the Librarian of Congress. The most liberal expressions also appeared first in regional, not national, publications: Corinne Bacon and Lutie Stearns first appeared in the *Wisconsin Library Bulletin* (though Miss Bacon was from the East). Granted the small sample and the oversimplification inherent in any schematization, it is possible to plot the distribution of attitudes toward popular culture and censorship as two separate attributes (see Figure 8.1). The typology is not exhaustive and must be qualified by the fact that three conservative critiques of popular culture are confined to children's literature of different kinds: yellow literature, standard classics, and Continental authors popular with adolescents. Moreover, Lutie Stearns is not classified adequately in terms of this scheme; her radical critique is both "right" and "left" of liberal, and her moral conservatism is still not accounted for.[25]

The typology nevertheless suggests roughly the complexity of attitudes that were involved in librarians' attitudes toward censorship and freedom at a time when censorship was still a prevailing ideology. Although a conservative populism was still important, as the ALA supplement showed, professional autonomy was being asserted in a different way. Where the "community" had been resisted in the name of exclusion, it was now resisted in the name of freedom, or the acceptance of minority views. The notion of consensus was being redefined so that it no longer meant a show of hands. It never had been accepted on those terms within an elitist perspective. But now, freedom was coming to connote a more abstract concept. It represented the larger society's ruling values or the public interest in the same way that censorship once had been accepted.

9.

WAR AND PEACE: 1914–1922

> "Once lead this people into war, and they'll forget there was ever such a thing as tolerance. To fight you must be brutal and ruthless, and the spirit of ruthless brutality will enter into every fiber of our national life, infecting Congress, the courts, the policeman on the beat, the man in the street."
>
> —Attributed to Woodrow Wilson.

In World War I, a deepening and ugly intolerance spread to attacks on library collections, rendering suspect pacifist and Socialist works and even scholarship that questioned the motives of the war. Many librarians acquiesced willingly, even eagerly, in this patriotic zeal. Putting the role of citizen above that of the professional, putting advocacy above their traditional neutrality, they happily censored their libraries and helped prepare lists of prohibited books. Others, however, to protect their collections, began to develop an ideology of freedom, resorting, for the first time, to First Amendment principles. Ironically, the defense of freedom itself cast into relief the rules of censorship that governed library service, norms that were not yet questioned.

ADVOCACY

By 1914, librarians saw themselves as part of an international community engaged, along with scholars, in the cooperative pursuit of knowledge and the "free trade" of ideas. Their internationalism was underscored at professional meetings and was supported by the surrounding culture—by Woodrow Wilson's vision of international harmony, reflected in his "conciliation" treaties with thirty countries; by Carnegie's Endowment for International Peace; by the peace movement, whose literature Nicholas Murray Butler and other intellectuals discussed with librarians in November 1912. That heyday of tolerance was short lived.[1]

As the European war erupted, the first response was fear and dismay at projects interrupted abroad, then concern with continuity in the international flow of ideas. From early 1915 on, librarians chafed at British maritime censorship aimed at German propaganda, which blocked the import of books that American librarians saw as merely educational.[2]

The war raised several issues in the freedom to read. First, could the international flow of ideas be maintained? The answer was an aggrieved acquiescence in British control. The second involved the definition of propaganda and its treatment in libraries. The third involved advocacy as the hopes of a once popular peace movement were blasted and Americans split into pacifists and defenders of war "preparedness." In 1915, George Bowerman, librarian of the Washington, D.C., Public Library, asked how far libraries could go in helping the "peace movement and similar propaganda." With the great University of Louvain library shattered, and American library budgets cut because of a war-induced depression, librarians had a vital stake in outlawing war. How could this commitment be reconciled with their neutrality?[3]

In a probing analysis, Bowerman defined the library's position as one of "interested neutrality" or "hospitable impartiality." By providing full information on all sides, along with "capable neutral criticism," in a spirit of free inquiry, it avoided becoming an instrument of propagandists. It could help the peace movement merely by treating the subject like any other controversy.

Beyond that, however, libraries had a special commitment to promoting international friendship. As agents of knowledge and democracy, they were linked to the entire world through their books and professional ties. And their survival was at stake. Money used for arms could not be spent on social projects. Not only did war and war preparation contradict the purpose for which the library existed:

War versus peace is no longer a controverted question of public policy at all. It is rather a question of fundamental ethics: Is the world willing to go on sanctioning a system that puts all the resources of modern technical sciences into commission for wholesale murder and theft?

The library advocating peace did not compromise its neutrality, for it would still furnish ample resources on both sides. It would act as a "leavening agent," as it had done in promoting tolerance, assimilating the foreign-born, and providing a balance to yellow journalism. Instead of remaining a "static institution simply responding to calls made upon it," it would become a dynamic agency advancing social movements.

Libraries could also help expand the range of published opinion. Merely by following publishing trends, they had helped foster warlike sentiments in fiction, history, and children's books. "I make no suggestion of a censorship that would eliminate such books." But they could furnish more antiwar books and encourage the writing of histories with "heroes of peace," doing for peace what *Uncle Tom's Cabin* had done for abolitionism. They could lend their rooms for debates that peace societies sponsored.[4]

The distinction between factional controversies and "fundamental ethics"—issues on which a society's value structure rested—had been raised before, but it had been used to defend the status quo and policies of censorship. Bowerman not only pushed the library beyond neutrality. He challenged the assumption that advocacy meant propagandizing one's own views and censoring the opposition.

But advocacy quickly showed its other face as it came to demand unquestioning allegiance. Once war was declared on April 6, 1917, President Wilson created a Committee on Public Information headed by George Creel, a journalist and politician, in what Walter Lippmann later described as the country's "most intensive effort to carry quickly a fairly uniform set of ideas to all the people of the nation." The press agreed to a system of voluntary censorship, and a host of lecturers, writers, actors, and scholars served as public relations counselors, press agents, and creative writers. More ominously, the first Espionage Act, punishing draft interference and aid to the enemy, also empowered the Postmaster General to deny use of the mails to material he saw as advocating treason, insurrection, or forcible resistance to the law. In October a Censorship Board was created and in May 1918 a stronger sedition law was passed. This national effort was underscored by state legislation and vicious vigilante activity.[5]

These new powers produced a rash of arrests and suppressions. The *American Socialist* was banned and the *New Republic* threatened. *The Masses* and *Milwaukee Leader* lost their mailing privileges, and the editor of the *Milwaukee Leader*, Victor Berger, was indicted for conspiracy with four other Socialists, although he had been nominated to the U.S. Senate on a Socialist platform promising a speedy and democratic peace. Eugene Debs was convicted for his Canton speech on June 16, 1918, and was not freed until Harding became president.[6]

As patriotic fervor mounted, citizens demanded that "treasonous" authors be removed from the shelves. Among them was Hamlin Garland, who had criticized his father for having left his family to fight the Civil War in an "overflow of sentimentality over a striped silken rag." "It does sound ghoulish," said the *PL* editor. "One cannot but feel that further and more drastic treatment is demanded." The Wisconsin State Library Commission reviewed its classic position of neutrality and concluded that in war its role as a public agency took precedence; it could not be aloof or "academically neutral." A policy of neutrality might have applied to the war issue before the war, but now the issue was settled "against the Central Powers by the decision of our representative government at Washington. . . . To be neutral now is to be disloyal." Libraries were to remove all books of doubtful patriotic character and center their efforts and funds on "material tending to awaken patriotism. . . . The library must remain above suspicion."[7]

The profession's main contribution to the war effort was the Library War Service, a project that brought books to men in military camps and kept them from sordid pleasures. Herbert Putnam, Librarian of Congress, headed the project, assisted by a long roster of the library elite. Part of their job was to help the War Department compile an Army Index of seventy-five to one hundred books that were allegedly harmful. Although most were anti-British or pro-German tracts, they also included pacifist and Socialist literature and scholarly books that were insufficiently critical of Germany. On the list were Ambrose Bierce, G. K. Chesterton, Henri Barbusse, whose prize-winning *Under Fire* was considered too lugubrious, Norman Thomas, Max Eastman, David Starr Jordan, and Frederic C. Howe, a Commissioner of Immigration. Howe's *Why War?* (Scribner's, 1916), dedicated to Woodrow Wilson, had interpreted the European war as the result of surplus wealth seeking privileges abroad and American militarism as the outcome of similar forces. As late as August 1918, Putnam advised camp libraries to remove Scott Nearing's *Open Letter to Profiteers* and Theodora Wilson's *The Last Weapon*.[8]

Though the Index was intended only for camp libraries, the Indiana *Library Occurrent* reprinted it, since the books might be "obsolete" or "inimical to morale," hence unfit for civilian consumption. "The civilian of today may be the soldier of tomorrow." Edmund Pearson later reprinted thirty titles, attacking their authors as "addle-headed pacifists, American-born professors, . . . their historical judgment corrupted with Wilhelm M. . . . What a crew they are!"[9]

Librarians were hardly alone in these positions. Nicholas Murray Butler, a pacifist while the war was confined to Europe, expressed the same logic as the Wisconsin Library Commission in his 1917 commencement address:

So long as national policies were in debate, we gave complete freedom. . . . So soon, however, as the nation spoke by the Congress and by the President, declaring that it would volunteer as one man for the protection and defense of civil liberty and self-government, conditions sharply changed. . . . What had been wrongheadedness was now sedition. What had been folly was now treason.[10]

Pressure may explain the likelihood of a response but does not determine it. Charles A. Beard, a war advocate himself, resigned from Columbia University in protest at Butler's dismissals; Harvard University resisted wartime censorship; the American Civil Liberties Union was born in the midst of this crisis. In Portland, Oregon, Mary Isom staunchly defended a pacifist worker who was to be fired. Librarians, trying to harmonize the conflicting claims of professional and patriot, defined their freedom to choose—and in the process, their notions of legitimate censorship.[11]

Late in 1917, John Cotton Dana resisted a patriotic author-artist group trying to censor his collection with the argument that "liberty of thought is a very desirable thing for the world and . . . can only be maintained by those who have free access to opinion." He was vindicated by his trustees. A month later, *LJ* defended the purchase of seditious and propagandistic books of historical value that would be unobtainable after the war, reserving them for students and for future use. Circulating collections had to exclude propaganda that supported enemy countries even indirectly, but that ban "should scarcely be extended to cover pacifist literature." (*LJ* later supported the pacifist librarian in Portland on the ground that she was not obstructionist.) The precedent for excluding propaganda already existed in library policies, wrote the editor, since many libraries did not circulate polemics for or against religious doctrines or sects.[12]

Ernest Richardson (Princeton University) ingeniously rooted the library's freedom in First Amendment freedoms without challenging library censorship. Free speech and press were aspects of the free exchange of ideas. Yet, just as any freedom was limited, free expression was limited by libel and by what in war would aid the enemy. Librarians could understand this censorship better than most, for

every library has practical experience in the forming of lists of books prohibited as injurious to morals. Most large libraries have been urged to prohibit classes of books which are contrary to the opinion of the majority of users on economic or political or religious subjects. Many have been asked to exclude books on Christian Science, books against Christianity, or against the Roman Catholic Church, or for the Roman Catholic Church.

No librarian, therefore, doubts that there is a limit, and hence a proper field for censorship.

Even well-written books that might damage "innocent literary tastes" were kept from immature readers. "There is no difference of opinion in this matter." [!] Similarly, seditious literature could not circulate freely. However, a competent tribunal—no mere patriot—was required to pronounce a book seditious, for every library received allegations of sedition and irreligion from the "most extraordinary variety of incompetent critics."

While seditious literature belonged only in the research library, borderline literature presented a subtler problem:

The fundamental right and absolute need of democracy is the right to know all that can be said for or against any question. There is no right, and rightly no right, of which we are so sensitive as this right of knowing both sides and of the right to know the truth. . . . This was no matter of theory with the founders of America or the framers of the constitution. In America the people are sovereign. They have a right to know, and information cannot be withheld from them which could be kept of subjects [under a monarchy].

The problem of censorship had been neglected. "It is a rich field for special research appropriate to libraries."[13]

PALINODE

By September 1917 the zeal for censorship was fading. On September 27, Creel wrote confidentially to Wilson's secretary that suppressing G. K. Chesterton and Ambrose Bierce was absurd and that he was refusing to release the Army Index for general publication. (This was a strange disclaimer, since large portions of the list had been published.) To give it to the public was to "work grave injustices to loyal people." Frederick Keppel, third assistant secretary of war, wrote to the Creel Committee that the index was widely discussed, and that War Secretary Newton Baker was being blamed for it. He thought someone should review it. "Fred Howe . . . writes more in sorrow than in anger on the subject [of banning his *Why War?*]," and books like Ambrose Bierce's were almost classics.[14]

Baker reversed the ban, complaining that it had been written and enforced without his knowledge by a censor in the lower echelons. American soldiers could be trusted to read what any citizen could read. He was annoyed at the ban of the book by Howe, his old Cleveland associate, and of Emily Balch's *Approaches to the Great Settlement*, a simple collection of documents and European party statements. *PW* hailed Baker's defense of freedom and criticized the newspapers' long silence; the Indiana *Library Occurrent* reprinted the editorial in January 1919, a year after it had published the Army Index.[15]

The timing of Baker's disapproval renders it suspect, for the titles had long been on the army list. Leaders did not share the fervor for censorship. Wilson allegedly had been concerned about intolerance. Creel, a Denver police commissioner when the IWW visited that city, had given them affable treatment, and he and his committee were unhappy with the postal censorship. Newton Baker and Frederick Keppel were hardly fanatics. Baker had been a pacifist, and both he and Keppel had cordial relations with the American Union Against Militarism. Yet all permitted official and unofficial repression, and when Baker repudiated the Index, the war was over. As soon as freedom of the press won official elite recognition, it was echoed quickly enough.[16]

As for Baker's claim to ignorance, Everett Hughes has spoken of the tacit mandate for illegitimate means—the collective unwillingness to know unpleasant facts or discuss matters whose open discussion threatens the group's self-conception and hence its solidarity. "To break such a silence is considered an attack against the group; a sort of treason." Among these taboos are the ways in which a society's agents for dealing with outgroups perform their "dirty work." The agents themselves may be "warped toward perverse punishment and cruelty," but they act "for the rest of us." We may not, for example, want prisoners to be cruelly treated or badly fed, but we also tend to feel "that they deserve something, because of some dissociation of them from the ingroup of good people. If what they get is worse than what we like to think about, it is a little bit too bad."[17]

NORMALCY

The wartime persecutions carried into the postwar years as hysteria over the new Bolshevik state and internal radicalism was expressed in the ruthless suppression of the IWW and the prosecution and deportations of thousands of political prisoners and immigrants. Palmer's Red Raids in 1920 were followed by state investigations and laws. Sacco and Vanzetti were arrested in 1920, tried in 1921. As patriotism deteriorated into nativism, Henry Ford's *Dearborn Independent* launched its attacks on Jews, while from the South, the Ku Klux Klan spread out into the Southwest and North with its messages of hatred of blacks and Catholics. Americanization programs were described as inadequate and immigration bans were demanded. New York State denied licensing to private schools whose curricula included seditious propaganda, while the president of Clark University barred Scott Nearing from speaking on its premises in 1921.[18]

Even Holmes's famous 1917 decision, remembered for its "clear and present danger" criterion for censorship, was repressive. Holmes's 1919 *Schenck* decision upheld the Espionage Act, and he upheld the Debs conviction. In some analyses, Holmes destroyed a long American tradition of unbridled criticism of public policy.[19]

The campaign of repression abated after 1921. Al Smith rescinded the Lusk legislation. President Harding freed Debs, whom Wilson had adamantly refused to pardon, though other political prisoners had to wait until 1933 and Roosevelt's Christmas pardon. The ACLU and lawyers also mobilized against legal violations by law enforcers. Zechariah Chafee wrote his *Free Speech in the United States*, Paul Brissenden his sympathetic portrait of the much-tormented IWW and its misunderstood notions of "violence." Norman Thomas described the treatment of conscientious objectors in World War I.[20]

The political controversies had little impact on library leaders. Intoxicated by the successful Library War Service, they launched a massive fundraising campaign for an "Enlarged Program," a naive venture that failed through public indifference and internal conflict. John Cotton Dana, resigning from the program committee, suggested shrewdly that the ALA might get its own bearings "before it asks the public for a sum that it may discover itself its own greatness."[21]

In a rare exception, Paul Paine, librarian of the Syracuse Public Library, gave an impassioned plea for freedom at the 1919 ALA conference. Sensing a "new kind of domination now threatening the world," Paine felt it urgent that people know more than either radicals or reactionaries about basic issues in democracy and social justice. The genius of self-government lay in weighing competing ideas. If librarians did not feel safe in providing competing opinions—on prohibition (passed in 1918), on labor, on socialism "as a widely held idea of the road to freedom, . . . if we dare not let them see what even bolshevism says of itself, then we are committing the sin of the buried talent." He ended with the invocation of John Milton, who had deplored " 'a fugitive and cloistered virtue!' "[22]

As president of the New York Library Association that year, Paine painted a gloomy picture of class war, the failure of the League of Nations, and the damage wrought by sincere Americans "hacking at the very roots of the Constitution. We hardly thought peace would be like this." He imposed on librarians, "custodians of good reading," the duty to make library service free and democratic.

He attributed to women, especially, a fear of providing both sides of a question, for example, John Spargo's and John Reed's works on Bolshevism, "one a merciless exposure, the other a defense." Letting the other fellow be heard was "the masculine view: it will be the feminine view when women have become more familiar with public affairs." (It was the year before women were given the vote.) He also deplored the suggestion of a trustee (of whose sex he seemed unaware) that the unpatriotic *New Republic* be removed from libraries. Any reader who was told the *New Republic* was not "wholesome" would only buy it and despise the library. If librarians did not present what critics of the League of Nations or advocates of the Soviet said of themselves, they dared not let libraries represent the community.

The library for a democracy . . . cannot have the full sympathy of the community if it is a milk-fed library surrounded by chicken wire and encased in glass. Its printed matter must be a cross section of the honest and sincere thought of mankind. It is too easy for us to be content. . . . There are social and economic wrongs which have long waited for a cure. A determined effort is going to be made to cure them without waiting any longer. Redress, not repress is the word. A new and surprising definition of democracy is to be presented. Librarians must recognize these things. Library service must be free.[23]

In contrast to this novel, abstract view of freedom and of the community, an *LJ* editorial on censorship could barely deal with the ideas involved. In Brookline, Massachusetts, the library trustees had refused to buy, or even accept as a gift, Zachariah Chafee's *Freedom of Speech*, claiming that it misrepresented "a contemporary trial." The editorial granted that the choice of a book was a matter for the local board to decide, but that local opinion was also to be consulted, difficult as it might be to sample. The editor compared the exclusion of Henry Ford's *Dearborn Independent* from the Lynn, Massachusetts, public library because of its anti-Semitic propaganda and the *Independent*'s charge of violation of free speech. The attack was not in order, for, as a complement of free speech and free press, "freedom of action on the part of responsible officials and local boards should be equally respected."[24]

The banning of the *Independent* raised the classic liberal dilemma of accepting all ideas, even repugnant views that undermine the very assumptions of tolerance on which that hospitality is based. The classic issues of authority vs. propaganda were embodied in works so different in principle as the scholarly Chafee study and the rabid, unauthenticated *Dearborn Independent*. But the issue was defined as bureaucratic or professional: the *right* to make a decision, without reference to the *principle* guiding the decision. Thus an editorial that balanced the trustees' right to decide with their responsibility to represent the community ended by defending their right to censor, though its intent had been to criticize and circumvent the trustees' action. The defense of the library's prerogatives against outsiders was confused with the defense of the community against those who professed to represent it. The formulation of the problem set limits on the possible conclusions.

THE NEW FICTION

The effects of political repression were lasting. Between 1919 and 1929 only ten "radical" novels were published, five by Upton Sinclair alone. A mood of private rebellion, or alienation, was expressed in the new literature: *Prejudices* (1919 on) by H. L. Mencken, a literary radical and social conservative; Sherwood Anderson's *Winesburg, Ohio* (1919), Sinclair Lewis's *Main Street* (1920) and *Babbitt* (1922), John Dos Passos's *One Man's Initiation* (1920) and *Three Soldiers* (1921), Eugene O'Neill's *Anna Christie* and *The Hairy Ape* (both 1921), F. Scott Fitzgerald's *This Side of Paradise, The Beautiful and the Damned,* and *Tales of the Jazz Age*.[25]

Ironically, as political repression mounted, the vice societies began to suffer defeats. When *Mlle. de Maupin* was brought into court in 1917, the judge ruled in its favor as a classic. Though a chapter of *Ulysses* in the *Little Review* was ruled obscene, favorable decisions were passed on modern works: Ludwig Bemelmans's *Madeline*, James Branch Cabell's

Jurgen, D. H. Lawrence's *Women in Love*, Arthur Schnitzler's *Casanova's Homecoming*, *Simon Called Peter*, and *A Young Girl's Diary*, and the *Satyricon*. Though the vice societies were still respected by most critics, authors, and publishers, they were criticized, even in court, for going too far. George Haven Putnam published his *Nonsenseorship* (1922), and Columbia law school Dean Harlan Fiske Stone urged lawyers to unite against literary censorship.[26]

Concern with the daring new literature prompted *LJ* to review fiction purchases. It found in 1921 that *The Moon and Sixpence*, "despite its rather strong condemnation in some quarters," had been bought by sixteen (out of forty-one) libraries, and *Jurgen* by three (St. Louis, Norwich, and Evanston). In 1922 it surveyed library policies on "questionable" books, discreetly omitting specific titles so that "salacious-minded" readers would not place "an embarrassing demand" on libraries. It covered three categories: suggestive fiction by prominent authors, books offering physiological information, and classics usually cataloged as "Erotica," "Facetiae," or "Curiosa"—for example, unexpurgated editions of *The Arabian Nights*. Some libraries declined to answer, one because "our present state of mind . . . is so chaotic and subject to change." Another feared that the report would make the "young intellectual" laugh. Several responded anonymously.[27]

The survey covered thirty-one public libraries and six library commissions. All respondents had restricted collections and privileged categories of readers. In closed stacks, locked cases, "reference" sections, teachers' or medical departments, or art anatomy collections, books were reserved for physicians, students, teachers, or "persons who will evidently use them legitimately" (St. Louis). The most liberal put restrictions only on youth. Often, works were bought only for the central library or a few branches and kept in custody of the librarian. Though the survey was confined to erotic literature, a few libraries volunteered information on other controversial subjects. The New Jersey State Library Commission rejected books that did not help solve social problems. In St. Paul, books on making alcoholic drinks were kept off the shelves on the district attorney's advice, and books on socialism were objectionable. Few libraries resisted outside censors categorically; only Chicago gave a firm "no."

A few libraries denied censoring, if sometimes apologetically. The Springfield, Massachusetts, library (Hiller Wellman) did not discriminate among adults, feeling it hardly a matter for the library to judge. In Washington, D.C., George Bowerman, restricting only the young, trusted his sophisticated constituency with disturbing popular books and works on Freudianism, despite his own squeamishness about "disgusting" books. He hoped the survey would not show that librarians had become prudes or public censors. Both the Denver and Chicago librarians, Carl Roden and Chalmer Hadley, bought sophisticated works by reputable authors and publishers. Hadley pointed out that once-taboo subjects were now discussed at clubs, public meetings, in the media and even schools. He dismissed self-appointed censors, who usually read through the books whose moral effects so disturbed them. Roden saw censorship as futile, since a large and often representative segment of the public had both "the taste and the maturity to appraise" works that were often by the best writers, even if they treated abnormal or pathological subjects. The young rarely sought such introspective works. To grant only large libraries the prerogative to buy all the best literature would be making a "sordid and sorry distinction," but large libraries did have the duty as well as the right to do so. Though he might deplore some of the trends, "we have felt no vocation to assume the role of Mrs. Partington, and to employ our little broom."[28]

The survey ended with a British librarian's astonishing version of conservative populism. It distinguished artistic issues, in which the librarian was to lead public opinion, from moral issues, in which he should follow it. Since culture belonged to a minority, whereas morality expressed majority opinion, a librarian could duplicate Conrad no matter how loud the public protest. But if 30 percent of the public objected to an immoral book, it was to be banned. By definition, a book in high demand could not be immoral.

Nor were literary masterpieces ever immoral—only "unsuitable" for certain readers. To restrict H. G. Wells was to judge not his morality, but the immorality of some who wanted *The New Machiavelli*. These writers were unsuited for degenerates needing books as aphrodisiacs, for the "physically, mentally, and morally" immature. Librarians could ease their anxieties as censors if they saw themselves as doctors, sterilizing their shelves, cutting away unhealthy and decadent books. Any author could treat any subject as long as his aim was constructive. But when a book only induced "morbid pessimism, we save our trust funds for better things."[29]

With evident approval, the *LJ* editor concluded that libraries with small budgets could solve the problem of censorship by buying only books "both healthy in tone" *and* superior in quality, leaving for serious students "the system of interlibrary loans, now so generously in operation, for books unnecessary or undesirable for public libraries." As the British writer had said, "we can save our trust funds for better things."[30]

THE ALA SUPPLEMENT AND THE FICTION CATALOG

The *ALA Supplement* for 1912–1921 reflected the important role that closed shelves now played.[31] Its recommendations for closed shelves were sometimes explicit. Jacob Wasserman's *World's Illusion*, depicting "chaotic depths of human misery and the extravagant and sensual use of wealth in modern Europe," was restricted to mature readers. So was Knut Hamsun's *Hunger*, about "slow starvation with its attendant demoralization; . . . powerful; of limited appeal." Sir Compton Mackenzie's *Youth's Encounter* and *Sinister Street* (1913, 1914), about two illegitimate children of wealthy parents, had the warning that the author's preoccupation with sex would offend some readers. *The Moon and Sixpence* was "unforgivably revolting" to some. Joseph Hergesheimer's "best work," *The Three Black Pennys*, was restricted because his heroes disregarded convention when it clashed with personal interest.

Even closed shelves, however, did not accommodate the still-prolific Anatole France. *The Gods Are Athirst* and *The Revolt of the Angels* were omitted, though he had won the Nobel Prize in 1921. Only Lewis Shanks's biography of Anatole France was listed—again an index of censorship. George Moore was still boycotted, and the continued omission of Upton Sinclair displayed a dedicated stubbornness. D. H. Lawrence, James Joyce, F. Scott Fitzgerald were not recognized. *Of Human Bondage* was left out. Among American radical novelists, Ernest Poole was included, but Abraham Cahan and Sholem Asch were not, though *The Rise of David Levinsky* had won critical acclaim and Asch's *Uncle Moses* had been well reviewed in ALA's own *Booklist*.

By contrast, Corinne Bacon, editor of the 1923 *Fiction Catalog*, indicated that she had included authors to whom libraries might object: Asch, Dreiser, Flaubert, Lawrence, Maugham, Moore, Nexö, Smollett, and others. The notes were phrased so that the careful reader might know the nature of the book.[32] The guide listed five novels by Anatole France and starred Upton Sinclair's *King Coal* and *The Jungle* for first purchase. It included D. H. Lawrence with *Sons and Lovers*. *Of Human Bondage* was listed with a quotation from the *Saturday Review* description: the work evoked "a sensation akin to nausea" yet was "arresting." Nexö's *Pelle the Conqueror* was listed with a Cleveland Public Library note stressing Pelle's labor activities and pointing out that the author "subordinates sex to its natural place in the life of a man who is waging the social struggle with all his powers." Neither catalog included *Jurgen*, James Joyce, or F. Scott Fitzgerald.

The most important reevaluation in both lists was the belated listing of Dostoievski, which was doubly significant for the ALA supplement since it rarely included older titles. The annotations suggest that more than neglect was involved in this delayed recognition. The author was "no amusing reading." He wrote for mature minds, relentlessly heaping "one shocking picture on the other," and never minced matters "in speaking on all themes, . . . including the most sordid."

The ALA supplement listed over fifty titles on labor and capital and the laboring classes. In addition, fourteen books on socialism and eighteen on Russia (largely on the 1917 revolution and its aftermath) showed

great range and variety, representing Robert Hunter, Frank Tannen-
baum, John Spargo, William English Walling, the Beards, the Ham-
monds, and Bertrand Russell. Writers on the Russian revolution included Kerensky, Kornilov, Basil Gourko, the former Russian chief of
staff, and American officials and academicians, as well as three journalists.

Especially because of that breadth, authority, and scrupulous balance, certain omissions are significant. Scott Nearing and Eugene Debs
were omitted. Brandeis's *Other People's Money* was left out, as was H.
G. Wells's *Russia in the Shadows* (1921), in which he held that much of
her fate depended on the response of other powers, especially the United
States. John Reed's *Ten Days That Shook the World*, which Paul Paine had
felt was so important, was ignored. And *The Communist Manifesto* was
listed for the first time—self-consciously, as an "important document
for reference, included here because of its use, although first published
before the date of this catalog." Even in this belated recognition, it was
relegated, as the word "reference" suggests, to closed shelves.

NEUTRALITY, AUTONOMY, AND FREEDOM:
THE WEBERIAN DILEMMA

The discussions of neutrality in World War I placed on the agenda
issues that have since become central to professions. A series of wars
and near-wars, the existence of Communist states, not mere ideologies,
and the many forms of repression we have witnessed, have sensitized
us to the limits of permissible dissent and the problems of professional
neutrality.

The norm of neutrality parallels the norms of disinterestedness and
universalism in science, which attempt to maintain scientific objectivity
and autonomy. They express a commitment not to allow science to "sell
itself"—to become the tool of extrascientific (e.g., political or economic)
interests, and to evaluate ideas for their scientific authority and not in
terms of the social or personal attributes of their proponents. Neutrality also resembles the value-free ideology that Max Weber developed
to depoliticize the university. As Alvin Gouldner has put it, the value-
free doctrine, as a "mode of ensuring professional autonomy," is not
unique to the social sciences. "Social scientists are akin to plumbers,
house painters or librarians. For most if not all occupations seek to elude
control by outsiders."[33]

Yet that norm operates against several compelling motives. On the
personal level, it can alienate the passionate idealist and create competent technicians or experts indifferent to the social consequences of
their work. Alvin Gouldner has called value neutrality a myth that masks
a truce between scientists and society: the abdication of an openly crit-

ical stance. On the institutional level, neutrality and autonomy depend on a social structure that will grant such autonomy. That degree of support can vary by regime and over time, as different value conflicts come to the fore. "Particularly in times of international conflict," says Merton, "when the dominant definition of the situation is such as to emphasize national loyalties, the man of science is subjected to the conflicting imperatives of scientific universalism and of ethnocentric particularism."[34]

That dilemma was apparent in the war, as librarians abdicated their traditional neutrality. Yet their work in the Library War Service demonstrated the benefits of advocacy: collective status enhancement as professional activity was geared to national priorities; the increase in efficiency and zeal that was possible when occupational and civic roles were fused. Censorship was a small price to pay when the overall benefits to soldiers were considered.

Accepting the primacy of the citizen's status did not imply a hypocritical ideology, for conformity embraced a variety of motives ranging from dedication through reluctant compliance to opportunism. It was natural for librarians to see social salvation in terms of the service that they, uniquely, could provide. Eliot Freidson sees this "occupational imperialism" as inherent in professions. Medical students do not merely want to heal, they want to be doctors. Professionalism itself "seems to transform the ideal responsibility to serve the good of the general public into limited concrete responsibility to serve the good of one's personal public." A profession fulfils itself through "occupationally defined . . . public service, to a particular occupation's view of correct knowledge and ethicality."[35]

Librarians were not intolerant, but they were not embroiled in issues that did not involve their immediate interests. Their self-interest *and* altruism were expressed, instead, in the choice of issues intimately tied to their status and achievement. Just as in medicine, self-interest will dictate exorbitant fees and idealism the extension of free medical care, idealistic librarians sought library extension to all, stressing service to underprivileged groups and Negroes. Freedom might contribute to these ends, but it was not a prerequisite.

To be sure, once the idea of freedom was attacked in war, its defense required ideological precision; it is in the face of challenge that ideologies become explicit. Yet Ernest C. Richardson linked the freedom to read with constitutional freedoms as if that connection were his private discovery. And he used it to vindicate only closed reference collections, not popular libraries.

The autonomy of libraries, which the norm of neutrality protected, was also limited by the potential conflict inherent in any profession as it develops its own set of values, interests, and commitments that may conflict with the public interest. For autonomy is granted on the assumption that experts serve the public good. When scientists become committed to the pursuit of knowledge for its own sake, without regard for its consequences, society rescinds that support and reacts back upon that specialist group. Today that conflict is apparent in the issues of nuclear power and genetic engineering, around which public movements have coalesced.

Censorship is one of these modes of external regulation. When the library becomes too dedicated to literature that threatens cherished social values, outside interests will intervene. Librarians may invoke the values of scholarship, which was a strong tradition at the time, or of diversity, which was not, just as scientists may appeal to the value of technological advance, to no avail. Librarians, whose activities, unlike those of scientists, are visible to the community, are especially vulnerable to such conflict.

Thus an implicit advocacy is assumed in the notion of the "public interest." Librarians had a tradition of presenting material on "both" sides within a limited range of tolerance. But even had they been given broader latitude, the question remains: how far can one go in presenting all sides? One may argue about a single title like the *Dearborn Independent*, but some value commitment is implied in balancing the collection. One does not allow a library to be filled with racist materials. Nor can one simply rely on the stream of publishing output to be sufficiently balanced. Bowerman had pointed out the bias toward militarism that such "balance" had produced, while critic after critic saw the library as a corrective to the biases of the press. That issue was hardly perceived by the editor who defended the banning of the *Dearborn Independent*. And it has not been resolved to this day. The Moral Majority contends that "neutral" textbooks have a liberal bias or liberals would be complaining. Liberals complain at any move that would produce what conservatives call "balance." Neutrality is not value-neutral.

The values endorsed in this period had remained the same over decades. Although librarians had gained far greater autonomy—"questionable" books were now reviewed by librarians themselves (in Washington, D.C., it was Bowerman or his wife who read them!)—their norms did not change. They were simply entrusted to carry out the same charge.

The code of ethics of 1922, an important earmark of professional development, showed that the profession was guided by the principles of neutrality, accountability, and mild censorship. Like many professional codes, it was largely a code of etiquette, a guide to the discharge of ethical role obligations to trustees, citizens, colleagues. It included the common agreement not to criticize colleagues in public. It counseled prudent personal behavior. The librarian was not to choose companions carelessly "nor indulge in habits and tastes that offend the social and moral sense." It included a promise not to use the public position of librarians to private advantage. The librarian would not buy books for his own interests, but would use catholicity and representation of community groups as a guide. He would not lend his name to a local faction or commercial enterprise (an acute temptation in a profession so close to the publishing industry). It counselled deference to trustees.

The code did not spell out the librarian's function or the public interest; they were assumed and expressed in other statements and guides. Nor did it assert his autonomy, being more concerned with the librarian's duties than his rights. It is clear from the statement, however, that his authority was assumed. Attempting to balance elitism and populism, autonomy and accountability, it urged the librarian to use his "power to guide" with discretion—that is, not to abuse his authority as a censor or gatekeeper.[36]

This extraordinary, lingering identification of the librarian's missionary function with censorship was so deep-rooted that even John Cotton Dana did not express the obviously liberal policies he carried out. He had resisted censorship in World War I, and a rare explosion in defense of exploited immigrants at the height of the Red Scare came from a worker in his library. Yet his language was colored by old debates. In an article entitled "The Librarian as a Censor," he also (like the code) criticized the "missionary" librarian who intruded his views into book selection and did not serve as expert for community-held books, as "keeper of the inn of all comers." He also urged the librarian to "guide" with discretion and eclecticism, yet "check his efforts by a skillful anticipation of what the community will quietly accept." Librarians' conflicts were generally produced by the community's refusal to grant representation to both sides, but the problem could be handled by the librarian who clearly saw "catholicity as the life blood" of his censorship and "tact its methodology."[37]

The tradition associating censorship with professional authority was coupled with deference to what today's obscenity trials call "local community standards." Yet the parameters of tolerance were changing, closing in on political expression, expanding the sphere of private morality. With communities pounding at these barriers, the collisions would produce a revolution in librarians' attitudes.

PART III

From Secular to Sacred: 1923–1939

10.

THE CRITICAL SHIFT: 1923–1930

In the 1920s the new literature confronted the old morality in city courts, state legislatures, and Congress. But censorship in this decade involved far more than the literary shocks of the Jazz Age. It was one of many eruptions of intolerance and campaigns for moral legislation: prohibition in 1919, the Scopes trial in 1925, the spread of the Ku Klux Klan, the Sacco-Vanzetti affair. The nativist hysteria was partially appeased by immigration curbs in 1924, which labor, even Socialists, supported, while business, an erstwhile champion of free immigration, resigned itself to machines as substitutes for foreign labor in keeping costs down. Political and literary censorship disputes persisted through the decade, and in 1929 the Customs Office added seditious literature to its roster of bans.[1]

Although some of these issues echo Progressive concerns, there was an important difference. First, the combination of moral liberalism and political conservatism of the 1920s was the opposite of the Progressive constellation. More important, the reform impulse itself vanished. Business was accommodated, involved as a friend of government, promoted in the mass media. The literary revolution, combining sexual liberation with a rejection of "commercialism," was largely apolitical and retreatist.[2]

As it came under assault, the library profession began to act as an interest group in defense of a limited freedom. As new strategies of defense were developed, the value of freedom came to replace censorship, and to supplement neutrality, in defining professional and social responsibility.

The profession now entered a new phase of sponsorship with new priorities, as the Carnegie Corporation, dropping its buildings program, focused on better library services and education, providing grants, scholarships, textbooks, and, most notably, a new research-oriented school at the University of Chicago, offering the first doctoral program in librarianship. These reforms were intended to put the field on a par with established professions.[3]

In some ways the new goals overlapped with traditional efforts to guide tastes away from trivial fiction. An important difference, however, lay in the Corporation's willingness to publish special materials, simply written books on serious subjects, to win readers. H. G. Wells's *An Outline of History* was considered a rare example of such a work. Moreover, the program sought to develop an informed public opinion rather than refined tastes. In the Carnegie study *The American Public Library and the Diffusion of Knowledge* (1924), William Learned echoed, though he did not cite, Walter Lippmann's concern in *Public Opinion* (1922) for a noncommercial source of sound information. Learned saw the library as a "community intelligence center," staffed by subject specialists on the level of college faculty, who would guide individuals' reading. Although some libraries employed readers' advisers, albeit with slimmer educational credentials, Learned's concept was much admired but seldom adopted.[4]

Indeed, the corporation created dissension among librarians. It established its programs through grants that were channeled through new bureaucratic structures—ALA boards for library education, adult education, and extension services—that strengthened the ALA staff bureaucracy and created new library elites with their own interests and competition for funding. Leaders of course embraced the new priorities, sometimes contending that they had been led astray by such goals as providing community centers and reading rooms. Even when they questioned the reforms, especially in professional education, they did not challenge the well-meaning encroachment implicit in foundation support, as did some college presidents who accepted philanthropy under protest, as it were.[5]

Nor did a strong concern with social issues emerge from these new directions. Only a few scattered references to propaganda, partisanship, or balance of opinion appeared over the decade. Librarians expressed, rather, the malaise of prosperity, discouraged by the passion for entertainment, the stereotyped mass media, the prevailing materialism. The lack of political consciousness was reflected in the avid interest in Russia's experiments with libraries. *LJ* ran twenty editorials on them between 1921 and 1925, all innocent of anti-Bolshevik sentiment or ideological discussion in lauding this professional expansion. Only Arthur Bostwick theorized on libraries under authoritarian regimes, seeing advantages in Russia's central control that freed it from local prejudice. The great drawback, he acknowledged, was the library blacklist; but then, that taboo did not extend to university libraries. Returning from a librarians' conference in Mussolini's Rome, he approved of the disappearance of beggars, dirt, and late trains, even though these changes had come about through discipline backed by ruthless repression. The tradeoff was "national efficiency or personal liberty." "You admit," he argued with an antifascist, "it has cleaned up the country."[6]

In line with the privatization of the literary revolt, the ideology of freedom among librarians emerged primarily in a literary context, part of a concurrent shift among authors, publishers, critics, and civic leaders who opposed the efforts of John Sumner, Comstock's successor as head of the New York Society for the Suppression of Vice. Smarting from his court defeats, Sumner tried to tighten New York State censorship with a law that would allow a book to be judged obscene on the basis of a single passage. The bill aroused so little opposition that it passed the New York State Assembly in March 1923. With only two months in which to act before the state senate voted, the publisher Horace Liveright, a main target of Sumner's crusades, hurriedly mobilized an opposition. It was not easy. The major publishing interest groups were neutral or even supportive of censorship, while Bliss Perry and other literary critics deplored both the new literature and the "alien influences" that produced it.[7]

The groups, however, were divided. Rabbi Stephen Wise, who had been a founder of the Clean Books League, soon defected from his own group. Though alarmed at the new literature, he could not sanction *legal* suppression, not even of the anti-Semitic *Dearborn Independent*. Harcourt and George Putnam left the National Association of Book Publishers because of its conservatism. A handful of literary critics, publishers, and New York newspapers opposed the bill (the press elsewhere favored it), and it was defeated on May 3, 1923. When a new version was unveiled later that year, an anticensorship rally was organized in Madison Square Garden. *Publishers Weekly* and the NABP, though still supporting censorship laws, opposed that particular bill and began to criticize vice societies on principle. In 1924, members of the American Booksellers Association heard a rousing defense of free speech by, of all people, the racist author Thomas Dixon, Jr., who was being victimized by bans on his *Clansman* and the film *Birth of a Nation*.[8]

The shift among librarians coincided closely with these events. In May 1923, at an ALA program on recent novels, Edith Tobitt (Omaha Public Library) disregarded the current debate over the best-selling *The Sheik* to defend serious literary efforts like Knut Hamsun's *Growth of the Soil* and Nexö's *Ditte*. They might "begin, continue, and end in sex," but they appealed to the intellect. "Should the librarian be a censor?" asked Mary Rothrock (Lawson McGhee Library, Knoxville) bluntly. The recent *LJ* survey showed ambivalence. Pleading that librarians "bring people the books that belong to them" and not censor on the grounds of immorality or coarseness, she asked for agreement to "keep open the channels of thought."[9]

Her paper touched off a dispute between George Bowerman, who lauded her paper as the "librarians' contribution to the [censorship] discussion," and *PL* editor Mary Ahern, who feared it might give publishers a "weapon." Miss Rothrock's paper appeared in *LJ*, while Miss Ahern went on to editorialize against these positions. Few, very few, librarians outside of cosmopolitan cities cared about intolerance, Ahern argued. The neurotic explorations in these works appealed to only a few erudite persons and made no contributions to man's happiness. Librarians, remembering their educational function, could "walk in lofty purpose and valuable service, unmoved by the roar of distasteful ideas around them."[10]

A year later, however, the American Library Association testified against the New York State censorship bill. And while *LJ* took no editorial position, it published a peppery critique by its former editor, Helen Haines, teaching in Los Angeles. She complained stridently about *LJ*'s "depressing" survey of questionable books and about the obsession of ministers, lecturers, trustees, and librarians with trashy novels by idle women. The most trivial reference question seemed more valuable, just because it was nonfiction, than the European and American novelists whose richness and variety far outweighed their iconoclasm and morbidity—novelists like Wasserman, Nexö, Hamsun, Couperus, Willa Cather, and Elinor Wylie.

Even worse was our "national disease of regulatory and supervisory fever," the pressures of local Women's Christian Temperance Unions, DARs, PTAs, "mentally limited busy bodies of every ilk." They weakened the librarian's morale, especially in small towns, where personal influence and the pressure for conformity were stronger. Librarians needed to gain independence in building collections yet had few strategic skills to resist the arguments of community censors.

Ideally, censorship might be sound, but it only excited more interest, could not be applied fairly, and prohibited free expression. Besides, censorship was not the librarians' province. Selection was, since it involved standards of quality, usefulness, timeliness, and legitimate demand. Censorship involved exclusion for reasons of orthodoxy or moral disapproval. There was no excuse for the stigma of the permission shelf, or for the practice of keeping works like *Anne Severn and the Fieldings, Sons and Lovers, Black Oxen,* and *Cytherea* in cupboards. These practices invested books with an illicit quality and made the adult reader of *Mme. Bovary* or *Portrait of the Artist as a Young Man* feel like a degenerate or a criminal. "Fiction is an adult art."[11]

The change in mood was reflected in state and regional discussions. "Minor label" books were debated in Oregon, yet both debaters confessed that they opposed labeling. An Albany library school instructor argued against the closed shelf: All books had to be within the reach of all; otherwise, how could the exceptional man, for whom they were apparently permitted, ever come upon them? A list of "principles" for library censorship unwittingly counselled the opposite—resistance to well-meaning community censors and tolerance of alien viewpoints in novels.[12]

In Belleville, Illinois, which before the war had had an English-language Socialist newspaper, a trustee and union leader lashed out at the banning of Upton Sinclair's novels by the Lisbon, Ohio, trustees and librarian. Trustees had the right to exclude books, but banning a man of Sinclair's eminence showed a lack of wisdom and justice. Even pagans had had their forums.

A sinister spirit of intolerance is stalking through our land. Various kinds of idiots are attempting to fashion all men and women after one pattern, pure and immaculate as the newborn babe. Prohibition, Blue Laws, antievolution, library censorship—for goodness sake what's coming next![13]

National library publications were less outspoken. In 1924 *LJ* gave more space to criticizing the New York library union's attack on Carnegie Corporation "censorship" (alleged control of policy) than to any other censorship issue. The Watch and Ward Society described its mild and "democratic" censorship to librarians and was praised at a national conference. Only one editorial on censorship, in relation to the anti-evolution issue, appeared in 1925.[14]

The prevailing concept of freedom was exemplified by Charles Belden, ALA president in 1926 and librarian of the Boston Public Library, praising the national system of interlibrary loans:

Neither specialization nor tradition must be permitted to destroy breadth of outlook. The appeal of the library is all-embracing; it exists for all sorts and conditions of human beings. It must give intelligent and just consideration to the needs of every user. The properly qualified reader or student (note carefully the words, "properly qualified reader or student") [parentheses in original] should and must be able, through some public, college, university, or institutional library which is within his reach, to lay hands on all recorded matter of expression, irrespective of its opinion or subject. The true public library must stand for intellectual freedom of access to the printed word.[15]

In that carefully parenthetical statement—the "properly qualified reader or student"—Belden spelled out, in the name of freedom, a policy of censorship, with immunities.

At that time, H. L. Mencken's *American Mercury* was mounting an attack on censorship, and a critique of "Three New England Libraries" was abstracted in the October 1, 1926, *LJ* with the editor's sardonic comment that, "weighed by the supreme test of their inclusion of the works of Dreiser," the libraries "were found wanting." The writer had objected to shelves crowded with books on Americanization yet deficient in the " 'real Americanization.' " In one library he had found no works by Carl Sandburg or Vachel Lindsay. Not one of the libraries had works by Flaubert, Gautier, d'Annunzio, Lawrence, Joyce, or Huxley.

"The writer," said the *LJ* editor, "propounds an interesting question: Will our libraries now mainly reflect the taste and patronage of a feminine public or, perhaps more accurate, the prejudices of their female staffs?"[16]

Imputing to women defects that were inherent in the profession, the question was misguided. The goal of Americanization and the norm of exclusion were not confined to small libraries, nor did they express female prejudices. They reflected values diffused from above, from professional leaders, selection guides, and the policies of large urban libraries headed by males, sometimes with elite educational backgrounds (Belden was a Harvard and Harvard Law School graduate).[17] Females were never in the vanguard of censorship, and they hardly trailed in its dissolution.

As censorship disputes continued, a new aspect added urgency to the ideology of freedom—the problem of retrospective censorship, or efforts to purge libraries of works that had long been accepted. Sometimes these efforts were isolated episodes; sometimes they were the culmination of attacks on the new literature. Their effect was to make more explicit the notion that free libraries meant more than the free distribution of accepted dogma.

By 1927, a craze had developed across the country, the *LJ* editor complained, for suppressing books on evolution and other subjects that could spread to religious, political, and social ideas. In fact, state laws might now be used to evade constitutional provisions. Libraries should be "free in a double sense," wrote the editor, apparently making a new distinction. "And in this sense free libraries like a free press are essential to our continuing progress as a free people."[18]

In Boston, a combination of new leadership in the Watch and Ward Society, and new zeal on the part of the local police, brought an abrupt end to the period of discreet censorship that had been maintained through cooperation between booksellers and the Watch and Ward Society, and supported by both the Brahmin stratum and the Catholic majority. These groups had quietly suppressed such works as John Dos Passos's *Streets of Night*, Sherwood Anderson's *Many Marriages*, Aldous Huxley's *Antic Hay*, and Floyd Dell's *Janet March*.

By 1927, however, the demand for "bad" books was increasing, and the urbane head of the Watch and Ward Society died. He was succeeded by Frank Chase, who lacked the same esteem and tact. When the *American Mercury* charged that Boston's censorship system had the consent of elites and Irish "immigrant morons," Chase banned the sale of the April 27 *American Mercury*, which carried a humorous story about a small-town Missouri prostitute. Unfortunately for him, the move backfired, for when a noncompliant dealer in Harvard Square was sued, he was acquitted by the court. Worse yet, the *American Mercury* lawyer, Arthur Garfield Hays, sued to enjoin the Watch and Ward Society from harassment. Newspapers suddenly reversed themselves and praised the court decision, and Chase was blamed for his handling of the case.[19]

The Boston police also became active censors. After suppressing Percy Marks's *The Plastic Age*, they banned nine new novels in early 1927. These novels had no particular distinction, but in April, the police banned three major works, Sinclair Lewis's *Elmer Gantry*, Theodore Dreiser's *An American Tragedy*, and Warwick Deeping's *Doomsday*. Publisher Horace Liveright, suing to protect *An American Tragedy*, lost his case. In May, a bookseller was arrested for selling Upton Sinclair's *Oil!*—an episode that produced more publicity when Sinclair peddled a "fig leaf" edition of the book.[20]

At first, *LJ* defined the issue as a popular culture debate, delivering a thoroughly conventional critique of the nine banned novels, blaming the press and not the censors, and pointing out that most libraries would not purchase those books although they had been issued by reputable publishers and were not intentionally salacious. It was better to refuse demand than be subject to moral criticism.[21]

In the next issue, the editor raised the dilemma of librarians faced with demand for censored books: they were bound to meet criticism by the press, whatever they did. Since libraries did have limited funds and policies that stressed enduring values, they were best off waiting until the "first ephemeral flush" of demand passed, or they would be left with worthless and unused books.[22]

On May 1, however, the polite repetition of bland formulae was checked. Boston had gone too far. Even the Massachusetts librarians were protesting. Censors were trying to ban *The Scarlet Letter*, *Adam Bede*, and *Tess of the d'Urbervilles*. Abandoning discretion, the editor even mentioned the test case of *An American Tragedy*. Libraries had above all to affirm "the responsibility of the shelves." One could not force them to throw out the classics.[23]

By then an anticensorship campaign was under way in Boston. In March a professor of English at MIT urged members of the Massachusetts Library Club to defend innovative, even "radical," books that were unpopular with the majority. In May librarian Hiller Wellman (Springfield) urged tolerance of literary innovation and a revision of the state obscenity law. He also tried to bring the ACLU into the debate, but the ACLU was too busy with civil liberties cases, particularly the Sacco-Vanzetti trial (the defendants would be executed in August). Hesitant librarians, still confusing elitism and censorship, conceded that it was not practicable to "elevate reading standards" by means of the law. In December, businessmen complained that Boston was a laughing stock and people were buying their Christmas books elsewhere. *PW* openly criticized private censors. As segments of the religious community also opposed censorship, a new consensus was formed.[24]

In Chicago, one city in which nativism took on anti-British tones, officials, inflamed by the *Chicago Daily Tribune*, scoured textbooks for their interpretations of the American Revolution. Mayor William J. Thompson fired his school superintendent for insubordination and un-American conspiratorial behavior, and in October 1927 charged the ALA and the Chicago Public Library with spreading pro-British propaganda. The offensive ALA document was a "Reading with a Purpose" booklist on Europe compiled by the historian Herbert Baxter Adams. The treasonous books in the library were also respectable scholarly works by David Muzzey, Arthur M. Schlesinger, and others.

Thompson threatened to remove a number of books and burn them. When he was threatened with a lawsuit, he disavowed the book-burning plan but sent his emissary, V. H. Herrman, who marched out of the library with four seditious titles discovered by the Patriots' League: Alfred Bushnell Hart's *The American Nation*, a work published in 1907; Willis M. West's *Story of American Democracy*; and two titles by Claude H. Van Tyne, who interpreted the American Revolution as a civil war between competing factions.[25]

Carl Milam, ALA's executive secretary, would not stoop to deny the charges, but the Chicago Public Library trustees rebuked the Mayor's anti-British attitude and defended both the ALA booklist (which they had not sponsored) and the library. As a depository of human thought, they maintained, the library had to contain contradictory contents. "This exchange of freedom of thought we consider the primary function of a library and in keeping with the American ideal of a free press. Any other course would lead to an arbitrary censorship as detrimental to American political liberty as to academic thought."[26]

The librarian's perspective was considerably different. A recent account has it that the Chicago librarian, Carl Roden, "strode into the room" where the Mayor's emissary was "piling" the proscribed books for removal. "Looming over the representative of City Hall, Roden ordered the man out of the library, never to return; he never did." Reports at the time, however, differ from this retrospective image. According to the *Chicago Evening Post*, Roden was "conciliatory" and, trying to save the books from the flames, suggested that they be removed from circulation instead. He added, however, that he would follow the orders of the board, even if those orders were to burn the books.[27]

Reconstruction of the event has imbued Roden with values appropriate to a later time and anachronistic in his own. Roden, who would be ALA president in 1928, was offering the classic compromise, discretionary circulation, when this was the norm for large libraries and their definition of freedom.

The critical shift of the decade had destroyed the overt commitment to censorship. Where in 1922 liberal leaders had had to defend, or at least explain themselves to their colleagues, they now exhorted others to move in the same direction. In Cleveland, Marilla Freeman defended *Elmer Gantry* and asked that librarians not allow the negative and "unlovely label of 'censorship' to attach" to their book choices. Did not debatable books belong in the library where readers could form their own views about them? If the library was to lead, not follow, public opinion, it would have to check intolerance through the eclecticism of its own collections. Elva Bascom, a former *Booklist* editor and a library school educator, argued for new courses and professors who were not so old or "spiritually isolated" as to be out of sympathy with the new generation and the startlingly different book world they entered. Greta Brown in New Britain, an industrial town with a large foreign population, urged librarians to "err on the side of inclusion," even if they were charged with "pandering to a decadent taste." Censors had to be reminded that the library served the whole community, sophisticated and thinking readers as well as lovers of simple stories with happy endings. Marjorie Bedinger stressed the librarian's duty to provide young people with all the information they would need to cope with new situations in a world of flux produced by technological change and shifting mores. And Margery Quigley (Montclair, N.J.) noted that, in the face of suburban maturity, the "meticulous censorship as practiced in all good libraries" only five years earlier had virtually disappeared.[28]

No longer was majority authority paramount, and no longer was heterogeneity the responsibility of large libraries alone. Literary standards had changed, said Miss Bascom, and a new candor about motivation was expressed in novels and biographies whose characters seemed to be "creations of a Freudian laboratory." Marjorie Bedinger thought it outrageous that the largest city library in her state had turned down a mature man's request for *Jude the Obscure* because it did not have the book. Changing public opinion, said Bowerman, had made acceptable Hardy's works, Dreiser's *Jennie Gerhardt*, and H. G. Wells's *Ann Veronica* (which he himself found "altogether too strong"). In New Britain, the younger generation and European readers insisted on the newest and most radical authors: Sherwood Anderson, Dreiser, James Branch Cabell, Proust, Rebecca West, Wasserman, Eugene O'Neill. Greta Brown, proud of not having removed the *Nation* in World War I, boasted of representing, despite criticism, works by Veblen, Scott Nearing, Upton Sinclair, Harry Elmer Barnes, Bertrand Russell's *Free Speech and Official Propaganda,* and Zechariah Chafee's *Freedom of Speech.*[29]

Librarians found their protectiveness superfluous. Margery Quigley, after reading *Point Counter Point,* had withdrawn it, feeling she had "no moral right to distribute it from the library." When it was assigned to a group of her most conservative clubwomen, she returned it to the collection with mild amusement.[30]

Even these statements carried residues of the old morality. Marilla Freeman advised librarians to wait before buying even some good sensational bestsellers; adding them would only satisfy the curious or salacious, then disappoint them! She resorted, however subtly, to the moralistic criteria of retribution for sin: "If we must have a definition of the 'moral' novel, it should be that novel which makes clear that the wages of sin is death. Allowing for the changing definitions of sin, the modes of dying, and the many ways of paying," the best current novels were as moral as *Anna Karenina* and *Tess,* which had once been kept off library shelves. Greta Brown saw Inferno collections as a matter of individual discretion and was proud that her own library, which had once kept Anatole France, George Moore, and Alexandre Dumas in a "special place," now had them in the stack "which is open to adults who ask the privilege." Another librarian, finding that young matrons, not young girls, demanded questionable books, offered this bold advice: "Buy it if the reviewers praise it enough; circulate it freely until someone objects; and in that event withdraw it from the open shelves but leave it in the catalog. . . . Only a pretty evil conscience will object to the asking."[31]

Only in Boston, a bastion of conservatism, did librarians advocate a "limited and negative censorship," and even that on different grounds— not moral guardianship, which was explicitly denied, but deference to the taste's of Boston's best families, who, it was maintained, were not prudes. To help identify offensive passages, a form was devised to characterize books for "Effect: Cheerful, Clean and Wholesome, Depressing, . . . Immoral, Moralizing, Sordid, Stimulating, Trashy."[32]

Most defenses of freedom, nevertheless, were limited, containing the implication that a judicious self-censorship was expected as part of the librarian's expertise in judging books and in assessing local community standards. This expectation became apparent even as librarians took sides against censorship through the decade.

In New York, John Sumner's targets in the late 1920s included Mary Ware Dennett's *The Sex Side of Life,* a work on sex education, originally written for her sons, that was being used by YMCA educators; Nan Britton's *The Strange Death of President Harding;* the delicate treatment of lesbianism in Radclyffe Hall's *The Well of Loneliness.* In Boston, action was taken against an astonishing group of well-known writers: Sherwood Anderson for *Dark Laughter,* John Dos Passos's *Manhattan Transfer,* William Faulkner's *Mosquitoes* (this before his controversial *Sanctuary*), Ernest Hemingway's *The Sun Also Rises,* H. G. Wells's *The World of William Clissold.* The June 1929 issue of *Scribner's Magazine,* which ran *A Farewell to Arms,* was banned. In September a stage performance of Eugene O'Neill's *Strange Interlude* was blocked. On October 30 *Lady Chatterley's Lover* was found obscene.[33]

As the Massachusetts Library Club mobilized to liberalize the state censorship law, Hiller Wellman defended its breach of political neutrality:

Organizations are sometimes criticized for interfering in legislative affairs with which, as a group, they have no immediate concern. But censorship directly affects librarians, and it appeared evident that their personal knowledge of the situation and their freedom from any selfish interest carried weight with the legislators.[34]

Opposition to legal banning left much room for professional censorship. *LJ* praised the New York court's vindication of *The Well of Loneliness* as not obscene, and especially its success in avoiding the publicity of the Massachusetts trial in which *An American Tragedy* was being appealed. *LJ* reported varying library practices on handling *An American Tragedy,* and deplored, in the name of "common sense," the Boston suppression of Voltaire's *Candide* and the New York prosecution of *The Sex Side of Life.* There was no need for court stricture, for "in this matter of censorship, such questions may fairly be left in most cases to the good sense of librarians."[35]

The assumption of self-censorship became equally clear when a new tariff bill came up in 1929. Two parts of the bill were opposed by Senator Bronson M. Cutting, a liberal who had attended Harvard with John Reed, T. S. Eliot, and Walter Lippmann. He was incensed at the banning of works like *Lady Chatterley's Lover* and the unexpurgated *All Quiet on the Western Front.* He also opposed a new sedition clause, intended to bring Customs regulations into line with the Post Office restrictions that had been in effect since World War I. The combined Customs and Post Office lists of banned books already included over 700 titles. The new clause banned any matter advocating insurrection, forcible resistance to law, or threat to the president.[36]

Librarians were urged to support the Cutting amendments along with protesting Harvard and Yale professors. Though Zechariah Chafee's libertarian arguments were part of the ALA's policy statement, the state associations' resolutions stressed the narrower appeal to scholarship, upholding, in effect, censorship by the courts and the doctrine of immunities. *LJ* also stressed that the sedition clause would lead to bans on Soviet literature important for record and research purposes and, if construed with the "prejudices of war," could also harm collections like that at the Hoover War library. With such a definition, even Charles Belden, who had defended censorship in the name of freedom, could lobby actively against the stricter censorship law.[37]

It is ironic that, with the many constraints in effect, female librarians continued to criticize female librarians for censorship, blaming their gentility, their cloistered background, their spinster's status, when male trustees and librarians with greater power endorsed the same restrictions. William Marcus, a prominent Montclair trustee (who would soon coauthor an ALA library handbook), excluded the bestselling *Strange Death of President Harding*—despite his advice to be "lenient" in censoring—as too sensational and irreverent about authority. A Seattle trustee ruled out obscene words, religious and ethnic slurs, and Socialist literature, arguing that freedom of the press was not violated by these restrictions. The issue was the legitimate use of public funds.[38]

The prevailing meaning of freedom is best reflected in George Bowerman's 1930 address, which was reprinted in a collection of his essays. Bowerman recognized that the problem of censorship was more than administrative, since the library was an institution that promoted new ideas and art. A librarian, nevertheless, excluded books on occasion, sometimes in response to pressure. Bowerman himself had retained a controversial biography of Mary Baker Eddy that many smaller libraries had removed, but allowed a professor at Catholic University to persuade him not to display, or recommend especially, Renan's *Life of Jesus*. "Note the mildness of the request."

More complex policies were required for D. H. Lawrence's books that were not legally banned and for *Ulysses*, which would soon be admitted by Customs. Bowerman held *Ulysses* to be most suitable for a library of medicine or abnormal psychology—or for Infernos or locked cases in public libraries, which held works by Havelock Ellis and Krafft-Ebing and "some extreme books on psychoanalysis" for the use of students. This popular plan met legitimate needs, though "aggressive" users might get the books and not the less persistent students with a better case. He blamed the lax legal and Post Office censors for creating the problem. The librarian had to exercise some minimal censorship in order not to alienate part of his constituency. Yet he could not be so weak that he made the library seem "an institution intended primarily for morons."[39]

Ultimately, the librarian as censor had to represent the most enlightened public opinion. "He should perhaps be a little in advance of his public, as an educational leader, but not so much in advance that it will lose confidence in his judgment and discretion. Certainly," Bowerman explained (with overwhelming modesty), "he should not be less enlightened than the average of the public which he serves." The librarian deferred to average or above average demands and above all to trustees. They were the censoring body. The librarian censored to "meet the approval of his board, which theoretically at least, represents the average opinion of the community."[40]

Reviewing Bowerman's book, Carl Cannon, who was active in the ALA anticensorship lobby, also warned that if librarians did not censor for themselves others would do it for them. William Yust, a former Rochester librarian, thought it better to maintain good relations with a community than to stand up for a principle. He resisted pressures to remove the Mary Dakin biography of Mary Baker Eddy and *All Quiet on the Western Front* by keeping them at the central library![41]

A few voices in less influential journals were more liberal. In *New York Libraries*, Paul Paine insisted that libraries would not be free until those in charge of them wanted it, and wished that laymen would demand what right libraries had to deny full information on the merits of bolshevism, the harms of the Eighteenth Amendment, or the mistakes of physicians. A large Missouri library had not bought Carl van Vechten's *Nigger Heaven*, not because it was lewd or offensive to Negroes, but for fear of criticism by the bigoted. "You know," said the librarian, "we are a border state."

In addition to the educational freedom of the open shelf, which was accepted library policy, the freedom of the soul, which was in conflict with censorship, required attention and always would. Communities, Paine maintained, could mobilize to resist censors. His own library had successfully retained *Nigger Heaven* through a program of public persuasion in which his board president, a minister, and other trustees had been active. They wrote reviews, offered debate, and spoke of the days when denominational journals had not been allowed in major college libraries. Paine closed with Milton's classic defense:

I cannot praise a fugitive and cloistered virtue, unexercised and unbreathed, that never sallied forth to seek her adversary but slinks out of the contest where that immortal garland [liberty] is to be run for, not without dust or heat.[42]

More ardently radical, Lutie Stearns, an elderly lady who had long since left active library work, tore into librarians' congratulatory meetings and bureaucratic absurdities: scrupulous inspections of returned books, no renewals for novels, a "guarantor's card to be signed by a banker, his landlady, and a greengrocer." Libraries failed to reach their communities because they denied patrons the books they needed, awaiting the proverbial "test of time," and finding it "dangerous if not disloyal to go outside the ALA *Booklist* or other mentors." A report to the Wisconsin Federation of Labor held that librarians did not have books the workers wanted. Had this problem been discussed with working people? Charles Kerr, the Socialist publisher, published books for working people, but she knew of no book of his that had ever appeared on the ALA or Wisconsin *Booklist*. (She was almost right; Kerr had been represented in the ALA catalogs only with *The Communist Manifesto* and Louis Boudin's *Theoretical System of Karl Marx*.)[43]

Libraries hastily sought "the other side"—but only when unpopular views were expressed. Why not have books on both sides of all questions, hold forums in library lecture rooms (as two Wisconsin libraries were doing)? "Why should women's clubs be the only users of your buildings?" Most of the population were "the great unreached" because librarians led "hermit lives," fussed over details and monthly reports to complacent library boards instead of "spending 60 percent of your time out hustling for new borrowers, attending and addressing all sorts of meetings of labor unions, businessmen's lunches (the supreme virtue), lodges, fraternities, store and bank organizations, welfare . . . societies."

Put the soft pedal on all this new patronizing chatter about Adult Education as if the lives of men were not filled with records of those like Edison and hosts of other who had educated themselves. As opposed to all this Adult stuff, which is really a confession that in the last 75 years you have never thought of him before, but have been putting in all your time on his offspring, just take a day off from this latter-day sweetness toward the grownups.[44]

Perhaps the most quietly scathing comment on the profession was a polite review of Bowerman's *Censorship* by Pierce Butler, a former research librarian who held a Ph.D. in theology and medieval history and had recently joined the Chicago library school faculty. The review appeared in the school's *Library Quarterly*. Praising Bowerman's eclecticism and experience, Butler observed, "One will find here, perhaps as the most striking quality, what at first may seem a cynical bias" (an extraordinary observation). But it was only the "moderation of enthusiasm tempered by contact with reality."[45]

If Paine reflected the commitment of an idealist firm in his consciousness of trustee support, and Lutie Stearns the conviction of an idealist without a material stake in a profession and hence no need to compromise, Butler reflected the scientific detachment of the scholar—the ivory tower distance, the theoretical bent, the stricter commitment to values that insulation from the conflicts of practical professional life permits. The distinction was itself expressed in Butler's charitable acknowledgment that Bowerman's work reflected the "large element of compromise" inherent in "every social institution."

THE NEW CATALOGS: REHABILITATION AND ACCOMMODATION

In 1926, the ALA issued a completely new catalog for the first time since 1904,[46] and a generation's change in values was reflected in its content. Its most striking feature was the rehabilitation of authors who had once been censored. Ovid was now represented with three works, Rousseau with *Émile* and *The Social Contract*, Voltaire, finally, with *Candide*. Tame as the latter selection may seem, it was to be a target of censorship in Boston just a few years later. Among novelists, Meredith, Hardy, and Henry James were now represented with their most controversial works, Anatole France with *Thaïs*, Flaubert with *Mme. Bovary*. George Moore and Oscar Wilde, formerly blacklisted, were now represented.

Some newer controversial titles were also included: H. G. Wells's *The New Machiavelli*, some of D. H. Lawrence's works, Dreiser's *Jennie Gerhardt* and *Sister Carrie*. The continuing preoccupation with appropriate retribution in novels is reflected in the annotation for *Sister Carrie*, which warned that the book had been criticized because its heroine was not punished. *An American Tragedy* was also listed, but it had not yet raised the furor that it would in 1927.

There were still several important exclusions of both old and current titles in the *ALA Catalog*, as there were also in the H. W. Wilson *Fiction Catalog* of 1923 (discussed in chapter 9) and the 1928 *Fiction Catalog Supplement*.[47] None of Zola's greatest works—*La Terre, Germinale, Nana*—appeared in either list. Among newer writers, James Joyce and F. Scott Fitzgerald (who by 1926 had written *This Side of Paradise, The Beautiful and the Damned*, and *The Great Gatsby*) were both missing. André Gide and Marcel Proust, whose works had begun to appear in translation, were not listed.

The ALA's *1926–1931 Supplement*[48] showed a similar mix of bold inclusions and important exclusions. Although the list was intended only to update the 1926 catalog, *An American Tragedy* was listed again—apparently to underscore its importance in the face of censorship. Other works (discussed in this chapter) that were included were *Point Counter Point, A Farewell to Arms, All Quiet on the Western Front*, which was offered in both Little Brown's censored version and the British Putnam's unexpurgated edition, and D. H. Lawrence's *The Virgin and the Gypsy*.

However, very important authors and works were omitted. Among these were *Lady Chatterley's Lover* and the works of Proust. Gide was represented with only one work, and that was an innocuous nonfiction title. Omitted also were Hemingway's *The Sun Also Rises* and—in toto— F. Scott Fitzgerald and William Faulkner, though Faulkner by then had written *The Sound and the Fury* (1929) and *As I Lay Dying* (1930) as well as the scandalous *Sanctuary* (1931). Two works laboriously defended by librarians were also omitted: *Elmer Gantry* and *Nigger Heaven*.

In the case of nonfiction, the "test of time" is of course harder to survive, since new scientific ideas and journalistic presentations replace old controversies. So it is ironic that, in view of the earlier exclusion of the most important muckraking works, Ida Tarbell's *History of Standard Oil* was now belatedly added. A few interesting new selections are *Since Lenin Died* by Max Eastman, an early Trotskyite who was already hated by American Communists; Trotski's *Lenin* (Minton, 1925) and Norman Thomas's *Conscientious Objector in America* (Huebsch, 1923).

Yet for a volume purporting to represent a significant spectrum of opinion, the following important titles were omitted: Havelock Ellis's *Little Essays of Love and Virtue* (Doran, 1922); D. H. Lawrence's *Psychoanalysis and the Unconscious*; Emma Goldman's *My Disillusionment with Russia* (Doubleday, 1923, 1924); Louis Brandeis's *Business—a Profession*, and Bertrand Russell's *Free Speech and Official Propaganda*, when twelve of Russell's works were cited. The Dakin biography of Mary Baker Eddy was omitted, though it had been on the ALA's list of best books of 1929, and *The Strange Death of President Harding*. (The last three titles had been explicitly cited as controversial by librarians quoted in this chapter.)

Among the most significant bans were those of politically radical nonfiction works: Bill Haywood's autobiography, John Reed's *Ten Days that Shook the World*, Felix Frankfurter's *Case of Sacco and Vanzetti* (Little, 1930), and Mrs. Frankfurter's edition of the Sacco-Vanzetti letters, certainly a documentary source. In fact, there was no book on the Sacco-Vanzetti controversy in the catalog or supplement, although documentary as well as propagandistic treatments were in print.[49]

The obstinate political conservatism of the ALA catalog also shows up for novels with political overtones. In contrast to the *Fiction Catalog*, the *ALA Catalog* still stubbornly excluded *The Jungle*, and it listed Upton Sinclair's *King Coal* with the careful explanation that "the story aims only to expose certain outrageous industrial practices, but it is in itself an admirable study of human character and motives. It is built around the experiences of a rich man's son as an investor in the coal mines." In the ALA supplement, Communist Michael Gold's *Jews without Money* (1930) was of course omitted, as were John Reed's stories edited by Floyd Dell. Upton Sinclair's *Oil!* (1927) was also excluded (the *Fiction Catalog* supplement did list it), as was *Boston*, Sinclair's novel about the Sacco-Vanzetti affair. Floyd Dell and Dos Passos, who had been represented in earlier works, were bypassed now. In 1930 Dos Passos had published *The Forty-Second Parallel*, with its bitter portrayal of the Sacco-Vanzetti affair and its parody of Andrew Carnegie, the patron saint of libraries, and of the library mythology of self-help for genius. "Thomas Edison only went to school for three months," wrote Dos Passos, because the teacher thought he wasn't right bright. His mother taught him what she knew at home and read eighteenth century writers with him, Gibbon and Hume and Newton, and let him rig up a laboratory in the cellar.

Whenever he read about anything he went down cellar and tried it out.

When he was twelve he needed money to buy books and chemicals; he got a concession as newsbutcher on the daily train from Detroit to Port Huron. In Detroit there was a public library and he read it. . . .

(This part is written by Horatio Alger).[50]

This distillation of the record of civilization was not a faithful witness to its age.

THE FREEDOM TO READ, CIRCA 1930

The norm of neutrality was still paramount in the librarians' culture. In the 1929–1930 code of ethics, librarians were advised not to express opinions on controversies, especially local controversies, and to give equal and "impartial service" with "no distinction of race."[51]

The striking change of the decade was the conversion to an ideology of freedom. An ideology of censorship no longer had strong defenders. Even those who carried out censorship policies affirmed an ideology of freedom, and only Boston boasted defenders of even limited censorship. (See Figure 10.1.) The appearance of journals in several columns shows the "conversion" that was characteristic of the time—shifts in opinion rather than the appearance of new members with new ideas. Thus, age is not important in the distribution of attitudes. Helen Haines, Hiller Wellman, Lutie Stearns, and George Bowerman had all entered the profession in the 1890s or around the turn of the century. Nor is sex. Women were predominant in the profession, but they were more than proportionately represented as advocates of freedom.

Among proponents of freedom, the more pragmatic statements appeared among national journals, the idealistic statements in state publications or research journals. The proponents also were outside the arena of direct community conflict; they were independent or at library schools. Public librarians reflected their communities: Paul Paine's idealism stemmed from strong trustee support;[52] Belden reflected Boston's conservatism. The freedom invoked was the institutional defense of freedom, in which trustees and librarians united against community censors—a defense consistent with ALA's courtship of trustees.[53]

To explain why this defense developed, rather than the defense of "academic freedom," one must step outside the time frame of this study. In a discussion of the origins and limitations of the idea of academic freedom, Walter Metzger has observed that it was formulated at a time (1915) when college faculty had little professional autonomy but the

Figure 10.1
LIBRARIANS' POSITIONS ON CENSORSHIP AND FREEDOM: IDEALISTIC
AND PRAGMATIC VERSIONS, 1923-1931

	CENSORSHIP	FREEDOM
ETHIC OF RESPONSIBILITY	Frank Chase (1924) Charles Beldon (1926) Evans, Boston Book Review Club (1931) Edward Allen (1932) LJ editor (1923-1927) PL editor Mary Ahern (1923) Carl Roden (1928) William Marcus (1931)	Edith Tobitt (1923) George Bowerman (1930) William F. Yust (1931) Carl Cannon (1931) Carolyn Jones (1924) Margery Quigley (1930) LJ editor (1927-1930) PL editor Mary Ahern (1929, 1931) Ethel Bacon (1929) Hiller Wellman (1927)
ETHIC OF ULTIMATE ENDS		Chicago Public Library trustees (1927) Mary U. Rothrock (1923) Helen Haines (1924) J. J. Gummerscheimer (1926) Mahlon Schnacke (1925) Paul Paine (1927) Lutie Stearns (1928) WB editor (1929-1930) (Pierce Butler) 1931 Margery Bedinger (1928)

college itself had relative institutional autonomy in relation to the state. It served a small constituency, was not central to the economy, and had a circumscribed relationship to the public sector on local and federal levels. Over the next decades these institutional relationships were transformed. Philanthropic innovation, public higher education, demands for practical curricula, and externally funded research projects robbed the university of its autonomy. It became a bystander in the distribution of rewards. As research became more opportunistic, the norm of neutrality was applied in a ritualistic, conforming way that permitted violation of the university's institutional integrity through secret research, sometimes secret agents, and the political use of student grading. Under these changed circumstances, the status defense of faculty against the administration no longer defines academic freedom adequately. Metzger asks for institutional resistance to outside repression to protect neutrality and openness of science.[54]

These descriptions have a direct bearing on the posture of libraries. Librarians were always more exposed to their communities, being tax supported and serving local communities. Moreover, a public agency is more vulnerable to outside pressure than a private institution. Trustees, who were at one remove from the community, were buffers against this encroachment and lent strength to the librarian's authority.

In their study of academic freedom after World War II, Paul Lazarsfeld and Wagner Thielens, Jr., found that feelings of apprehension among social scientists were stronger in state-supported than in privately supported universities, since the former were more vulnerable to outside pressures.[55] This does not mean that private universities are bastions of liberty. But if even private institutions with long traditions of academic freedom capitulate or compromise, it is unlikely that librarians in public agencies just developing an ideology of freedom would have defended their autonomy against both their superiors and the community at large.

Although the shift in ideology came about because publishers organized as an interest group to challenge the law, that process took place in an environment in which older values had already been attenuated. From the Comstock law of 1873 through the crusades of the 1920s, censorship activists tried to restore norms as a conscious goal in the face of the publishers' secularization, their defection from old religious and moral standards. On one level, these movements seem to be "normative reactions to normlessness," as Howard Becker describes them. However, as Becker saw, secularization was only one aspect of the total "historical process."[56] Émile Zola, Upton Sinclair, Theodore Dreiser represented not only a loosening of the old morality but new values as well.

Moreover, another debate was also involved in these activities. The debate centered on the role of the state in regard to private morality. Opponents of censorship laws did not necessarily support the new literature or oppose its control. They objected to the *mode* of control, feeling that the issue did not belong in the political arena. At the same time, state coercion was deflected from the private or moral sphere to the sphere of the citizen. The shift was reflected in the continuation of wartime legislation into normality, in the free speech cases throughout the 1920s,[57] in the extension of the Customs law to cover sedition. In this legal shift, the threat to social cohesion lay not so much in individual immorality as in political disloyalty. It involved a redefinition of the sacred.

11.

WITHOUT DUST OR HEAT: 1930–1935

U.S.A. is the slice of a continent. U.S.A. is a group of holding companies, some aggregations of trade unions, a set of laws bound in calf, a radio network, a chain of moving picture theatres, a column of stock-quotations rubbed out and written in by a Western union boy on a blackboard, a public library full of old newspapers and dogeared historybooks with protests scrawled on the margins in pencil.
—John Dos Passos, *U.S.A.*

The 1930s began in depression and ended in war, and the turmoil and despair of that decade were reflected in professional conflict and disorientation. Many of the conflicts and the changes were rooted in the past: the review of priorities, the debate on library education, even the quest for sponsorship. Combining with depression-induced self-criticism, they produced new role definitions as librarians pushed aside the old elitist-populist debate. Freedom began to supplant neutrality as the core professional value.

Unlike the insular professional concerns of the 1920s, the public perceptions of the 1930s mirrored the external world. But that reality was refracted in different ways in the professional journals. The *ALA Bulletin* furnished the socially approved images, though diversity was provided in reports, letters, and symposia. Coverage of censorship was skimpiest in this publication. The *Library Journal*, with the greatest range and variety of coverage, also mirrored the professional elite, but its "open round table" invited comment from the rank and file. Although criticism often appeared in its pages, the editor rarely took an adversary posture. Censorship was covered more frequently than in the *ALA Bulletin*, but not in editorials. The *Wilson Bulletin* combined conventional information with columns by young librarians and news that provided a systematic opening to the library world. Exuding a liberalism so complete and un-selfconscious that it needed no formal affirmation, the *Wilson Bulletin* gave heaviest and most varied coverage to the censorship issue. Its editor, Stanley Kunitz, debated with his readers about

Ulysses, Cytherea, Sean O'Casey, sex books in the library, social problem novels, the troubles of little librarians, conscientious and put upon. Though personally outside the mainstream of library activity (he attended only the New York conference in 1937 and rarely met any of his contributors),[1] Kunitz was the herald of change.

These contrasts set a problem for this study. Once the flurries over Customs censorship subsided in 1930, the problem of intellectual freedom was not a central concern, except in the youngest, least prestigious, most dissident publication, the *Wilson Bulletin.* Yet when the Des Moines library bill of rights was announced in 1938, it was heralded simultaneously in the three journals and adopted by ALA soon afterwards. How did the idea move from the periphery of attention to command formal commitment? What was the meaning of the comparative attention in the three journals?

The late 1920s and early 1930s saw a resurgence of radical literature, sparked in part by the Sacco-Vanzetti affair, which alienated writers like John Dos Passos. This political radicalism was reflected in new journals, criticism, publishing, and literature: the *New Masses,* founded in 1927; critics Michael Gold, Granville Hicks, the brilliant and abstract Kenneth Burke; a host of proletarian novelists. Some of the works raised new problems in literary taste and obscenity. Erskine Caldwell's *Tobacco Road* (1932) was barred as a play. *God's Little Acre* (1933) was sued for obscenity in 1933 but acquitted. James T. Farrell's *Young Lonigan* (1932) was published with the notice that it was "limited to physicians, social workers, teachers, and other persons having a professional interest in the psychology of adolescence"—a criterion well-known to library censors.[2] Yet the ideology of freedom, unlike the idea of freedom in the 1920s, did not spring directly from these literary controversies. It emerged as a byproduct of professional concerns.

By the early 1930s librarians had most of the conventional attributes of a profession: accredited schools in universities, a code of ethics, a doctoral program, a research journal. Yet the profession was hardly a community within a community. It was shot through with conflict. ALA members assailed ALA for its bureaucracy, its foundation-dictated priorities, its incompetent and uncontroversial reading lists, its "trivial" *Bulletin.* Jesse Shera, a young bibliographer with the Scripps Foundation (he had not yet attended library school) deplored the profession for demanding academic status but not the opportunity for research. While *LJ* sought endowments from "undiscovered millionaires" and grants from "friendly corporations," a disgusted Lutie Stearns urged librarians to "refuse to send a penny to the ALA Endowment for the Preservation of the Status Quo," and communities to rebel, elect their trustees, and get the radical books they wanted. Morse A. Cartwright, executive secretary of the American Association for Adult Education, told librarians that they had adopted the trappings but not the substance of a profession.[3]

Above all, the profession fought over whether librarianship was an art or a science. The problem was crystallized in the Chicago school, with its outsiders (its first deans, including Douglas Waples, had no library experience) and pretensions to scientific status. For opponents like C. Seymour Thompson, its research was absurd and irrelevant— for example, Waples's studies comparing people's reading tastes and actual reading. Worse yet, Waples sought to offset the mass media treatment of issues like militarism, crime, business ethics, and sex by giving college students adequate treatments of these subjects to compare and analyze. This approach, said Thompson, merely fought propaganda with propaganda, forcing librarians to promote books rather than base "our open-shelf, best-book collections" on cultivating the appreciation of books. The new science could only destroy the love of books and of people that made library work a joy.[4]

In true academic fashion, Waples answered with the textbook definition of a profession. A learned profession could be safely practiced only by those who knew more than ordinary laymen, who earned public confidence through "ceaseless research, a diligent checking of factual observation, and a constant striving to discover new and better tests of service efficiency." Having won that confidence by providing good books on many needs, librarians could use the new science for more systematic knowledge of readers and their needs. The studies that Thompson derided could identify and remove conditions, like lack of readability, that kept people from reading about what interested them.

More important, Thompson had misconstrued his view on propaganda. There was nothing amiss in the conclusion Thompson found so preposterous,

namely, that college libraries should have well-balanced collections and that it is possible by the methods described to find out how well balanced they are, with respect to highly controversial issues not covered in the regular college curriculum.[5]

It is not surprising that Thompson and Waples should have been talking past each other. They invoked different frames of reference— not antagonistic ideas, but different, and potentially competing, emphases.

Thompson echoed the old elitist-populist debate. His references to "the diffusion of knowledge" of good books carried the aura of a cultural professionalism that was decades old, a belletristic orientation to the reader's taste and cultural uplift. Best-book, open-shelf collections reflected the librarian's decision to expose, rather than to dictate tastes. By providing varied materials and endorsing none, the library avoided authoritarianism and maintained its neutrality. Since freedom meant not intruding these censorious views—authoritarianism in aesthetics, or partisan opinion—taking a position or cultivating an opinion seemed one-sided. To promote some materials and reject others violated the librarian's neutrality to make him an advocate.

Waples addressed completely different issues. Concerned with the development of opinions rather than taste, and engaged in a more active educational role, he cared more about the balance of ideas than of collections. If the commercial media were biased, the library provided an alternative. Moreover, in terms of the library's objective—to reach readers, not merely expose them—it had to intervene more actively. His studies showed that people did *not* read about what most interested them because readable materials were not available. Thus, the library as educator had to provide them. This perspective did not solve the problem of neutrality; but it transformed the terms of the discussion, and it dealt with the elitist-populist dichotomy in a different way: The library did not cater to the reader with trivial material, but neither did it provide only the best and allow him to wend his way. It sought, in a far more literal sense, to educate and not leave the reader to his own self-education.

Although Waples, in the next few years, would become less optimistic,[6] the position he took here was developed by an entire school of thought stemming from, but not confined to, the Chicago school. Spurred by the Depression, the New Deal, and the threat of fascism, the demand for a more active educational role would become an insistent theme.

DEPRESSION

He would be marched out into a street still cold and dark at seven o'clock of the late autumn morning; he would go out with the army of men in baggy trousers, ragged coats, and worn shoes, the new men of leisure, without duties and the whole day before them.

How should a man pass his day pleasantly? My large, barrel-chested friend Smith told me he always felt weak and a bit sleepy from lack of sufficient food, though the fare he got was "good enough for what you pay for it." Where to go? He and the others liked to promenade about the city and its squares of parks. "The public libraries are a God-send!" he remarked with feeling. But sometimes, out of fatigue, one fell asleep over a book or magazine and was ejected. . . .

I . . . had the thought that, though they seemed good and useful men, quiet and shy in manner, they were doomed.

—Matthew Josephson, *Infidel in the Temple*

By 1931 the Depression had hit with a vengeance. The ALA conducted emergency meetings and mobilization campaigns. Competing for funds, facing unemployment in their ranks, libraries sought sponsors and allies, trustees and citizens, publicity and platforms.[7]

Reflecting the creeping sense of disaster, the themes of the ALA presidents gradually moved from questions of mass culture and commercialism to a greater political awareness. By 1932 Josephine Rathbone (Pratt library school) voiced the solutions of the Hoover era. Libraries would provide for "greatly increased leisure"—the popular euphemism for permanent unemployment. They would provide information on social problems, maintain morale, create home projects, give unemployed professionals socially constructive activity. "For unless they are employed discontent will express itself in social revolt."[8]

Some librarians revived memories of the 1890s depression. And, indeed, many of the same issues arose. Early on, kindly Gratia Countryman brought books to men in rooming houses. As the problem of tramps increased, a symposium was asked, "Is the library for all?" "Yes!" said Jennie Flexner, reader's adviser with the New York Public Library. "No!" said Milton Ferguson (Brooklyn Public Library) and quoted Dana's 1896 address, with the same contempt as Dana for "those often so unfortunate as to be without a job, even in good times, whose coats, soaked in the rain, in mass formation give off an odor so unlike the perfumes of Araby." Ferguson contended that libraries were neglecting financiers, manufacturers, and college students.[9]

As in the 1890s, this was a minority view. But now, idle men were seen as victims of an enforced leisure that might be a permanent feature of the new economy, and their needs were important levers in the thrust for public support. Besides, librarians, especially new graduates, were themselves unemployed in large numbers. The futility of these questions forced Carleton Joeckel, a forty-six-year-old instructor at the University of Michigan library school, to explode in impatience at the endless and vapid value-demand debate. Librarians, he charged, had no sense of purpose to justify their activities. As a result, the present crisis found librarians still debating

whether the library is for all the people or only for some of them, whether it shall supply books of ephemeral interest to its readers or leave such books to the tender mercies of the rental library, and so on. Am I going too far when I say that I doubt whether any other activity of government is as vague, as indefinite, and as generally inarticulate in defining its purpose and proper field of service?[10]

Coming when the profession faced a crisis in legitimation, his complaint was well received. Carl Milam, executive secretary of the ALA, praised, then echoed him: "We seem to be a strangely inarticulate profession when it comes to express objectives in terms somewhat more specific than 'education, recreation, information.' "[11] Efforts to develop a platform appeared in all the major publications.

Joeckel's influential critique converged with even sharper professional attacks. Jesse Shera sneeringly dismissed ALA's "babbling" about libraries in a changing world. Pierce Butler of the Chicago library school developed a professional theory based on a sociology of knowledge that was earnestly discussed, especially by young librarians. Philip Keeney, no youngster himself (he was born in 1891), and Sydney Mitchell (UCLA library school) deplored the lack of creative opportunity for young librarians and the selfishness of their superiors. Mitchell called for a more aggressive, socially concerned librarian and for a new, "less emasculated" code of ethics.[12]

In the midst of this floundering, new promise seemed to lie in adult education. Lyman Bryson, who was heading the Carnegie Corporation-sponsored Des Moines Forum project, described some of its problems. The first was reaching the community. In the case of involved and well-informed participants, including radical groups, the library's job was "to give them more weapons with which to fight their cause, and, of course, give their opponents more weapons to fight against them." He praised the city librarian, Forrest B. Spaulding, for the "new tradition of free speech" he had fostered, something unusual in towns in the central states. Spaulding had invited the organized Communists of the city to use the library for their Sunday meetings, then had given the library on alternate Sundays to the only ones who objected, the Socialists. These radicals, though suspicious that the Carnegie Corporation was "trying to ram capitalism down their throats," were now vocal participants in the forums.

The problem was more difficult with those who did not read but might be interested in the issues. They needed materials that they could read in an evening—not articles, whose authority they distrusted, but summaries. These sources would have to be provided if educators were to succeed in "this magnificent project of salvaging democracy that we are all talking about."[13]

The question of neutrality arose. Bryson felt it better to state his bias, which could then be discounted, than pretend "to be inhuman enough not to have an opinion about the question I am talking about." John Studebaker, the Des Moines school superintendent who had initiated the forums, took the same view. The leader needed academic freedom in order not to defer to partisan opinion and to retain the public trust. He could, however, state his bias yet remain tolerant enough to leave his opponents "unembarrassed" and help discover all opposing facts. When Studebaker became U.S. Commissioner of Education very soon after, he planned to expand these forums into a national system of adult civic education that would replace the ·"cracker barrel forums of the country store and the New England town meetings," as an alternative to the mass media and political parties.[14]

THE STATE AND DEMOCRACY

Adult education dovetailed with the mood of the New Deal, whose heightened political consciousness was caught by Gratia Countryman (1934): "We feel that we stand at an historical moment in civilization, . . . but in the drama we are participants and not spectators." The President's friendly voice came through "that most marvelous invention, the radio." (Radio was barely ten years old.) People were discussing industrial conditions, sweat shops, race problems. Workers awaited the daily paper to learn the President's next plan. These last dark years had ended political apathy. Young people were questioning the social order that denied them work and opportunity. They were faced with the "crude and vulgar," with commercialized and vicious recreations, "and now"—in a despairing reference to the repeal of Prohibition—"the licensed saloon." The library, addressing the interest in public issues, would be a corrective to "propaganda in the newspapers, over the radio, . . . among walking delegates" (union leaders) and would prove itself a store of material "on every side of every question, without bias or partisanship."[15]

The rhetoric of this elderly lady, who had lived through the 1890s depression, was tinged with old concepts of social reform, but it caught the mood of the time. An *LJ* editor praised her emphasis on civic education. "The early statesmen of this country" had based democracy on a citizenry of high intelligence; the times now demanded "a reemphasis of this function."[16]

The theme had not been continuous in librarians' concerns. It reappeared in times of crisis and suspicion of the social order, and it could be linked with justification of the status quo. But civic education, as Miss Countryman had discerned, was now linked to a quasirevolutionary ideology. Though the notion of a strong state was not new, the notion of planning (outside of war) was. Hence Roosevelt's experiment in state control invited comparison with totalitarian regimes, and the government, to disarm resistance, had to prove the compatibility of strong government with popular control. Its efforts to do so ranged from the TVA's grass-roots strategies to the public forum concept itself, which, by a subtle circularity, attempted not only to raise civic consciousness but to validate federal policy through mass participation: Because of the "widespread ignorance about public questions," said John Studebaker, "we do not even know how to give our assent to the amount of federal control that we are willing to submit to." It was "to enlighten our-selves" that adult civic education was needed.[17]

Librarians were soon caught up in national planning—in the TVA, the Civilian Conservation Corps, and other programs; their new job, in anticipating planning information needs, would soon supplant the older tasks of dispensing fantasies or classics, said William Ogurn, the University of Chicago sociologist.

Yet despite the programs and promises of federal support, the ALA could not get its members to endorse the first step in library expansion under federal support—a national library agency to administer federal funds. In a debate that lasted through 1935, partisans of local auton-omy charged that libraries would be exposed to both political influence and bureaucratic censorship. Frank Kingdon, president of Dana Col-lege, feared that the concentration of power would produce conditions like those in Germany, Italy, and Russia, and he saw that trend appar-ent in the current efforts of state legislatures to check the free speech of teachers. The issue so split the 1935 ALA conference that a vote had to be postponed.[18]

Censorship, however, was hardly confined to federal control. De-fenders of federal aid pointed out that local political history showed worse corruption, "more censorship, more petty politics," that an ef-fective if unacknowledged censorship was usually exercised, even in normal times. In the World War, could public libraries have been any more effectively censored had they been under federal control? Some standardization was "part of the very warp and woof of our present age; it can't be escaped under any form of control." And it was on the local level, a law librarian pointed out, that librarians kept *Leaves of Grass* out of branches and refused to read *Strange Interlude*. If librarians were to foster a pioneering spirit, they themselves would have to read "wise-ly and daringly."[19]

The debate over federal control heightened sensitivity to the mean-ing of freedom. Librarians had seldom questioned philanthropic influ-ence or trustee control. But when budget constraints created sharper dilemmas, the desire for a "cosmopolitan" system of libraries assisted by the government forced librarians to reconsider the premises of local control and freedom.

These doubts were given scholarly confirmation with Carleton Joeck-el's landmark doctoral thesis at the University of Chicago, *Government of the Public Library*, published in 1935. Studying the social class distri-bution of boards of trustees to find heavy elite representation and few members of unions or the lower strata of the community, Joeckel helped to destroy the premises of institutional unity that had defined the lim-ited notions of freedom. A few librarians like Mary Rothrock began to ask for union members, or younger members, to broaden the representation of boards of trustees.[20]

TERROR ABROAD

From the start, the rhetoric of the New Deal was affected by Nazism, a parallel and opposite response to economic chaos that heightened the self-consciousness of all democratic regimes. In that process democratic freedoms took on new symbolic meanings. Librarians were not initially sensitive to these implications. It was outsiders who spelled them out.

Librarians' neutrality was evident at the 1933 meeting of the International Federation of Library Associations at ALA, for most discussions by foreign librarians were studiously technical (e.g., a German librarian spoke on interlibrary loan). A few gloomy references crept into several speeches. If democracy was more than victory in a conflict of ignorant clamors, said Arundell Esdaile (British Museum), it meant a society that thought and discussed, whose judgment and not blind loyalty directed its ends. "Such a society cannot exist without free access to books." Frederick Keppel, head of the Carnegie Corporation, saw civilization as a thin veneer over savagery, kidnapping, book burning. Public opinion was molded by flashy Congressmen, films, Hearst, and the *Chicago Tribune*. Perhaps value change required literature rather than information, required a vehicle more powerful than conscious thought.[21]

In a striking departure from his stilted conference assignment, Howard Mumford Jones, president of the University of Chicago, delivered an impassioned manifesto of freedom. Over most of the earth, he saw violent movements molding men's minds into "a single set of ideas about the state." Bolshevism, fascism, communism, Hitlerism shared one technique: to destroy the circulation of the opponents' ideas and propagandize one's own. The barbarities of Hitlerism were matched only by its stupidities, its book burnings. That "bald return to the methods of the Inquisition" evoked Spinoza's flight, Bruno's execution. "The most celebrated theoretical physicist of our day is in exile with a price set on his head; the most liberal minded authors of Europe are in exile; fundamental dissent is dangerous or impossible in Italy, in Austria, in Ireland, in Turkey." In America, too, the drive to regiment men's minds was gaining ground.

That men should everywhere have access to ideas was a fundamental decency of civilization.

The charter of our freedom is that the people shall have the right freely to receive and freely to discuss ideas regarding themselves and the state to which they belong; and the frail shield which we have to interpose between this hard won political platitude and the storm of absolutism which is sweeping the world is the thin and perishable leaf of the printed book. . . . We do not desire to be bound to the chariot of any form of government which is despotic in the empire of the mind; we believe . . . that the records of the human past shall be freely open to all men whatsoever; that the ideas of critics of the existing order shall be as readily accessible to our people as the ideas of the proponents of the existing order; that it is within the power of no government of ours and no form of the state to burn our books, to close our libraries, to dictate what our schools may teach, to muzzle our public press, to exile our philosophers. Our record as a nation is, we know, not spotless; . . . but so long as we can, we shall struggle to keep faith in the axiom that a free and enlightened people may freely read and freely discuss the ideas which have come to them through the printing press. . . .

What is the place of books and reading in modern society? I reply that libraries and the ability to read books are fundamental guardians of popular liberty in a diseased and desperate world.[22]

If library leaders did not discuss the international crisis and confined their resolutions to matters of tenure, it was not by accident. At the 1933 conference, Henry Lydenberg received a letter urging some response to Hitler's book burnings. The executive board considered the matter but took no action. At the end of that conference, it considered a request to endorse the Roerich Peace Pact, an agreement to safeguard artistic, scientific, and cultural institutions in time of war. It decided that, "except for matters which directly concern the operation of libraries, the board does not adopt resolutions commending the activities of other organizations." This rationale, notes a biographer of Carl Milam, was often used by the ALA to decline joining with other groups on "anti-censorship or civil liberties issues." In this case, it declined to support cultural institutions as well.[23]

Leaders were slower to pick up the new themes than were outsiders or the rank and file. The German book burnings of 1933 received no comment in the library press. In *LJ* a brief note in 1934 announced the opening in Paris of a library of the books that had been burned in Germany. In the *Wilson Bulletin*, however, Arthur Berthold compared the role of the library in democratic and totalitarian states, and his theory provoked extended commentary. At the 1934 conference, Lyman Bryson, by then at Columbia University, urged librarians on professional grounds—their training and their "responsibility as custodians of the public mind"—to exercise the difficult but clear public duty to see that all people had access to all ideas. Even pernicious ideas deserved a chance in free competition. Libraries were the "invention of modern democracy," and librarians had a duty to defend that liberalism against both Marxist and totalitarian critiques.[24]

WB writers took up these themes. Gretchen Garrison (NYPL) asked how librarians might cultivate internationalism in the face of rising intolerance, chauvinism, and "the false lure of war." Arthur Berthold warned that the United States was drifting toward fascism and the fascistic concept of the library. The library might have to drop its traditional liberality as "neutral ground" where all schools "meet and mingle" in order to deal with this new intolerance. Kunitz objected: Who would do this calculating?

Before the librarian surrenders his classic (tho sometimes illusory) position of "entire liberality and absolute impartiality"—and there is no point in denying that if the state in a crisis of government should demand it, he would have to comply or lose, at the least, his job—before, I say, the abdication is made with patriotic gladness, it behooves the librarian to study and attempt to understand the forces at work in modern society, and learn how to separate the friends from the enemies of life, in order that truth and the clean heart and human dignity may not perish from the earth.[25]

The neutral internationalism of librarians was also questioned. When the *ALA Bulletin* innocently described a Friends of the Library program at the University of Denver, one of its readers charged them—in the pages of the *Wilson Bulletin*—with helping to spread fascist propaganda because of their friendly ties with the Italian consulate. The university librarian, Malcolm Wyer (Wyer would be ALA president in 1936–1937), never answered Kunitz's request for a comment.[26]

At this time, the idea of freedom as a defining feature of American libraries was proposed by Leon Carnovsky, a thirty-one-year-old graduate and faculty member of the University of Chicago library school. Carnovsky had just visited Germany, where he had been struck by its banning of Communist literature and all non-Nazi newspapers, and by the forbidden literature in its libraries that was kept on isolated shelves and allowed only to students with letters from professors, who promised in writing not to use any material for propaganda purposes. Americans had placed the wrong emphasis on the democracy of libraries. They prided themselves on making no class distinctions and providing impartial service to all. Yet no country in Europe made such class distinctions in library service, not even Germany.

But we may, I think, point with pride to our policy of allowing all voices a hearing, of giving equal opportunity of expression to both the supporter and reviler of the established order. With the surrender of this prerogative, democracy in the library is at an end. Though this may be a truism it cannot be repeated too often, for it impregnates the very character of American librarianship.[27]

But did it? That policy might hold, objected a reader, in a large university library with "a well-defined community, a student body." Otherwise, controversial material was ruled out, "not by official restriction, but by an unwritten code of courtesy and ethics." According to that code, public funds were not used to buy propaganda, certain members of the governing board were not to be offended, and influential community groups were not to be antagonized. Almost all library heads would rather admit slick magazines "than allow the public mind to be polluted by the excellent, living *New Masses*" and similar journals. True, the restrictions were not *ordained* by government bodies.

But he must indeed be unintelligent who does not see that our real government is composed of those donors, board members, and offended portions of the community whom the librarian must propitiate. They rule by virtue of their divine guidance and support, and so their ire must be appeased.[28]

The critique was an understatement if anything. Librarians had generally affirmed a freedom without dust or heat. Deference to trustees and to respected community groups, restrictions on propaganda, had been endorsed by librarians and documented in their policy. Their code adjured them not to express opinions on controversial subjects. What the writer uncovered was an anomaly that had not generally been recognized: the degree to which these policies of deference and neutrality subverted the notion, now advocated, of the public library as defender of the freedom to read.

12.

FACING ARMAGEDDON: 1935–1939

Now that your learning is abused:
Now that the fighting's at your door:—
Now are you peaceful in your house?
Now are you neutral in this war? . . .

I say the guns are in your house:
I say there is no room for flight.
                    —Archibald MacLeish, "Speech to Scholars"

In the second half of the decade, the ideology of uncompromising freedom passed from outsiders, dissidents, and idealistic neophytes to the professional library leaders. This movement occurred when the value of democracy, challenged from abroad and assailed from within, was embraced with increasing fervor. Yet these factors do not alone explain the adoption of the 1939 Library Bill of Rights. To them must be added pressure from a segment of the profession upon its leaders.

By 1935 America was becoming a haven for exiles. In 1933, the New School for Social Research had set up its University in Exile for emigré intellectuals, who included Albert Einstein, Thomas Mann, Arturo Toscanini, Paul Hindemith, Kurt Weill, and George Grosz. At the same time, Fascists and Jew-hating organizations were growing, among them Father Coughlin's Christian Front, while sedition bills were passed or considered in a number of states.

Demands for loyalty oaths and other challenges made academic freedom an issue in universities and schools and a major dispute at the 1935 National Education Association conference. In spring 1935 John Strachey was deported from the United States for his Socialist views. James T. Farrell's *A World I Never Made* was tried for obscenity and acquitted. Uniting against fascism, liberals and Communists joined forces in the Popular Front.[1]

TECHNICAL NEUTRALITY AND SOCIAL RESPONSIBILITY

A mood of self-questioning swept the professions. Even federal officials questioned the notion of the technically competent, neutral expert, detached from social responsibility. In totalitarian countries, asked
Oscar Chapman, Secretary of the Interior, had professionals—librarians, students, writers, research people—"so lost themselves in their
own fields of service that they failed to understand the social forces
preparing to destroy their work?" He urged professionals to turn from
technical problems to help solve the social and economic problems of
their time; librarians in particular could bridge the gap between experts
and the public. John Studebaker, U.S. secretary of education, linked his
public forums to a critique of intellectuals and elites: "We can no longer
depend upon the understanding of college and university graduates,
trickling down to the masses of American citizens."[2]

From a more radical perspective, professional leaders were accused
of betrayal. An anonymous young librarian, "Jay Otis," charged that
the library profession was dominated by executives whose philosophy
and interests were closely linked to those of the business world and
who deplored the "overproduction" of librarians when four tenths of
the people lacked library service. Publicists puffed the library "as a social safety valve serving to drain off militancy and any desire to struggle collectively for better immediate conditions and a better social order." Library executives sabotaged libraries and culture with their
ruthless economies and "secret censorship":

Librarians seldom admit that they practice censorship. When hard pressed, they
call it "a proper choice of books with a limited book fund." Anything not in
keeping with the ideas of the library board (which is usually composed of business and "professional" men and almost never includes a "working man") is
ruled out. John Strachey's works are usually considered dynamite and it would
probably be hard to find the works of Langston Hughes in southern libraries.
As one prominent administrator said, "In this whole matter there is need for
opportunism and compromise. The librarian as censor must try to represent
the best and most enlightened public opinion. He should *perhaps* [italics in Otis]
be a little in advance of his public," but not very much—and only *perhaps*. The
"best and most enlightened opinion" which he strives to represent seldom
reaches as far as the works of Marx, Lenin, Strachey, and Dutt.[3]

Otis was quoting George Bowerman only five years earlier.

It was a good point. Librarians prided themselves on their liberties
yet did not recognize censorship where it occurred. Charles Compton,
ALA president, returned from a librarians' conference in Madrid real-
izing that where political criticism was suppressed, libraries might serve

useful educational and recreational functions, but they were not free. Yet he decided, as he told the trustees' section, not to treat this problem in his president's address, but only with the trustees. Although thought suppression in the United States had not yet involved libraries, he advised, it was "well for trustees to be on their guard." Without denying the librarian's "responsibility in this respect," he considered trustees to be far better equipped to protect libraries. It was they who officially represented the public and were recognized for their judgment and opinions.[4]

Compton made the flattering assumption that neither trustees nor librarians had restrictive policies. The fallacies of that assumption became patently clear at the meeting on "so-called radical periodical literature." (Not mentioned by title, the major publications were very likely the Communist *New Masses* and the fledgling *Partisan Review*.) The title of the symposium betrayed the liberal sentiments of the discussion leader, Samuel Ranck, as did his guiding comment (another echo of the 1890s) that "things that are radical today are reactionary tomorrow."[5] However, his panelists, who represented large public, research, and college libraries, coupled lip-service to liberalism with unambiguously restrictive policies.

Anne M. Mulheron (Portland Public Library) knew of no library that excluded radical material and hoped she never would, "though that is not a very popular thing to say." She would never exclude a radical work "if it is good literature—and there is where we draw the line. We do not keep out *Nation* and we do not keep out *New Republic*—and they are pretty radical at times—and we did not keep them out, except in the hysteria of war." As for the "cheap propaganda stuff," she did not know if readers of the *Nation* and *New Republic* read it; she thought they would be bored. She nevertheless would accept such materials if they were offered as gifts, rather than say that the library could not admit them—provided they were clearly set off and marked "Gifts." She had done this with a gift of Soviet periodicals. The designation showed that the library did not buy it with public funds, so that it was "perfectly legitimate to have it, if it passes our standards in literature."[6]

For George Utley, librarian of the Newberry library, the library's "nonpartisanship and impartiality" meant that it was "neither Democrat nor Republican," whatever the librarian's personal view might be. However, not all "wild and perhaps dangerous" propaganda would necessarily be respectable some day; some yardstick was required. His own library included radical material "within the scope of the library, provided it is capably written and printed on paper that will be reasonably long lived." Large reference libraries had a duty to collect radical propaganda but limit its use to scholars and serious students who were known to the library or who presented "satisfactory recommendations"—remembering always that much of it might be conservative tomorrow.[7]

F.L.D. Goodrich (College of the City of New York) also accepted all views; besides, nothing incensed a student so much as censorship of his reading. Restrictions were based on the grounds of preservation against mutilation and theft and never on the claim that the material was subversive. The library could accept propaganda as gifts, but could never buy any with public funds. Unfortunately, publications with excellent literary and academic standing, but of "a delicate shade of pink," could rarely be obtained as gifts. They were sometimes dropped when the color deepened, but at a distinct loss to the reference collection, since they included many unbiased articles on noncontroversial subjects. Even in a college with "a noisy group of extra-liberal students," the library could not pay for or advertise radical literature, though it would provide shelf space. In the end, the problem involved the college itself; the librarian followed administration policy.

The audience seemed to echo: All "so-called radical literature" of adequate literary standards could be accepted as gifts. To allow such material on the shelves, however, depended entirely on community and board policy.[8]

There were parallels here to Nazi libraries, albeit with the important difference that Americans allowed a two-party system and censored only radical literature. In Bavaria, forbidden literature encompassed all books catalogued under Socialism and Communism—except for works opposing these doctrines—as well as literature with Marxist, internationalist, pacifist or atheist tendencies. Restrictions, however, were similar. Censored works were allowed only to users whose purpose was "especially demonstrated" as not objectionable, or for serious scientific work by persons who were politically reliable.[9]

Although such parallels were not pointed out, Kunitz did assail the specious liberalism of the conference: the failure to mention gag laws, the stifling restrictions even on gifts when presenting both sides meant getting them, not buying up the ideas of one side and forcing the other to fend for itself. Since propaganda existed in all material, the issue was not propaganda at all but the propaganda of unpopular causes. Calling on librarians to defend their liberties, he proposed a Liberal Library League and named himself first member. He was soon joined by a retired librarian identifying herself only as the "Stormy Petrel," by Jesse Shera, by Gretchen Garrison. Others joined over the year.[10]

Marion Harmon applauded him. Many "young librarians (and some older ones too)," she said, had been sore in spirit at the symposium's "sham battle of the rubber swords," but fearful for their jobs. If these censors sought literary merit, they would not ban journals publishing Auden and Odets, Rolland and Barbusse, Nearing and Strachey, Hacker and Josephson. She contrasted the ALA meeting with the youth, vigor, and social consciousness of the rank and file at the Pacific Northwest Library Association conference two months later, at which resolutions had been put on the agenda protesting fascism and war preparation, supporting federal aid, and endorsing the democratization of ALA.[11]

Over 1935–1936, liberal ideology spread to other journals. *LJ* solicited the report on the Tübingen conference, published protests against gag laws and defenses of buying radical literature, ran Harold Laski's speech to the British Library Association. Laski urged librarians to defend the rights of readers to Lenin or Hitler, D. H. Lawrence or Boccaccio, Freud and Wycherley, to all "knowledge of the human adventure." The single criterion of inclusion was "the test of significance."

Do not let us be ashamed to be advocates of freedom. The librarian is in charge of the tradition of civilized man. He is required by his office to be a militant about its rights. He is, as Heine said, a soldier in the liberation war of humanity. Let him earn his reward for valor in that noblest of all conflicts.[12]

Librarians were now asked to practice what they preached. Leroy Merritt objected to restrictions on the use of meeting rooms, to receive an indignant retort that the library excluded only religious or political meetings. Leon Carnovsky (Chicago library school) exposed the disingenuous policies of a large city library that locked up *New Masses* but displayed, in the main library and in all branches, the *National Republic*, "the worst periodical usually found in library reading rooms." This Hearst-type publication was full of "hysterical articles demanding deportation of alien communists" or attacking "Carnegie Money and Communist Propaganda." Librarians might well reject it on the literary grounds they loved to invoke. He would not suggest denying it space as a gift, but he questioned the easy acceptance of anything that seemed patriotic and the censorship of unpopular minority views. When an organized group had offered gift subscriptions to the *New Masses* for each branch, the librarian had insisted on a three-month experiment to determine whether its popularity justified making it available. Of course it did not, and the journal was now held only at the main library and "carefully kept" on closed shelves. One might demand that journals justify their keep, but not use that argument to discriminate against unpopular titles.

I object to the supine acceptance of the censorship principle when there is nothing more behind it than the false fears of certain groups, made articulate by a reactionary press. Let us continually affirm and reaffirm that as librarians we propose to stick to our guns; that the principle of free speech shall not be throttled in the American Public Library.[13]

The *New Masses* was a case in point, for it had long been noted for its quality, relevance, and sensitivity to the fascist menace. Although the library, to justify its inclusion, used the old populist criterion of demand (rather than the elitist criterion of quality), Carnovsky showed that the principle it used was really censorship. Earlier, a college librarian had asked how the *Readers' Guide*—whose invaluable indexing made it a selection guide for libraries as well—could index a fascist sheet like the *National Republic* and not the *New Masses*. The *Readers' Guide* never added the *New Masses* to its coverage, but the *National Republic* was dropped by 1937.[14]

As witch-hunts were conducted in schools and colleges, an anonymous school librarian complained of "Red hunts" in the schools. Librarians were asked to oppose the University of Montana's censorship of Vardis Fisher's *Passion Spins the Plot*, for they might some day be directly implicated. Jesse Shera complained that he had encountered more resistance to the Liberal Library League among librarians than among any other group, and asked liberals to lobby against the sedition bill in Congress.[15]

It was becoming clear to many that neutrality might no longer be compatible with a commitment to freedom. In fact, it might militate against it. Neutrality, said Jesse Shera, had kept librarians from resisting encroachments on academic freedom. "'There are times when silence is not neutrality but assent.' " They who "so prided themselves on their objectivity and detachment, what have they done to prevent the growth of those very forces that now threaten civil liberties and academic freedom?" He demanded that college librarians unite with other professionals to protect civil liberties, particularly in the AAUP. There could be no tolerance of intolerance. Sidney Ditzion, a New York City college librarian (he, along with Shera, would later write the classic histories of public libraries), analyzed the advertising content and editorial bias of magazines, concluding that the category "propaganda" magazine—a criterion for exclusion—did not exist.[16]

A new perspective meshed freedom with the advocacy of a host of democratic values—civil liberties, pacifism, antifascism, racial equality. A relatively unknown librarian, William Carlson (Vanderbilt University) crystallized this attitude. The international fellowship of librarians was worthless, he felt, if its technical cooperation only supported the work of suppression and its conferences ignored the issues of book-burning and libraries in totalitarian states. He invoked Bowerman's 1915 discussion of neutrality and pacificism, along with the recent PNLA resolutions opposing war, as admirable precedents in reevaluating the traditional goals of impartiality and reevaluating tolerance. As "soldiers in the liberation war" (the words were Harold Laski's), librarians would have to oppose a social order that threatened their freedom. When Father Coughlin could deluge the Senate with forty thousand telegrams overnight, "even the most optimistic of us must admit that there is thunder on the horizon."[17]

More dramatically, Stanley Kunitz's editorial "Specter at Richmond" exposed the accommodations of the ALA leadership to segregated facilities at the site of its 1936 conference. Kunitz did not make the statement without risk. Soon after the editorial appeared, he was asked by the company president, Halsey Wilson, to subject his writings to management review or resign. Kunitz wrote his letter of resignation and prepared to leave. Wilson backed down in the end, however, and Kunitz remained, with the guarantee of complete editorial freedom.[18]

The most ardent advocates of the new perspective included, though they were not confined to, the Chicago library school faculty and even its future students. Its dean, Louis Round Wilson, expressed that perspective as ALA president in 1936. Criticizing the belletristic and vocational emphases of traditional library service, he called for a bolder educational role and broader social responsibility. By an extraordinary process of "anticipatory socialization," he was echoed by young librarians—Jesse Shera, Lester Asheim, Lowell Martin, Bernard Berelson, Leroy Merritt—who would later attend the Chicago library school.[19]

Throughout the decade, this perspective was opposed by old-line ALA presidents. Malcolm Wyer (1937) recalled the 1877 conference and resurrected the issues of recreational reading and the appropriate proportion of fiction in the library. Harrison Craver (1938) called attention to "the forgotten men"—businessmen, doctors, engineers, amateurs—who made a greater contribution to national development than other groups. Similar criticisms were made in 1936 by Ralph Munn, who would be president in 1939, and by others. Milton Ferguson, president in 1938, criticized "adult education," one earmark of the new school.[20]

The old-line librarians were not always conservative. Helen Haines, opposed to a library "science," expressed a humane liberalism, and her *Living with Books* (1935) was gratefully received as a weapon against censors. Nor were economic conservatives supporters of censorship. Milton Ferguson would be a strong defender of freedom in 1938. But they defined freedom within a different framework of values. Moreover, supporters of the "new" school could still be confused enough to make excuses for censorship. Clarence Sherman (Providence), for example, wrote a sympathetic comparison of the Chicago library school's "revolutionary" theory of librarianship with the older "censorship" and "sponsorship" theories. Yet he defended the Salt Lake City library's closed-shelf policies when they were criticized by Bernard De Voto, editor of the *Saturday Review of Literature*. De Voto regretted having to attack libraries when they were in such desperate financial straits, but he could not condone the librarian's keeping Vardis Fisher's books in a locked case and refusing to circulate them. (This editorial was one of several *Saturday Review* articles opposing libraries' closed-shelf policies.)[21]

Sherman defended exclusion with the old elitist arguments. In many libraries, he maintained, Vardis Fisher was not purchased at all. Moreover, public demand was neither predictable nor legitimate enough to dictate book selection. It was the librarian's prerogative "as a public servant" to "determine, subject to trustee approval," books of sufficient value to purchase. In the same address he lauded the common interests of librarians and publishers in "united opposition to censorship."[22]

Was it the librarians' inherent conservatism that kept them from opening their collections? Marian Scandrett, instructor of the Baltimore Public Library's training class, attributed the profession's negligible social significance to its exclusion of works like James T. Farrell's novels and its neglect of the class that Studs Lonigan represented. The prevalence of censorship was also reflected in the Western Writers of America's resolution against library censorship. On the other hand, the Chicago Public Library in 1936 refused demands by Polish and Russian groups that it remove "communistic or pornographic" works from the library.[23] It was a trustees' decision, in line with Chicago's tradition of liberalism, and this fact creates a functional identity between Chicago's liberalism and Salt Lake City's conservatism. Librarians were simply agents of their sponsors.

If librarians were to carry out their mission, then, they could not simply do so under orders. They might have to challenge the structure of authority that made them neutral experts carrying out the policies of others, policies that might contradict the democratic principles to which libraries were dedicated.

STRATEGIES OF INDEPENDENCE

With continuing depression and insecure status, professional elites were suspect for having wedded themselves to the interests of their sponsors, for what Julien Benda, in his popular critique (which Lyman Bryson and Stanley Kunitz cited), called "the treason of the intellectuals." That betrayal, for Benda, had lain in the involvement of intellectuals in "political passions" and propagandistic causes—whether fascistic, bolshevik, or bourgeois. Benda's was not a doctrine of neutrality, for he saw the intellectual's role as that of social critic, upholding values when they were violated in the political process. Like Voltaire, Spinoza, Zola in the Dreyfus case, the true intellectuals affirmed a disinterested morality.[24]

As the unreliability of patronage scarred the image of professional and functional unity, particularly among the rank and file, the erosion of loyalty to sponsors and to elite colleagues produced what Reinhard Bendix calls "strategies of independence"—allegiances that competed with managerial power, that challenged the functional dependence of librarians on their sponsors. Marx has described this functional dependence in another context: the relationship of literary and political representatives to the class they represent, and their identification with their sponsors' interests. They themselves may have backgrounds, education, and social positions that differ from those of their sponsors. But "in their minds they do not go beyond the limits which the latter do not go beyond in life. . . . They are consequently driven theoretically to the same tasks and solutions to which material interest and social position practically drive the latter."[25]

Jesse Shera, who had criticized professional leaders and colleagues, now attacked library sponsors—the "Friends of the Library" groups, whose friendship was interpreted in terms of " 'checks and balances,' " and the governing boards of trustees, "that nondescript agglomeration of big businessmen, lawyers, prelates, and politicians, obsessed with moneymadness, destitute of any qualifications for the offices they hold." Until their stultifying influence was lifted, he contended, there was small hope for educational advance.[26]

As the characteristic age-consciousness of this decade was transmuted into class consciousness, lower professional strata organized into nonexecutive staff associations and unions. In professional debates, unions were opposed because they violated the neutrality of public servants, which permitted no class allegiances, and because they put self-interest above the public interest. Union defenders pointed out the no-strike policy of the American Federation of Teachers and the fact that salaried physicians and actors had unionized without jeopardizing their professional status. The librarians' vaunted impartiality, they argued, concealed an "adamant" antiunion bias.[27]

Contrary to critics of the time and to sociological theorists, both unions and staff associations pursued more than material class interests. On the contrary, the *ideal* interests of these movements—their concern with censorship and social responsibility—spurred them to challenge neutrality in the name of professional conscience. The Washington Library Discussion Group, formed in May 1935 to exchange ideas on professional problems and work conditions, was behind much of the ferment of the 1935 PNLA resolutions.[28] Moreover, unionization itself was identified with social consciousness, with concern for clients. The distinguished social worker Mary Van Kleeck of the Russell Sage Foundation told the year-old Staff Organizations Round Table how professionals were becoming involved in social programs and legislation, "indeed affiliating with the labor movement" as an "organized source of power for human rights in conflict with the destructive . . . acquisitive forces which defend the status quo." If professionals overcame their detachment and their lack of responsibility for the social uses of their own discoveries, they could ally themselves with organized workers in support of democracy and peace.[29]

In 1937 the issues of professional tenure and professional freedom, which had been discussed separately by different proponents, were suddenly fused, as an open letter took the ALA to task for its evasions of civil liberties issues.

[May 8, 1937]

Mr. Malcolm Glenn Wyer
President, American Library Association

Last October the writer suggested to one of the staff at ALA headquarters the desirability of placing on the program of the New York convention an adequate discussion of civil liberties from the librarian's point of view. It was further suggested that perhaps no one would be in a better position to present the case than Mr. Roger Baldwin of the American Civil Liberties Union, whose authority to speak on such a subject, and whose ability as an orator, were unquestioned. The recommendation died aborning because it "might simply start the American Legion and the DAR in full cry on the library trail, without accomplishing very much that is constructive."

The suggestion was made, not with any desire to foment dissension, to embarrass the national officers, or even to excite the animosity of those revolutionary daughters, . . . but rather it was the sincere conviction that an impending future would witness repeated attacks upon those liberties that should be librarians' by right. Unhappily, the apprehensions of that warm October day have been confirmed. Librarians fleeing in terror from an unpleasant anticipation can now harvest the fruit of their timidity as an accomplished fact. . . .

In the capital city of . . . Iowa, professional ability and tenure have been relentlessly sacrificed before the brazen image of political favoritism. Contemptible as the proceeding has been, librarians are content to pass it by with but a word of regret. . . .

So the blow has fallen again, this time in Montana, where Philip O. Keeney, librarian and ranking professor for the past six years on recognized permanent tenure, has been asked to purge the campus . . . of his presence because his "philosophy of librarianship" was diametrically opposed to that of the university administration.

Jesse Shera
Oxford University
Miami, Ohio

The official reason for the firing was Keeney's "philosophy of librarianship"; the real reasons, said Shera, were his reputation (he was a Socialist) and his apparently successful efforts to organize a teachers' union on campus. Keeney had requested an ACLU and AAUP investigation, and Shera asked ALA to appoint a civil liberties committee so that it also could act.[30]

Malcolm Wyer responded that the ALA already had a committee on salaries, status, and tenure. It was investigating both the Keeney affair and the Iowa issue, in which a lawyer had been appointed state librarian.[31]

Milton Ferguson (Brooklyn Public Library), who had been writing *LJ* editorials on tenure, a question of material interest, now reported on the Keeney affair. Keeney was a Socialist, "is greatly interested in human rights and liberties, and abhors censorship in all its phases." His collection in economics and politics was the best between Minneapolis and Seattle. But his six years on annual appointment had not been renewed because he and the university president disagreed on "the philosophy of library administration." According to the university president, Keeney had promised no more trouble if he were granted another contract, but had threatened otherwise to call in the ACLU, AAUP, and AFT, and spread his case in "every radical sheet." What was the "ethical right of a librarian," Ferguson asked, "to ignore the opinions and wishes of higher authority?" How far did academic and free speech freedoms permit a faculty member "to project his personal convictions into college affairs and the administration of his library?"[32]

With the issue of loyalty to the administration—the classic academic freedom question—finally on the agenda, reformers explicitly linked fighting censorship to improving the *status* of librarians. Self-interest, which might have suggested loyalty to trustees, was subordinate to values in these discussions, just as the AFT and the AAUP, a union and a professional association, both pursued the academic freedom issue raised by the Keeney dismissal.

The question of obedience to trustees, which Ferguson had interpreted as one of neutrality, was now raised for the first time by the Committee on the new Code of Ethics. In summer 1937 it finally sought collective opinion on the classic academic freedom issue:

Is a publicly supported library, as a nonpartisan institution, obligated to purchase books representing all phases of opinion and interest? If true, should the librarian endeavor to secure impartiality in opposition to a policy established by his employing body?[33]

Debating an ALA representative, Marion Harmon of the PNLA asked if ALA was really helping the profession. It opposed staff associations because they had economic platforms. It had neglected to protect and extend the freedom and status of librarianship because it never opposed:

abridgement of the library's freedom in the censorship activities of many library boards. There is no blinking the fact that many libraries are subject to acute limitations on their choice and display of reading matter. It should be evident that the evil cannot be conquered successfully, just as a local matter, even if the fundamental principles of our profession did not insist on its treatment as a national problem. Has the ALA done anything to improve this unhappy situation?[34]

The answer was a nonanswer: Charles Compton had spoken to the trustees, who as recognized authorities and public representatives were better prepared to protect libraries. However, the delegation of responsibility to trustees itself made censorship a local issue. It permitted trustees to censor. The thrust of reform, meanwhile, as Miss Harmon made clear, was to define the defense of freedom as a *national* professional responsibility. Would the national association define this as a problem transcending local discretion?

Miss Harmon also asked why ALA had produced no report and announced no action on another prominent case (obviously Keeney's) involved with "improving the status of librarianship and directly concerned with the question of library freedom"—the protection of tenure. The answer: the old committee on salaries, staff, and service had just become a board on tenure and academic freedom.[35]

The AFT and the AAUP did undertake that study. It was the teachers' union, Keeney told his sympathetic friends, who would be responsible for his reinstatement. In spring 1938 the AAUP vindicated Keeney, and in March a district judge ordered his reinstatement. The university appealed the verdict. In summer the ALA board on staff, salaries, and tenure passed a resolution supporting Keeney. So did the Staff Organizations Round Table, in a more adamant attack on censorship and fascism.[36]

Keeney, whose three articles in *WB* in 1938–1939 showed Kunitz's unique sponsorship, now challenged a number of professional myths. The "people's university," he held, was a fiction; the homogeneous and unadventurous boards of libraries hardly represented the "best citizens," as Chalmers Hadley maintained. He thought this elitism strange for a public institution, since it was anathema to the public school. Hadley promptly responded that, true, trustees should represent their communities, but did they have to represent the "87 percent of the population who own barely 10 percent of the wealth?" Few would assume the responsibility of trusteeship, and those who did had keen civic awareness. There was a difference between public opinion and popular clamor—witness 1917, when librarians at popular demand had withdrawn Goethe and Schiller from the shelves.[37]

Even more challenging was Keeney's open letter to ALA suggesting a mechanism to defend librarians who were unfairly dismissed (he gave two cases). Keeney urged sanctions, not merely studies—a procedure that would warn librarians of libraries in which ethical standards were violated, the adoption of a vote of censure (the AAUP's "most condign punishment"), and organizational refusal to recommend a member for a position until conditions were improved. A comparison of the ALA and AAUP budgets would show that ALA had no financial problems in investigating such cases. The AAUP had spent $1,600 in 1937, or about the same amount as its cash balance, to study fifty-eight cases. Had the ALA spent the equivalent of its own cash balance, it would have disbursed $13,000.[38]

Even more significant are figures that Keeney tabulated but did not discuss. The ALA had a slightly larger membership than the AAUP—14,103 as against the AAUP's 13,930. The AAUP's 1937 budget had been $47,433, with all except for $1,310 derived from members' dues. By contrast, the ALA had a budget of $391,623, of which only $72,400 came from members' dues. The ALA membership dues alone were one and a half times the entire AAUP budget yet only one fifth the ALA budget. And, although both organizations spent about the same percentage of their budgets on administration (50 percent for the AAUP, 51 percent for the ALA), *the dollar amounts on administration alone were $23,000 for the AAUP against a staggering $190,000 for the ALA.* Roberto Michels's iron law of oligarchy posits that an organization's leaders develop their own vested interests that are independent of, and may conflict with, their members'. That law had a sound financial base in the ALA organization and virtually no countermechanism.[39]

DEMOCRACY AT BAY

As the Spanish civil war, Mussolini's Ethiopian venture, and Hitler's expansionism took their toll, the commitment to freedom intensified. "Freedom of speech is becoming our almost unique and most treasured possession," wrote Marilla Freeman, "certainly the possession for which free public libraries must fight to the death." The press at last aimed its potent ridicule at even the suggestion of censorship, while censorship from inside was also declining. Books were judged less by passages and language than by what the author was trying to say. In a world assailed by "isms," she found neutrality an "afraid" word—"negative, colorless, ineffective. Why should a librarian be neutral, forsooth?"[40]

In spring 1938 Stanley Kunitz's monthly literary notes were a *cantus firmus* of disaster. Chinese librarians, victims of Japan's "undeclared war of aggression," were appealing for help. Exiled Vicky Baum was becoming an American citizen. Thomas Mann's papers were deposited at

Yale. Storm troopers were in Vienna; Jewish writer Egon Freidel had jumped to his death through a Vienna window; Freud had been put in "protective custody." Little, Brown established an award for a manuscript by a German exile. As the Austrian Nazis began their purge, Brooklyn Borough President Ingersoll wired the chief librarian of the Austrian National Library in Vienna, offering to buy the banned books.[41]

ALA President-elect Milton Ferguson (Brooklyn) took up the theme. Surveying the turmoil around the globe, he praised librarians for having "for the most part" provided "information on all subjects, even those whose advocates seek to destroy our liberties." It was a strangely ineloquent statement. Censorship could produce its opposite. "A bad case thrives, for a time, on martyrdom. Burned books, phoenix-like, will rise from the ashes, if they be real books; but if they lack soul their destruction is little loss. Besides, that whole show is such an asinine trick the wonder is anyone should pause momentarily to observe it." Most controversies had "at least two sides though one of them be ever so wrong."[42]

Ferguson also touched off a dispute by praising librarians for not having identified themselves with unions. Before Hitler could burn the books, Maurice Leon of Milwaukee and William P. Tucker (Washington state librarian) reminded him, he had had to crush the unions. But even objectors praised Ferguson's stand on censorship.[43]

Censorship was salient to many at that conference, and especially to the Staff Organizations Round Table, which passed resolutions supporting Keeney, opposing his administration's censorship, urging library and book groups to protest against fascist regimes. Most important, it defined bias in book selection and in library administration as "breaches of library ethics" and resolved that SORT affiliates watch for and report such breaches to the ALA, with recommendations for action and publicity."[44]

In that frenzied atmosphere, critics of neutrality saw a false dichotomy between neutrality and advocacy. Presenting all sides of a question was a necessity, but only a start, said Bernard Berelson (University of Washington). On certain values the library could hardly be neutral— not on education, prejudice, the public interest, or war. The "duty of library impartiality" was keeping them from a "vital and neglected function." Libraries lacked influence because they did not see themselves as part of a social process of educating citizens in the face of propaganda—a more crucial if less worthy cause than individual education. Given that responsibility, a library's program followed naturally: to resist all censorship and protect the freedom of librarians to 'teach' what they believe. Librarianship must pay more attention to this educational program than to . . . methodology and mechanics, . . . to be better trained in the social sciences and in adult education."[45]

Could librarians adopt this role, Marian Scandrett questioned, when they were so conservative? They were functionaries, not thinkers, and evaders of controversy. They stacked their meetings with worthy educators and pleasant authors, and were so out of tune with the twentieth century that they thought of unions only in terms of strikes.[46]

Accepting propaganda began to seem a democratic duty. Ralph Esterquest outlined a policy for choosing propaganda on all sides; Sydney Mitchell claimed that the *Saturday Evening Post* was as propagandistic for some readers as the *New Masses* was for others, and he praised a student who had argued with a trustee to include Earl Browder's book on communism—and won. For public librarians, this was a major advance: the librarian need not accept a trustee's word as sacrosanct; policy was negotiable.[47]

Leon Carnovsky flatly denied the conventional ethical wisdom:

I most certainly do not subscribe to McColvin's dictum that "the library should have no opinions, no motives, no religion, no politics, no morals."

I know this seems to fly in the very face of the cherished principle that the librarian should not permit his personal predilections to dictate his policy of book selection. This is generally true; but what I am arguing for is a librarian whose predilections are for established truths and who then bases his book selection upon those truths. . . . The principle of wide representation . . . should never be applied to justify the equal provision of established truths and their denials.[48]

"The equal provision of established truths and their denials." With that statement Carnovsky laid bare the fallacy of the norm of neutrality. The statement did not imply censorship, for by "established truths" Carnovsky did not mean orthodoxy. Quite the contrary, for he specified: Should the library lend its considerable prestige to unpopular truths? "I do not see how this can be avoided if the library is to take seriously its educational prerogative. Indeed, if such truths are unpopular, the reason is all the greater for the expounding, for their lack of acceptance implies the need for education." The criterion of intellectual authority and the "principles of logic and reason" were to be set against "the shifting tides of sentiment manipulated by clever demagogues."[49]

It was a question-begging statement, in a sense, just as the term "established [but unaccepted!] truths" was question-begging. But it tried to grapple with the problem of authority in the way that the norm of neutrality did not. And it resurrected the passion and educational ambitions of the forgotten library leaders of the 1890s who had also actively sought leadership in the development of a critical public opinion that would be immune to demagoguery and propaganda. That passion was accompanied by a concern for scholarship, which would lend them the authority they sought.

In winter 1938, a policy statement that had been adopted by the Des Moines Public Library was submitted to the major library publications by Forrest Spaulding, the librarian, in response to two anonymous writers in *WB* who had despaired at the conservatism of librarians. Spaulding blamed trustees for conservative policies and praised his own trustees for the liberality of the policy statement. "Must the fire-eating Juniors swallow, little by little, all their fire" to protect their jobs from reactionary trustees? lamented Kunitz.[50]

Published in the three major journals in December and January of 1938–1939, the Des Moines Library's Bill of Rights was heralded in *LJ*, printed on the inside front cover of the *ALA Bulletin*, reprinted with Spaulding's comments in *WB* (Document 12.1). It had four clauses:

DOCUMENT 12.1
THE DES MOINES LIBRARY'S BILL OF RIGHTS

The Library's Bill of Rights

Now, when indications in many parts of the world point to growing intolerance, suppression of free speech, and censorship affecting the rights of minorities and individuals, the Board of Trustees of the Des Moines Public Library reaffirms these basic policies governing a free public library to serve the best interests of Des Moines and its citizens.

1. Books and other reading matter selected for purchase from public funds shall be chosen from the standpoint of value and interest to the people of Des Moines and in no case shall selection be based on the race or nationality, political or religious views of the writers.

2. As far as available material permits, all sides of controversial questions shall be represented equally in the selection of books on subjects about which differences of opinion exist.

3. Official publications and/or propaganda of organized, religious, political, fraternal, class, or regional sects, societies, or similar groups, and of institutions controlled by such, are solicited as gifts and will be made available to library users without discrimination. This policy is made necessary because of the meager funds available for the purchase of books and reading matter. It is obviously impossible to purchase the publications of all such groups and it would be unjust discrimination to purchase those of some and not of others.

4. Library meeting rooms shall be available on equal terms to all organized nonprofit groups for open meetings to which no admission fee is charged and from which no one is excluded.

Adopted by The Des Moines Board of Trustees—Nov. 21, 1938.

SOURCE: *American Library Association Bulletin* 32 (December 1938), inside front cover.

1. It stipulated that books and other reading matter were to be chosen for their value and interest, and never for the race or nationality, or political or religious views, of the writers.

2. All sides of controversial materials were to be represented equally in the selection of books on disputed subjects.

3. Official publications of organized sects, societies, and similar *propaganda* groups were to be *solicited* as gifts and made available to all. This policy was necessary because of the meager funds available for books and the reluctance to purchase just some of these materials and not others.

4. Library meeting rooms would be open to all organized nonprofit groups for open meetings for which there was no charge.[51]

A new code of ethics was adopted by the ALA Council at the Midwinter meeting of 1938–1939. The first Library's Bill of Rights was adopted in summer 1939 (Document 12.2) through a motion presented by Ernestine Rose, a New York branch librarian and chairman of the

---

DOCUMENT 12.2
THE AMERICAN LIBRARY ASSOCIATION LIBRARY'S
BILL OF RIGHTS

Adopted by the Council of the American Library Association, ALA Annual Conference in San Francisco, 1939

Today, indications in many parts of the world point to growing intolerance, suppression of free speech, and censorship affecting the rights of minorities and individuals. Mindful of this, the Council of the American Library Association publicly affirms its belief in the following basic policies which should govern the services of free public libraries:

1. Books and other reading matter selected for purchase from the public funds should be chosen because of value and interest to people of the community, and in no case should the selection be influenced by the race or nationality or the political or religious views of the writers.

2. As far as available material permits, all sides of questions on which differences of opinion exist should be represented fairly and adequately in the books and other reading matter purchased for public use.

3. The library as an institution to educate for democratic living should especially welcome the use of its meeting rooms for socially useful and cultural activities and the discussion of current public questions. Library meeting rooms should be available on equal terms to all in the community regardless of their beliefs or affiliations.

SOURCE: *American Library Association Bulletin* 33 (15 October 1939): P60–P61.

ALA board on adult education. At the same conference, the Supreme Court order mandating Keeney's reinstatement was announced.[52]

Both events were obscured by a far greater controversy, the appointment, as Librarian of Congress, of a nonlibrarian, Archibald MacLeish. Decades after the bookman-librarian had been forgotten, librarians complained that MacLeish was not qualified. He was not an administrator, and librarianship was not a literary pursuit.[53]

Both the code of ethics and the code of freedom concealed important ambiguities. The code of ethics stressed the "final jurisdiction" of the governing authority (trustees), though the library was held to exist for the benefit of its constituency. It endorsed a "spirit of loyalty" and "impartial service" to users. "Provision" was to be made for "as wide a range of publications and as varied a representation of viewpoints as is consistent with the policies of the library and with the funds available." Thus the standard dilemma and the criteria for exclusion remained untouched. And, after that brave question of trustee control, the code was silent on the matter of divergence between trustees and the library's public when that divergence resulted in censorship.[54]

So, too, the ALA Library's Bill of Rights, though following the Des Moines statement almost verbatim, made a quiet omission. The bill affirmed freedom in collections, free use of meeting rooms, and the selection of materials on the basis of value and interest irrespective of the author's race or creed. But it left out clause 3 of the Des Moines statement, which solicited propaganda as gifts:

This policy [requiring gifts] is made necessary because of the meager funds available for the purchase of books and reading matter. It is impossible to purchase the publications of all such groups and it would be unjust discrimination to purchase those of some and not others.[55]

The Des Moines clause committed the library actively to seek out propaganda on all sides. The national organization chose to treat that as a local issue, hence one it did not have to confront.

SUMMARY AND EPILOGUE: THE POPULAR FRONT

The omissions and vagueness in the code of ethics and the code of freedom were the price of consensus, bringing together an array of disparate groups: those committed to balanced enduring collections, the pivot of the populist-elitist debate; supporters of conservative trustees; liberals who sought an active educational role; radicals who should have wished to challenge trustee censorship. Like the Popular Front, this coalition concealed its internal differences in order to take a stand, and even then only after internal resistance.

As the hypothesis in Chapter 5 suggests, leaders will hesitate to invoke norms in situations of conflict, since this strategy can arouse opposition as well as support in the community. That posture was explicit when the ALA rejected Jesse Shera's civil liberties agenda and resisted Mary Harmon's probing questions about censorship as a national professional problem. It is not youth alone that will adopt a Weberian ethic of ultimate ends. The leadership, however, will more likely adopt the pragmatic ethic of responsibility.

As external crisis made the affirmation of freedom more popular, however, leadership resistance broke down. Between 1938 and 1939, Milton Ferguson spoke out several times against censorship. Although one hesitates to attribute opportunism to him, it seems clear, from Ingersoll's offer to buy banned books from Austria, that when Ferguson, chief librarian in Ingersoll's borough, advocated freedom, he acted with solid political support. And, though one cannot logically equate eloquence with sincerity, there is a lack of imagination and intensity in his words that contrasts with the precise and focused affirmations of Carnovsky, Shera, and Berelson.

To those who voted for it, the Library's Bill of Rights may have had many meanings. But one thing it did not affirm, in the context of that time, was the norm of neutrality. Commitment to democratic teaching and advocacy was urgent after Hitler's march into Czechoslovakia. At the 1939 conference, a message was broadcast from Jan Masaryk, exiled in London. Soon after, Carl Milam, executive secretary of the ALA, summoned libraries to the active defense of democracy, calling upon them to stress programs in propaganda analysis. Milton Ferguson stated that libraries might have to establish propaganda departments. By then Britain was at war, and even Roosevelt, pronouncing a reluctant neutrality, confessed to neutrality only in action, not thought.[56]

It was a fragile consensus. The Progressive Librarians Council was formed that year, with Keeney among its active leaders. In a year, advocacy itself would mean different things. It would mean pacifism to the Progressive Librarians Council, as it still did to both Communists and isolationists; to individuals like Mrs. Beatrice Rossell, who resigned as editor of the *ALA Bulletin* when she saw ALA leaders adapting themselves to war aims; to less militant librarians like Hiller Wellman. To others, like Archibald MacLeish, pacifism would connote a craven neutrality while commitment to values would mean war against Nazism.[57]

Nor were notions of freedom transformed by the statement. The country was troubled in 1939 with censorship episodes involving *The Grapes of Wrath* in California, Kansas, and Buffalo. There were complaints but no organized protests.[58]

If the vagueness of the new codes was the price of consensus, that bargain was hardly unique to the time or the profession. Staughton Lynd has made that point about the Declaration of Independence. Because the revolution's manifesto had to appeal to all, it was vague on the issue of human and property rights and slavery. As the submerged conflict erupted in abolitionism, that coalition, in turn, was silent on the kind of economic system that would supplant slavery. Lynd sees, within the framework of a surprisingly consistent Utopia, "a dialectical process of ideological response to changing social conditions, such that each sharpening of social conflict calls forth a clarification of ideas previously ambiguous." The more diverse the coalition, the more ambiguous the ideology justifying its action.[59]

More generally, Philip Selznick points out that "language used for self-protection and for exhortation develops terms which are unanalyzed, and persistently so, for their effectiveness depends upon the diversity with which they may be invested." They may be linked to symbols like democracy. Since unanalyzed abstractions cannot guide action, behavior will be determined not so much by professed ideas as by immediate pressures.[60]

This does not mean that unanalyzed abstractions serve as empty rhetoric. They give a sense of unity and bind together technical experts who would otherwise confine themselves to their special professional interests.[61] These abstractions can also set into motion the process of ideological clarification that Staughton Lynd describes and that may be dictated by the perceived discrepancies between ideals and reality.

That process became apparent as the year progressed: in Carl Milam's hint that the ALA would soon engage more actively in disputing censorship; in his reference to *The Grapes of Wrath* banning as a violation of freedom; in *LJ*'s questioning of the right of trustees to keep such a book from taxpayers rather than delegate selection to the librarian. Some librarians proudly pointed to precedents in freedom. Others, like Jens Nyholm in 1940, maintained that librarians violated that value.[62]

The pride and self-criticism were not set in motion by the Library's Bill of Rights. They stemmed, rather, from the same heightened sensitivity and solidarity that had already produced the code of freedom itself. Moreover, freedom had become more than a functional norm required for the exercise of librarians' duties. Those duties were themselves set in the service of freedom.

When Archibald MacLeish addressed the librarians in 1940, he offered that code as his solution to the problem they had never solved: finding an adequate definition of their unique professional role. As he reviewed the social purposes that had been proposed over the past century—recreation, equal opportunity for ambitious men, even the condescending missionary impulse to improve the masses—he found them inadequate as goals for a profession. But if librarians saw themselves as more than agents whose responsibilities were ended when readers received their books, their problem could be solved. If they saw themselves as selecting from the record the books that people needed for their decisions, they could, in this "impending democratic crisis," validate a way of government and a way of life.[63]

It was not a new solution that he offered. There were precedents enough, dating back to the 1890s, repeated in the praised but admittedly neglected Learned report, urged by the Chicago school and by friends like Alvin Johnson, author of the gratefully received *The People's University* (1938). But that orientation had produced no tradition. MacLeish could thus offer as his contribution his rediscovery of a professional mandate:

To subject the record of experience to intelligent control so that all parts of that record shall be somewhere deposited; to bring to the servicing of that record the greatest learning and the most responsible intelligence the country can provide; to make available the relevant parts of that record to those who have need of it . . . and in a form responsive to their need—surely these are not difficulties beyond the competence of the men and women who have constructed in this country one of the greatest library systems the world has seen.

There are dangers in such an undertaking. But there are dangers also—even greater dangers—in refusing to attempt it. And the rewards of success are rewards worth seeking. Not only would the cause of democracy, the cause we believe to be the cause of civilization, be served. But it is conceivable that the profession to which we belong might find in the process the definition of its function for which it has sought so long—a function as noble as any men have ever served.[64]

For a while, it would be enough.

13.

CONCLUSIONS AND THEORETICAL IMPLICATIONS

This study has traced the way in which librarians' attitudes toward censorship changed in line with changing concepts of the public interest and of the library's democratic function. When the first large public libraries were established, free educational institutions were seen as guardians against religious and class discrimination. The knowledge relevant to their goals was certified and useful knowledge, while policies of neutrality through exclusion, mirroring the separation of church and state, respected strong religious identifications. These functions of the library were compatible with censorship. At the end of this study political identities were paramount, free education had been taken on by other institutions, and education on political issues and mass media propaganda had become an important function.

What models of social change are suggested by these patterns? One is nationalization—the cosmopolitan "intrusion" on local and rural communities with the growth of national markets and centralized government. This process explains the changing nature of the conflicts in this study. For, contrary to the nostalgic evocations of a later age, the earlier, "traditional" period of this study was no era of harmony, homogeneity, or "community," but one of sharp partisan conflict. The portraits of past social cohesion were created by participants in a conflict on a larger scale.

What changed were the social identities that underlay the conflicts—religious vs. political, local vs. "cosmopolitan." The Comstock law of 1873 was a national law that affected state and local communities as well as large cities. The mass media and controversial new literature were also introduced through a national system of distribution and advertisement and the mass marketing of literature. The Scopes trial erupted when secondary education, incorporating state-level curricular changes, spread to lower social strata in small communities. But these were not rural-urban conflicts. Censorship conflicts existed in New York, Boston, and Chicago as well as small towns. What differed between rural and urban communities were the degree of homogeneity and the balance of power, hence the outcome.[1]

The process of secularization also sheds light on these changes. Secularization refers to the decline in salience or power of religious concepts, values, and institutions in a society's culture, social structure, or individual motivation. Secularization, however, was a many-faceted process. In the early nineteenth century, church-state relations were caught at a stage when a change of function—state responsibility for education—entailed a promise not to challenge religious values. The policies of exclusion respected the importance of religious identities. Thus, even as secular law replaced religious authority as the censoring agent, religious values were carried into the secular sphere. Just as the blue laws reflected religious values, the antiobscenity law of 1873 was a secular version of religious morality. Its sanctions cannot be said to have conflicted with, and checked, publishers' economic interests, for they made it economically expedient as well as morally desirable to adhere to the rules. It *was* in the publishers' economic interests to conform to the laws, for individuals, schools, and libraries purchased books in terms of a publisher's reputation.

Over time, these notions of propriety were deinstitutionalized. Risqué literature appeared more often, was less frowned upon, and came daringly close to the legal boundaries of permissible expression. In the meanwhile, the growth of the publishing industry itself provided the resources to challenge the censorship laws.

These changes did not signify a simple breakthrough of economic interests, of commercialization. Accompanying the literary changes were changing moral criteria. The presumed harmful effects of improper literature were questioned. On the level of values, new distinctions were made between sin and crime, between private and public morality, while values like freedom and honesty became more important than propriety in depicting social relations.

The publishers' ideology of free speech—another sacred value—may have justified their economic interests. But the ideological arguments themselves were culturally constrained. In the entire time period of this study, First Amendment freedoms were not claimed by publishers in their defenses of so-called obscene literature. Such legal arguments would be raised only after World War II. Thus, even the way in which one's interests are expressed reflects existing social values.[2]

Perhaps the most important aspect of this change involves the shifting of intolerance from moral to political bases. Not only were religious values secularized; other values became sacred. The long-term trend is toward greater freedom of expression in sexual matters, or private morality, but greater control of political expression, in which the freedom of the 1930s was only an interlude. That long-term trend is shown in increasing legal suppression at the national level, from the deportation laws of the late nineteenth and early twentieth centuries to the wartime legislation of World War I, which was never repealed, and the formation of committees and groups on un-American activities. This shifting of intolerance continued, after the time period of this study, in legislation during and after World War II in the Smith and McCarran acts.

This is quite the opposite process from that described by Coser, in which political and moral censorship tend to go hand in hand.[3] The most relevant factor in explaining it are the increasing salience of the citizen's status and the importance of loyalty to the state, which involved a redefinition of the spheres of private and public morality. The laws are the key indicators of this shift. The move of sexual morality to the private sphere is reflected in the weakening of the Comstock law. The salience of the citizen's loyalty is shown in the increasingly stringent legislation barring deviant political action and expression.

With this separation between society and government in the modern political community, such distinctions as *Gemeinschaft-Gesellschaft* become less significant in defining modern society than the Weberian distinction between private groups and the formal authority of the state. "The growth of citizenship and the nation-state," Reinhard Bendix comments, may be "a more significant dimension of modernization than the distributive inequalities underlying the formation of social classes." The nineteenth-century class conflict that Marx theorized about was replaced by class accommodation and the welfare state.

Sigmund Diamond describes a similar pattern in the changing criteria of American loyalty. Political loyalty came to be equated with loyalty to an economic system and citizenship came to mediate class conflict by fostering common loyalties and identities over the divisive loyalties of class.[4]

THE ROLE-SET MODEL

The development of the profession, which forms the background of this study, was irregular. The victories of the turn of the century—the appointment of professional librarians to the key Library of Congress and New York Public Library posts—contrast with the professional defeat of 1939, when Archibald MacLeish was named Librarian of Congress. Yet the intervening years had seen sharp advances in professional education, research, and the development of ethical standards. In the 1930s, despite these advances, positions were scarce and tenure subject once more to political manipulation. The reason was the market situation of the Depression.

This irregularity of development is not peculiar to librarianship. In nineteenth-century America, resistance to professional monopolies created a period of deprofessionalization before the Civil War, a trend that did not block marked intellectual advances. In recent years, academia has seen a similar regression, and a wave of rebellion has mounted against belief in professional expertise. Many features of professions— their goals and functions; the level of required expertise; their autonomy and concepts of the public good—are not givens. They change with the social situation and reflect changing social support of their activities.

Because the model of professionalization seemed too narrow for purposes of this study, the more abstract model of the role-set was used to probe the structure of occupational relationships. A triangular relationship was isolated; the relationship between professional expert, sponsor, and client. The value and role conflicts involving the choice of literature stemmed from these relationships.

The *elitist-populist* dilemma involves the conflicting demands of sponsor and client, or professional and client, with respect to high and popular culture. These demands were particularly acute for librarians, because the library's clientele is not guaranteed, as with many other public services; hence the client is relatively powerful.

The *neutrality-advocacy* dilemma involves the librarian's need to serve all groups impartially, without allowing dominant groups to dictate policy or book choice. Librarians at first avoided religious and political literature in line with church-state separation, just as schools forbade sectarian texts or prayers. Later this impartiality insulated them from political encroachments. These policies changed over time to admit more and more controversial material.

Neutrality was challenged when the central values of the state or society itself became primary. In times of war or crisis, librarians advocated, or were sometimes expected to advocate, pacifism, patriotism, or democracy. These values did not themselves dictate censorship or freedom, but they led to policies that might endorse either censorship, as in 1917, or freedom, as in the 1930s.

The third dimension, *censorship-freedom*, relates to these borderline problems, for it involves literature with little social support, literature embodying morally or socially subversive views or relationships. Here librarians moved from positions endorsing censorship to positions endorsing freedom, but they lagged behind the literary changes, censoring what was most modern and controversial. With religious and political radicalism, librarians shifted between more and less hospitable positions. The boundaries were broader during the Progressive era, when socialism was spreading, narrower in the 1920s, a period of political conservatism, and broader again in the 1930s.

Although censorship seems to imply repression of innovative ideas, the problem of censorship encounters the classic liberal dilemma: the

responsibility of a democracy to allow free expression to the most repugnant ideas, even those that deny the very principles of freedom on
which that hospitality is based. Fascistic literature, racist children's literature, crime, sadism, pornography, and child pornography present
these problems. It is not possible to exclude them all on the basis of
aesthetic principles alone. To represent them on the basis of what publishers choose to issue is to beg the question. Yet even the most liberal
library will hesitate to allow deviant views to appear as more than occasional curiosities. Although the inclusion of radical literature seems
to raise different problems, the analogies between all themes that undermine what a society holds sacred must also be recognized.

Librarians assert their autonomy so that they can realize these values, but the nature of autonomy is not self-evident. It can be used to
justify deference to the client, or to the sponsor, or to resist them—
one, or the other, or both. In the nineteenth century, moral censorship
in the name of the public interest transcended the keenest populist solicitude.

Moreover, the question of accountability raises an entire range of issues about how the public is to be defined—in terms of majoritarian
considerations or a superior elite representing the public interest? Here
the elitist-populist distinction requires refinement. At first the community was defined in majoritarian terms and the demands of minorities
had little legitimacy. In the twentieth century, minority rights were
granted more legitimacy and conflict itself became increasingly acceptable. Finally, the abstract notion of a society transcending local communities became the context for defenses of intellectual freedom.

The triadic professional-sponsor-public relationship also implies that
the assertion of autonomy against one role partner is likely to be a defense of the other. Autonomy cannot be considered in abstract terms
but involves an implicit coalition: professional and sponsors against
outside control; professional and client against hierarchic control. From
this implicit coalition are derived the two forms of professional autonomy: *institutional* and *status* autonomy.

This study traced four such coalitions. In the 1880s, several librarians
challenged trustees in defense of the value of censorship, asserting status autonomy. In the Progressive era, librarians and trustees, asserting
institutional autonomy, defended censorship against outside efforts to
liberalize the library. In the 1920s, trustees and librarians united to defend freedom against censorship pressures from the community. In the
1930s, the status autonomy of librarians was invoked in the name of
freedom, as liberals, unionists, and Socialists claimed independence of
trustees in the name of clients and the public interest.

Partly because the public library never had the institutional autonomy of the older college and university, the institutional defense of

freedom preceded the status defense of freedom. Although deference to sponsors shaped librarians' choices of clients, statuses and issues, these influences permitted a range of possibilities. Choosing among them, librarians were hardly aware of the constraints they accepted. Eventually sponsorship itself was a liberating force, as the Carnegie Corporation projects show.

Even with the client advocacy of the 1930s, however, professionalism was never asserted in terms of a populism that equated service with public demand; in that sense, professional leaders were always elitist. But elitism does not connote censorship, nor does populism connote freedom, for a conservative populism was an important ideological strain for almost the entire period under review. Professional leaders, though sympathetic to the public, sought to improve public taste or public opinion. They differed in the *way* they saw libraries as educational forces.

Thus, there is no development from elitism to a democratic acceptance of the public taste, as has been claimed by some sociologists and historians. The tension between elitism and populism is endemic, though the content of debate may change and though the language of censorship may be drawn into the discussion. The dime novel of yesterday is replaced by the bestseller and tabloid of today.

Nor can the 1939 code of ethics, with its deference to the public, be legitimately interpreted as an abdication of professional autonomy to popular taste. Librarians had long asserted their obligation to educate the public; they *had* risked unpopularity in asserting censorship; they *had* dismissed lay opinion as irrelevant and incompetent.[5] Superiority to the client and loyalty to trustees in defending censorship were common as late as 1937. What the 1939 code of ethics meant was a renunciation of censorial control, the tradition from which librarians were still breaking away. Solicitude for the client was doubly significant in a decade when professionals themselves were under suspicion as betrayers of their clients.

Like populism and elitism, loyalties to sponsors and clients are endemic sources of conflict. The relative emphases change with the historical situation, as the struggles of the 1930s (not to mention the 1960s), make clear.

Thus the professional rarely challenges his entire role-set but implicitly mobilizes one part of it against the other even in asserting autonomy. He takes sides between them. That implicit coalition underscores the precariousness of professional autonomy.

The role-set model also clarifies the presumed conflict between professions, which stress peer control and autonomy, and bureaucracy, which rests on line authority and hierarchic control. The conflict is said to occur when the professional works in a bureaucracy—in a hospital, law firm, or corporation—and must subject himself to supervision by laymen. Taking issue with this view, a critical school argues that professionals function very well within bureaucratic confines—indeed, that professionalism makes their behavior predictable to bureaucrats.[6] We have seen both modes of behavior in this study.

The question slices deeper, however, than conflict or accommodation between professional and bureaucrat—as these empirical findings should indicate. There is a theoretical convergence, however, between profession and bureaucracy that Weber caught and that the role-set model clarifies. Bureaucracies in Weber's classic essay have the *same features* as professions: specialized expertise; a service orientation; recruitment based on competence; rules that ensure impartial service "without regard to person." Thus they raise the same role-set conflicts and values: elitism-populism, neutrality-advocacy, and the assertion of autonomy.

Neutrality—and tenure—protect the civil servant from arbitrary rule from above and from outside political interference. He retains his position through changes in administration. Officials protect themselves from outside lay and political interference by asserting their superior knowledge and the right to act upon it. On the other hand, not wanting to be arbitrary, bureaucrats may enlist advice from outside parties. Here is the elitist-populist dimension: assertion of superiority when threatened by clients versus a sense of accountability to the public.

Finally, professionals and bureaucrats are both technical experts carrying out policies they do not create, seeing to it that the "societally exercised authority is carried out." Hence the structurally based motivation for experts to conform to their superiors or sponsors.[7]

However, the execution of policy itself involves discretion and choices among alternatives, hence a sphere of autonomy that carries bureaucrats through political changes while the leaders are shuffled. As a result, bureaucracies develop independent vested interests, and a conflict can result between rulers, staff, and subjects in which bureaucrats have power because of their expertise.

Thus the structural dynamics of professions and bureaucracies show strong parallels. The common values are expertise, public service, neutrality, technical execution of policy determined by others, and autonomy. On the structural level, the ruler-staff-subject (citizen) triad parallels the sponsor-professional-public triad. These parallels are obvious when they are assimilated to the abstract model of the role-set.

The two ways of looking at bureaucracy, in terms of its functioning from above and of the development of autonomous interests, produce the respective claims to institutional autonomy and to status autonomy. And the dilemmas that bureaucrats face parallel the three major themes of conflict of this study: populism-elitism, neutrality-advocacy, and the assertion of institutional and status autonomy. These value dilemmas are derived from parallel role-set relationships.

The convergence between profession and bureaucracy hardly rules out conflict between them. But that conflict does not stem from any attributes *specific* to professions. It is produced by different role orientations and structural relationships *within* the same profession. Specialists in the same profession may serve poor or rich clients, public or private agencies.[8] Or conflict may stem from peer-oriented, status-specific interests, as they challenge organizational loyalties.

Status-specific interests are not confined to professionals in bureaucracies. They can emerge in collegial organizations or in the form of unions, groups considered antithetical to professions. Whether these strategies take the form of academic freedom or union consciousness is less important than the fact that both crosscut the functional ties producing loyalty to an organization. Both, moreover, support both material and ideal interests. In this study, unions were militant champions of academic freedom and union advocates were among those most completely committed to the code of freedom.[9] Thus, the conflict between profession and bureaucracy has less to do with the problems of autonomous expertise than with the values that expertise is made to serve.

An unexpected finding of the study was that, though women were not more prudish than men, they were blamed for its restrictiveness— by both women and men—as they were blamed for other faults of the profession, including its love of fussy detail. They seemed literally to be scapegoats, not only assigned the dirty work but blamed for it. Their standing and function shed light on semiprofessions.

Semiprofessions are occupations that have a service ethic but not the requisite expertise and autonomy and prestige of the full professions; they are also centered in bureaucracies and tend to have a high proportion of women. Peter Rossi has suggested that the status of librarianship could be raised if the division of labor were made "as radical as that accomplished in medicine where nursing is the female occupation and doctoring the male." Amitai Etzioni, by contrast, holds that it hardly pays for librarians to aspire to professional standing, since the intellectual qualifications do not exist and/or are not needed.[10]

These studies seldom question another theoretically relevant dimension of reward: pay. Women provide a cheaper work force for a *comparable* level of education. Men entering the field are not likely to change these conditions; in the 1930s, men entered librarianship because of the retrenchment of opportunity. On the contrary, once the pay scale in a field improves, men are likely to move into it.

Moreover, the fact that librarians aspired to different goals requiring different levels of education suggests that the question is misplaced. It should be: What kinds of material rewards accompany what kinds of professional investment?

This question sheds light on the librarians' never-ending claim that the library is no longer a storehouse of books but has become an active educational force. The active pursuit of this valuable objective would have required extensive preparation, as its advocates from the 1890s on saw. The problem was the investment, a problem raising the question: What level of competence, proficiency, even vision will a society support? The public interest is generally defined by the powerful. The resources required to fund such a free, nonprofit, tax-supported institution are not likely to be ample.

The problem is illustrated by another occupation engaged in the diffusion of knowledge: journalism. The reporter's objectivity does not ensure reportorial responsibility. Quite the contrary. Journalistic objectivity has been codified as a technique and not a perspective. By quoting highly visible authorities who can define the situation, reporters avoid responsibility for knowing what they write about.[11] An academic background would be desirable in a reporter. That it is not is not due to the occupation's low standing. Given the expected profits for such input, publishers (and journalists) will not foot the bill. Similarly, the function that MacLeish prescribed for librarians, and that many sought, was socially valuable. But it was not likely to provide the economic rewards to warrant the investment.

The socially defined social contribution of a profession depends on factors that are not easily separable from the profits to be derived for given levels of competence and service to particular social strata. These are causes, and not consequences, of a given level of intellectual competence.

IDEALS AND IDEOLOGY

The findings of this study support the notion that the professional values of neutrality and autonomy entail a tacit agreement not to be too critical of society. Librarians exercised autonomy within limited spheres and through careful client-status, status-selection, and issue-selection that focused on uncontroversial roles. This argument is not confined to capitalism. Capitalist society, or any society, may permit a range of activity that is not repressive and may be quite generous in the case of literature, if its separation from action is stressed. Moreover, aspiring professions with modest goals should not be criticized in the same terms as established professions.

These findings also confirmed a variable relationship between values and interests. Ideas do not survive on their own merits. They require receptive environments and sponsors who will urge them. Nor are they likely to survive unless they appeal to the particular interests of their advocates. However, while ideas and values require the spur of economic or political interests in order to become impulses to action, the two are mutually interdependent. Where interests are pursued, ideology develops to justify them. However, ideology is no spurious by-product of these interests. It may react back upon them and change their nature. Throughout, the Weberian coupling of "ideal and material interests" was used to indicate this complex interweaving.[12]

Values are also expressed broadly enough to be interpreted in several ways that may be opportunistic or idealistic. They may compete with interests, not merely express them. Such potential conflict is inherent in all situations, since values are seldom bolstered so completely by a system of rewards and punishments that conformity exacts no toll. It is a paradox, moreover, that to the degree that values are institutionalized, they are structured *into* material interests so that values and self-interest are not distinguishable. Given such structurally induced motivations and the institutional control of a wide range of motives, commitment to values, or integrity, is consistent with conformity. But integrity, strictly speaking, is undetectable under such conditions. It is *discernible* only when it costs.

Thus, only a few idealists will rise above apologetics to criticize their own self-interest. Such disinterested thinking characterizes scholars rather than sages, prophets rather than priests—those not completely part of this world. Professionals, however, are part of this world and must make the compromises of the marketplace. As a group, librarians were not characterized by uncomfortable definitions of the situation.

Nevertheless, their responses showed a variety of relationships between values and interests and a range of ideological functions. The defenses of freedom (or censorship) ranged from self-serving and conventional affirmations, to moderating mechanisms of accommodation, to severe and honest self-questioning. Particularly in times of crisis, the quest for new values, functions, and definitions was clear.

Are there ways, then, to detect the few who were idealists and who applied standards critically to their own groups? Although the major factor in most cases was trustee support—in which case *idealism, strictly speaking, is undetectable*—several structural bases of integrity seem tentatively definable:

1. Strong extraoccupational commitments, which might be scholarly pursuits, or political or religious identities. Early leaders with scholarly interests were more altruistic and tolerant, although they may have reflected the needs of scholars rather than the rights of the public. These examples include William F. Poole, Worthington C. Ford, and Lindsay

Swift. In the 1930s, university librarians were vocal in defending professional freedom, influenced by academic freedom issues affecting their organizations. In addition, librarians with strong religious or political convictions or commitments carried some of their passion into library work. Examples are Frederick B. Perkins, Frederick Crunden, John Cotton Dana, the younger George Bowerman, Jesse Shera, and Philip Keeney. Such identities, particularly political identities, surface in times of crisis.

2. Insulated positions: Financial independence or positions in professional schools. Schools provide a structural basis for idealistic orientations because the pressures for accommodation are absent. Professional educators did enunciate and foster more altruistic role definitions and interpretations of freedom than did practicing leaders, even in the early stages of professional education. Library educators include Corinne Bacon, Mahlon Schnacke, Carleton Joeckel, Pierce Butler, Leon Carnovsky, as well as several young reformers who later went on to the University of Chicago and careers in professional education, rather than in practical work: Jesse Shera, Bernard Berelson, Lowell Martin, Leroy Merritt. Those who retired from the field or earned their living in other ways were less subject to occupational sanctions and demanded adherence to principle. Examples are Helen Haines and Lutie Stearns.

3. Demographic factors, such as sex and age. Women as a group were more idealistic than men. In their writings, the tone of accommodation so common among male leaders of large public libraries is virtually absent. Among these women are Tessa Kelso, Lutie Stearns, Helen Haines, Mary Plummer, Marilla Freeman, and Mary Rothrock. Although some were educators or financially independent, Tessa Kelso, Marilla Freeman, and Mary Rothrock were public librarians. Until the 1930s, in fact, the profession seems to have recruited a long line of glorious women and pedestrian men. Although these cases seem to challenge the generalization that women are less committed to work than men with comparable attainment, the factor to which the generalization is attributed—marital status—seems borne out in these women's lives, for they were single. Marriage under many circumstances produces role conflict for women. The single woman has fewer structured statuses to compete with her work role. A secular nun, she is available for dedication.

Age was also an important factor in the 1930s, although not before then. The findings in this study support the view that occupational altruism is conducted mainly by younger professionals in behalf of have-nots, and, more specifically, by a coalition of younger members, largely students, and the faculty of professional schools, against the leadership and local organizations in which professionals work.[13]

In the 1930s, as a coalition of young librarians, especially in university libraries, library school faculty, and participants in Carnegie Corporation projects, expressed deepest involvement in the issue of freedom. This pattern supports the hypothesis posed in chapter 5, that professional leaders are not likely to adopt an ethic of ultimate ends.

However, the historical circumstances of the 1930s were critical factors. Reform groups polarized several professions: law, where liberals Morris Ernst and Frank P. Walsh set up the National Lawyers Guild as a rival to the anti-New Deal American Bar Association; medicine, in which a reform movement formed long before the Depression drew especially strong opposition from the American Medical Association; academic and even secondary schools, with conflicts over academic freedom and loyalty. Sharp polarities in government were reflected in the conservative antisedition bills and the liberal Lafollette Committee (1936), formed to investigate violations of free speech and assembly and interference with labor's rights.[14]

Without such historical factors, structural factors or age and group coalitions do not explain reform movements. Age does not explain the conditions under which, in situations of scarcity, youth will be more easily coopted, more prone to internal competition, or more likely to unite in solidarity and develop strategies of resistance and reform.

The code of freedom adopted in 1939 was the expression of an ideology rather than a norm. It was not backed up by a reward structure. But that dichotomy is neither exhaustive nor subtle. If an ideology is distinguished by its function of justifying value or norm preferences, that function may be variously conceived. An ideology may function as a Machiavellian rationalization or as the "romantic-utopian" expression of a wish. Individuals and groups look for morally sustaining ideas to support decisions that must rest on compromise and restraint. At crucial times they engage in an effort to close the gap between what they wish to do and what they can do. "It is natural that . . . the struggle should be resolved in favor of a reconciliation between the desire and the ability, . . . in ideas which reflect a softened view of the world."[15]

Yet an ideology does not always gloss over a situation; it cannot be defined by its dysfunctions. It can function, like the Sorelian myth, to give meaning to individual efforts. At its best, it will, like prophecy, call for greater adherence to values. It may express no more than self-deception. In its most invidious form, it represents hypocrisy. But, as hypocrisy is the tribute that vice pays to virtue, ideology, even in its most pejorative meanings, is not the invalidator of, but a witness to, the value system.

NOTES

1. Cf. Robert H. Wiebe, *The Search for Order, 1877–1920* (New York: Hill & Wang, 1968), on nationalization.

2. Talcott Parsons, *The Social System* (New York: Free Press, 1951), pp. 349–354. Cf. also Weber's ethic of responsibility and ethic of ultimate ends, in Max Weber, "Politics as a Vocation," in *From Max Weber: Essays in Sociology*, ed. H. H. Gerth and C. Wright Mills (New York: Oxford University Press, 1946), pp. 120–127.

3. See Bibliographical Essay.

4. Robert K. Merton, *Social Theory and Social Structure*, 1968 enl. ed. (New York: Free Press, 1968), pp. 432–433 (hereafter *STSS*).

5. William J. Goode, "Librarianship: From Occupation to Profession?" *Library Quarterly* 31 (October 1961): 316–318.

6. Mary Furner, *Advocacy & Objectivity: A Crisis in the Professionalization of American Social Science, 1865–1905* (Lexington: The University of Kentucky Press, 1965), pp. xiii-xiv.

7. Cf. Merton, *STSS*, pp. 422–438; Merton and Elinor Barber, "Sociological Ambivalence" [1963], in Robert K. Merton, *Sociological Ambivalence and Other Essays* (New York: Free Press, 1976), pp. 3–31.

8. Herbert J. Gans, *People and Plans* (New York: Free Press, 1974), pp. 97–98.

9. Thomas S. Kuhn, *The Structure of Scientific Revolutions*, 2d ed. enl. (Chicago: University of Chicago Press, 1970); Schmuel N. Eisenstadt with M. Curelau, *The Form of Sociology—Paradigms and Crises* (New York: John Wiley, 1976).

10. Eisenstadt, *The Form of Sociology*.

1. PROLOGUE: KNOWLEDGE AS A PUBLIC UTILITY: THE MOVEMENT FOR FREE LIBRARIES

1. Quoted in Jesse Shera, *Foundations of the American Public Library: The Origins of the Public Library Movement in New England, 1629–1855* (Chicago: University of Chicago Press, 1949), p. 205n. (hereafter *Foundations*).

2. Ibid., pp. 16–18, 26, 204; Lawrence Cremin, *American Education: The Colonial Experience, 1607–1783* (New York: Harper, 1970), p. 398.

3. Cremin, *American Education*, pp. 398–399; Edwin Wolf II, "Franklin and His Friends Choose Books," in *An American Library History Reader: Contributions to Library Literature*, ed. John David Marshall (Hamden, Conn.: Shoe String Press, 1961), pp. 117–119.

4. Vinnie J. Mayer, "The Coonskin Library," in Marshall, *Reader*, pp. 45–46.

5. Letter, 1818, quoted in Esther Jane Carrier, *Fiction in Public Libraries, 1876–1900* (New York: Scarecrow Press, 1965), p. 46.

6. Shera, *Foundations*, pp. 108–109; Gwladys Spencer, *The Chicago Public Library: Origins and Backgrounds* (Chicago: University of Chicago Press, 1943), pp. 328, 349–359.

7. Robert E. Spiller et al., eds., *Literary History of the United States*, 3d ed., rev. (New York: Macmillan, 1963), 1:293 (hereafter *Literary History*); Boston Athenaeum, *The Athenaeum Centenary: . . . 1807–1907* (1907; reprint, Boston: Gregg Press, 1972), pp. 10, 40–41 [quote].

8. Letter to Thomas Wren Ward, quoted in Walter Muir Whitehill, *Boston Public Library: A Centennial History* (Cambridge, Mass.: Harvard University Press, 1956), p. 21.

9. Richard D. Altick, *The English Common Reader: A Social History of the Mass Reading Public* (Chicago: University of Chicago Press, 1957), pp. 195–201, 205; Philip S. Foner, *History of the Labor Movement in the United States*, vol. 1, *From Colonial Times to the Founding of the American Federation of Labor* (New York: International Publishers, 1975), p. 115n.; Sidney Ditzion, "Mechanics' and Mercantile Libraries," *Library Quarterly* 10 (April 1940): 202, 205.

10. Elfrieda B. McCauley, "The New England Mill Girls: Feminine Influence in the Development of Public Libraries in New England, 1820–1860" (doctoral dissertation, Columbia University, 1971), pp. 1, 23–55, 104–151 (hereafter "Mill Girls"); Vera Shlakman, *Economic History of a Factory Town: A Study of Chicopee, Massachusetts*, Smith College Studies in History, 20, nos. 1–4 (October 1934-July 1935): 59, 107ff., 97, 120, 121.

11. Shera, *Foundations*, pp. 234–236.

12. McCauley, "Mill Girls," pp. 137, 140, 154; Shlakman, *Factory Town*, pp. 107–108, 119–121.

13. McCauley, "Mill Girls," pp. 54ff., 133, 153; Shlakman, *Factory Town*, pp. 60–63 (poem [1834] quoted on p. 61), 110–113; Thomas C. Cochran and William Miller, *The Age of Enterprise: A Social History of Industrial America* (New York: Macmillan, 1947), pp. 18–23.

14. Robert K. Webb, *The British Working Class Reader, 1790–1834: Literacy and Social Tension* (London: Allen & Unwin, 1955), pp. 36–40, 63; Altick, *English Common Reader*, pp. 69–71, 189.

15. Altick, *English Common Reader*, pp. 189–205; David Craig, *The Real Foundations: Literature and Social Change* (London: Chatto & Windus, 1973), pp. 97–101.

16. Foner, *History of Labor*, 1:115; Shera, *Foundations*, pp. 222–223.

17. Sidney Ditzion, "The District School Library, 1835–1855," *Library Quarterly* 10 (October 1940): 564–569.

18. Ibid., pp. 570–573, on policies of exclusion.

19. Ibid., p. 569; Shera, *Foundations*, pp. 233, 196–197, 239.

20. Shera, *Foundations*, pp. 73, 181n., 161–169, 206–241; Spiller et al., *Literary History*, 1:233, 531; Hellmut Lehmann-Haupt, *The Book in America* (New York: R. R. Bowker, 1951), pp. 117–130; Edward G. Holley, *Raking the Historic Coals: The ALA Scrapbook of 1876* (n.p.: Beta Phi Mu, 1967), p. 5.

21. Michael H. Harris, ed., *Charles Coffin Jewett and American Librarianship* (Littleton, Colo.: Libraries Unlimited, 1975), pp. 20–25, 49 n.71; Phyllis Dain, *The New York Public Library: A History of Its Founding and Early Years* (New York: The New York Public Library, 1972), p. 6.

22. *Report of the Trustees of the Public Library of the City of Boston, July 1852* (Boston: J. H. Eastburn, City Printer, 1852), pp. 8–9, 16–20 (hereafter *Ticknor Report*); Stephan Thernstrom, *Poverty and Progress: Social Mobility in a Nineteenth-Century City* (1965; reprint, New York: Atheneum, 1975), pp. 72–73.

23. *Ticknor Report*, pp. 15–17.

24. Boston (Mass.) Public Library. *Proceedings at the Dedication of the Building for the Public Library of the City of Boston, January 1, 1858* (Boston: City Council, 1858), pp. 53–54.

25. Oscar and Mary Handlin, *The Dimensions of Liberty* (1961; reprint, New York: Atheneum, 1966), pp. 141–143; Samuel Haber, "The Professions and Higher Education in America: A Historical View," in *Higher Education and the Labor Market*, ed. Margaret S. Gordon (New York: McGraw-Hill, 1974), pp. 240–265; Cremin, *American Education*, pp. 469–470.

26. Michael Harris and Gerald Spiegler, "Ticknor, Everett and the Common Man: Fear of Social Unrest as Motivation for the Founding of the Boston Public Library," *Libri* 24, 4 (1974): 249–275; David B. Tyack, *George Ticknor and the Boston Brahmins*, (Cambridge, Mass.: Harvard University Press, 1967), p. 44, ch. 6; Anna Ticknor, ed., *Life, Letters and Journals of George Ticknor* (Boston: Houghton Mifflin, 1909), 1:29, 36–37, 140–141, 212, 266–267; Dumas Malone, ed., *Dictionary of American Biography* (New York: Scribner's, 1936), on Everett (hereafter *DAB*).

27. Rush Welter, *Popular Education and Democratic Thought in America* (New York: Columbia University Press, 1962), pp. 2–5; this perspective characterizes Welter's entire work.

28. See, for example, Felice Flannery Lewis, *Literature, Obscenity, and Law* (Carbondale: Southern Illinois University Press, 1976), ch. 1 (hereafter *Obscenity*).

29. Howard K. Beale, *A History of Freedom of Teaching in American Schools* (New York: Scribner's, 1941), pp. 97, 104–105; Richard A. Hofstadter and Wilson Smith, eds., *American Higher Education: A Documentary History* (Chicago: University of Chicago Press, 1961), 1:435–440.

30. W. Phillips Davison, James Boylan, and Frederick T. C. Yu, *Mass Media: Systems and Effects* (1956; reprint, Holt, Rinehart and Winston, n.d.), pp. 11–13; Michael Schudson, *Discovering the News* (New York: Basic Books, 1978), pp. 4–5, 15–18.

2. THE CENTENNIAL CONSENSUS: 1876

1. S. R. Warren and S. N. Clark, eds., *Public Libraries in the United States* (Washington, D.C.: Government Printing Office, 1876), 1:xi–xxvii (hereafter *1876 Report*).

2. Holley, *Raking the Historic Coals*, pp. 4–10.

3. William F. Poole, "Organization and Management of Libraries," *1876 Report*, p. 489.

4. Josiah P. Quincy, "Free Libraries," *1876 Report*, pp. 389–390; William F. Poole, "Some Popular Objections to Public Libraries," *LJ* 1 (30 November 1876): 45–51.

5. Quincy, "Free Libraries," p. 401; Poole, "Organization and Management," p. 478; Samuel S. Green, "Sensational Fiction in Public Libraries," *LJ* 4 (September-October 1879): 350; William I. Fletcher, "Public Libraries in Manufacturing Communities," *1876 Report*, pp. 404–405.

6. William I. Fletcher, "Public Libraries and the Young," *1876 Report*, p. 416; *1876 Report*, p. xiv.

7. Fletcher, "Manufacturing Communities," pp. 403, 411.

8. Ibid., pp. 407–408.

9. Fletcher, "Public Libraries and the Young," pp. 412–414.

10. Poole, "Organization and Management," p. 477; Frederick B. Perkins, "How To Make a Town Library Successful," *1876 Report*, p. 421; Justin Winsor, "Free Libraries and Readers," *LJ* 1 (30 November 1876): 65–66; Justin Winsor, "Reading in Popular Libraries," *1876 Report,* p. 432; Poole, "Some Popular Objections," p. 50.

11. Quincy, "Free Libraries," p. 396; Kate Gannett Wells, "Responsibility of Parents in Selection of Reading for the Young," *LJ* 4 (September-October 1879): 326.

12. Quoted from Quincy, "Free Libraries," p. 395; William Rose Benét, ed., *The Reader's Encyclopedia*, 2d ed. (New York: Thomas Y. Crowell, 1965), on Ainsworth, *Rookwood*; Frank Luther Mott, *Golden Multitudes; the Story of Best Sellers in the United States* (New York: Macmillan, 1947).

13. Green, "Sensational Fiction," p. 347.

14. Perkins, "How To Make a Town Library Successful," p. 421; Poole, "Some Popular Objections," p. 50.

15. Eric F. Goldman, *Rendezvous with Destiny: A History of Modern American Reform* (New York: Knopf, 1952), ch. 3; Sigmund Diamond, ed., *The Nation Transformed: The Creation of an Industrial Society* (New York: Braziller, 1963), pp. 3–22; William C. Todd, "Free Reading Rooms," *1876 Report*, p. 463.

16. Paul Boyer, *Purity in Print: The Vice Society Movement and Book Censorship in America* (New York: Scribner's, 1968), pp. 3–31; Fred W. Paul and Murray C. Schwartz, *Federal Censorship: Obscenity in the Mails* (New York: Free Press, 1961), pp. 20–24, 343–344.

17. Perkins, "How To Make a Town Library Successful," p. 421.

18. Lewis Coser, *Men of Ideas: A Sociologist's View* (New York: Free Press, 1970), pp. 90–91.

19. Boyer, *Purity in Print*, ch. 1.

20. Perkins, "How To Make a Town Library Successful," pp. 422, 425; Todd, "Free Reading Rooms," p. 462.

21. Poole, "Some Popular Objections," p. 47.

22. Quincy, "Free Libraries," pp. 400–402.

23. Quoted by Talcott Williams, "Newspaper Exclusion at the Philadelphia Library," *LJ* 13 (September-October 1888): 288.

24. Sidney Ditzion, *Arsenals of a Democratic Culture: A Social History of the*

American Public Library Movement in New England and the Middle States from 1850–1900 (Chicago: American Library Association, 1947), pp. 60–61; "General Notes," *LJ* 5 (March 1880): 90–91.

25. Richard Hofstadter and Walter P. Metzger, *The Development of Academic Freedom in the United States* (New York: Columbia University Press, 1955), pp. 335–338.

26. Frederick B. Perkins, *Best Reading: Hints on the Selection of Books, on the Formation of Libraries, Public and Private, on Courses of Reading, Etc.*, 2d ed. (New York: Putnam, 1877).

27. Boston Athenaeum, *Catalogue of the Library of the Boston Athenaeum* (Boston: Boston Athenaeum, 1874–1882), 5 vols.

28. Winsor, "Free Libraries and Readers," p. 66; Fletcher, "Manufacturing Communities," p. 411.

29. Charles A. Cutter, Frederick B. Perkins, and Frederick Jackson, "Restriction Labels," *LJ* 3 (April 1878): 60.

30. Green, "Sensational Fiction," p. 347.

31. Ibid., p. 350; Whitehill, *Boston*, pp. 84–85.

32. Details from *DAB* and *Dictionary of American Library Biography*, lst ed. (Littleton, Colo.: Libraries Unlimited, 1978), under relevant names (hereafter *DALB*)—*DAB* only for Fiske, Whitney.

33. Cf. Wiebe, *Search for Order*, ch. 5, for the new occupational model, unlike Richard Hofstadter's notion of the status anxiety of a displaced elite in *The Age of Reform* (New York: Random House, 1955), ch. 4. See Garrison, *Apostles of Culture: The Public Librarian and American Society, 1876–1970* (New York: Free Press 1979), pp. 18–21, takes a different view of the early librarians from that presented here.

3. DEBATE AND DIVISION: THE 1880s

1. Lead quotation from Frederick B. Perkins, "Free Libraries and Unclean Books," *LJ* 10 (December 1885): 396; Josephus Larned, "Public Libraries and Public Education" (1885), reprinted in his *Books, Culture, and Character* (Boston: Houghton Mifflin, 1906), p. 150; Mellen Chamberlain, "Report on Fiction in Public Libraries," *LJ* 8 (September-October 1883): 209.

2. Whitehill, *Boston*, pp. 104–108; editorial, *LJ* 1 (31 July 1877): 395.

3. "Libraries and Politics," *LJ* 8 (January 1883): 7; James A. Ward, "Public Libraries and the Public," *LJ* 7 (July-August 1882): 167; Charles Cutter, "Address of the President," *LJ* 14 (May-June 1889): 149.

4. Editorial, *LJ* 5 (January 1880): 5, 11; Melvil Dewey, "Secretary's Report," *LJ* 11 (September-October 1886): 343; Cutter, "Address of the President," 1889, p. 150.

5. Samuel S. Green, "The Library in Its Relation to Persons Engaged in Industrial Pursuits," *LJ* 14 (May-June 1889): 215, 217; James M. Hubbard, "Are Public Libraries Public Blessings?" *LJ* 14 (October 1889): 407; Minerva A. Sanders, "The Possibilities of Public Libraries in Manufacturing Communities," *LJ* 12 (September-October 1887): 397.

6. Sigmund Diamond, *The Reputation of the American Businessman* (Cambridge, Mass.: Harvard University Press, 1955); Merton, *STSS*, pp. 189–193.

7. "Notes," *LJ* 10 (May 1885): 111–112.

8. Sanders, "Libraries in Manufacturing Communities," p. 397.

9. William F. Poole, 1885 ALA proceedings, *LJ* 10 (September-October 1885): 296.

10. William F. Poole, "Address of the President," *LJ* 11 (August-September 1886): 203; William F. Poole, "Address of the President," 1887, *LJ* 12 (September-October 1877): 314.

11. Spencer, *Chicago Public Library*, pp. 328, 349–359, 371, 398.

12. Whitehill, *Boston*, pp. 116–117, 12l–122; James M. Hubbard, "Bibliography," *LJ* 6 (January 1881): 14–15.

13. James M. Hubbard, "Fiction in Public Libraries," *International Review* 10 (February 1881): 168–178; "Memorial," *LJ* 6 (February 1881): 28; "Bibliography," *LJ* 6 (March 1881): 45.

14. "Bibliography," *LJ* 6 (March 1881): 45–46.

15. Ibid., p. 46 and *LJ* 6 (May 1881): 162.

16. "Mr. Hubbard," *LJ* 6 (July 1881): 205–206.

17. Boston Public Library, *Annual Report*, 1881, excerpted in *LJ* 6 (August 1881): 225.

18. Ibid., pp. 225–226.

19. James M. Hubbard, *The Public Library and the Schoolchildren: An Appeal to the Parents, Clergymen, and Teachers of Boston* (Boston, Mass.: 21 October 1881); "Boston Public Library," *LJ* 6 (December 1881): 319; Boston Public Library, *Annual Reports, 1882*, pp. 15–16; *1883*, pp. 13–14; *1884*, p. 14; *1885*, pp. 18–19; Whitehill, *Boston*, pp. 118–119.

20. Perkins, "Free Libraries and Unclean Books," pp. 396–398; "'Odd Fellows' Library Association," *LJ* 6 (September-October 1881): 264.

21. Perkins, "Free Libraries and Unclean Books," pp. 397–399. Quotation on p. 398.

22. Justin Winsor, "Address of the President," *LJ* 6 (April 1881): 64; Samuel Green, *The Public Library Movement in America* (1913; reprint, Boston: Gregg, 1972), confirms Winsor's reference to Hubbard; editorials, *LJ* 6 (March 1881): 39–40; August 1881, p. 223.

23. News story, *LJ* 6 (June 1881): 183.

24. Hubbard, "Are Public Libraries Public Blessings?" *North American Review* 149 (September 1889): 339–346; reprinted in *LJ* 14 (October 1889): 407–409; William Fletcher, "The Inferno in Libraries," *LJ* 14 (December 1889): 480; William Howard Brett, "The Public Library Assault," *LJ* 14 (December 1889): 475–477.

25. Editorial, *LJ* 14 (October 1889): 399.

26. "The Popular Sale of Objectionable Books," *PW* 37 (3 March 1890): 350; "Modern Censorship," *PW* 38 (6 September 1890): 381; editorial, *LJ* 14 (September 1889): 367.

27. ALA "Report on Exclusion," *LJ* 7 (February 1882): 28–29; Mott, *Multitudes*, pp. 245, 263, 321–323.

28. Hubbard, *Appeal*.

29. Ibid., pp. 10, 17, 6, 11, 15, 17.

30. Patricia Meyer Spack, review of Elaine Showalter, *A Literature of Their Own*

(Princeton, N.J.: Princeton University Press, 1977), *New York Times Book Review*, 27 March 1977, p. 14; see also Garrison, *Apostles*, pp. 75–88.

31. Bernard Barber, "Function, Variability, and Change," in *Stability and Social Change*, ed. Bernard Barber and Alex Inkeles (Boston: Little, Brown, 1971), pp. 254–255; William York Tindall, *Forces in Modern British Literature: 1885–1956* (New York: Vintage Books, 1956), pp. 121–128; Ditzion, *Arsenals*, p. 185.

32. "Why Mark Twain Is Happy," *LJ* 10 (April 1885): 131; Mott, *Multitudes*, pp. 112–113, 249.

33. Spiller, *Literary History*, p. 953; see also note 26.

4. PIVOT OF CHANGE: 1890–1900

1. Cf. Reuben Gold Thwaites, "Address of the President," *LJ* 25 (August 1900): C1–6, for one overview of the decade; quotations at beginning of chapter from Josephus Larned, "Address of the President," *LJ* 19 (December 1894): C2, and John Cotton Dana, "Hear the Other Side," *LJ* 21 (December 1896): C2.

2. Larned, "Address," p. C2. Wiebe, *Search for Order*, describes these shifts much as Larned perceived them.

3. Ellen Coe, "Fiction," *LJ* 18 (July 1893): 250–251; "Common Novels," *LJ* 19 (September 1894): C14.

4. "Common Novels," pp. C14–22.

5. Paul Leicester Ford, review of William Fletcher, *Public Libraries in America*, *LJ* 19 (July 1894): 237; S. W. Cattell, ALA conference proceedings, *LJ* 17 (August 1892): C89.

6. "Supplying of Current Daily Newspapers in Free Library Reading Rooms," *LJ* 19 (December 1894): C42–49; questions are abstracted from A.W. Whelpley's response, pp. C42–43; Whelpley quotation, p. C43.

7. Tessa Kelso, "Some Economical Features of Public Libraries," *LJ* 18 (November 1893): 472–474.

8. ALA conference proceedings, *LJ* 19 (December 1894): C143–145.

9. Lutie E. Stearns, "Report on Reading," *LJ* 19 (December 1894): C85; see also pp. C81–84.

10. William H. Brett, "The Present Problem," *LJ* 19 (December 1894): C7; Larned, "Address" (1894), pp. C3–4.

11. Larned, "Address" (1894), pp. C1–4.

12. Brett, "The Present Problem," pp. C5–7.

13. 1894 conference proceedings, pp. C157–159; quotation from Dana, p. C139.

14. Ibid., p. C159; "Improper Books: Methods Employed To Discover and Exclude Them," *LJ* 20 (December 1895): C36.

15. Dana, "Hear the Other Side," pp. C1–4.

16. Cf. Larned, "Retrospect and Prospect in the Last Years of the Century," *LJ* 21 (December 1896): C5–13.

17. "A Word on the 'National Spirit,' " *LJ* 22 (January 1897): 6.

18. Frederick M. Crunden, "What of the Future?" *LJ* 22 (October 1897): C5–11.

19. Frank Kingdon, *John Cotton Dana: A Life* (Newark: The Public Library and

Museum, 1940), pp. 48–62; Chalmers Hadley, *John Cotton Dana, A Sketch* (Chicago: American Library Association, 1943), pp. 31–33.

20. Editorial, *LJ* 22 (January 1897): 477.

21. *Locomotive Firemen's Magazine* (February 1890), and *Coming Age*, 10 February 1894, quoted in Herbert Gutman, *Work, Culture, and Society in Industrializing America* (New York: Knopf, 1976); "Perils of the Republic," *Reformed Church Review*, quoted in Samuel Ranck, "Libraries as Agents of 'the Money Powers,' " *LJ* 23 (June 1898): 228.

22. Ranck, " 'The Money Powers,' " p. 228.

23. Ditzion, *Arsenals*, pp. 154–157, 159, 164; Carnegie quotation from "The Public Library Movement in Brooklyn," *LJ* 22 (January 1897): 19; Herbert Putnam in "The Library and the Laborer," *LJ* 25 (March 1900): 112.

24. "Why There Was No Strike," *LJ* 22 (September 1897): 437; A. L. Peck, "Workingmen's Clubs and the Public Library," *LJ* 23 (November 1898): 612–614.

25. Gratia Countryman, "Shall Public Libraries Buy Foreign Literature for the Benefit of the Foreign Population?" *LJ* 23 (June 1898): 229–231.

26. Abram Kardiner, personal interview, 30 May 1979.

5. FREEDOM OF ACCESS: 1890–1900

1. Bernard Steiner and Samuel Ranck, "Report on Access to the Shelves," *LJ* 19 (December 1894): C87–98; C. Knowles Bolton, "Bettering Circulation in Small Libraries—The 'Two-Book System.' " *LJ* 19 (May 1894): 161–162.

2. William York Tindall, *Forces in Modern British Literature*, pp. 5–8, ch. 5; Spiller, *Literary History*, pp. 953–957; Mott, *Multitudes*, pp. 181, 188–190; Alice Payne Hackett, *Banned Books* (New York: R. R. Bowker, 1970); Alfred Kazin, *On Native Grounds: An Interpretation of Modern American Prose Literature* (1942; reprint, New York: Doubleday Anchor, 1956).

3. John Tebbel, *A History of Book Publishing in the United States*, vol. 2 (New York: R. R. Bowker, 1975), p. 622.

4. Ibid., pp. 622–623; "The Los Angeles Libel Suit," *LJ* (October 1894): 340, 329; editorial, *LJ* 20 (May 1895): 161–162; *LJ* 21 (March 1896): 105–106, 92.

5. "A Question in Library Censorship," *LJ* 20 (May 1895): 162; Frederick Crunden, "Concerning Literary Censorship," *LJ* 20 (June 1895): 198.

6. Cf. "Selection of Books," *LJ* 19 (December 1894): C30–42.

7. Charles F. Adams, Jr., editorial, *LJ* 18 (April 1893): 107 (see also pp. 118–119); "Improper Books: Methods Employed To Discover and Exclude Them," *LJ* 20 (December 1895): C32–35.

8. Lewis, *Obscenity*, ch. 1; "In re Worthington Co. Court, Special term, New York County, Supreme 22 June 1894," in *Censorship Landmarks*, comp. Edward de Grazia (New York: R. R. Bowker, 1969), p. 44.

9. Hall Caine, *Critic*, n.s., 29 December 1894, p. 453, cited in Carrier, *Fiction*, p. 133.

10. "Chicago," *LJ* 19 (November 1894): 389–390; "Crerar Library To Be a Library of Science," *LJ* 20 (March 1895): 86.

11. Editorial, *LJ* 20 (March 1895): 76; Mary Ahern, *Public Libraries* 1 (December 1896): 216 (hereafter *PL*).

12. "Improper Books," p. C32.

13. Ibid., p. C36.

14. U.S. Bureau of Education, *Catalog of "A.L.A." Library: 5000 Volumes for a Popular Library* (Washington, D.C.: U.S. Government Printing Office, 1893); Walter Fuller Taylor, *The Economic Novel in America* (Chapel Hill: University of North Carolina Press, 1942); see also note 2 above.

15. Editorial, *LJ* 21 (September 1896): 306.

16. "Fiction Discussion," *LJ* 21 (December 1896): C142–144; *DALB* on Hewins, Wellman, Green, Hosmer, Eastman.

17. "Fiction Discussion," pp. 144–146; Tindall, *Forces*, p. 13l; on Peck, "Common Novels in Public Libraries," *LJ* 19 (December 1894): C137.

18. Robert K. Merton and Harriet Zuckerman, "Institutionalized Patterns of Evaluation in Science," in *The Sociology of Science*, ed. Norman Storer (Chicago: University of Chicago Press, 1973), pp. 489–490; Everett C. Hughes, *Men and Their Work* (Glencoe, Ill.: Free Press, 1958), pp. 88–10l; Merton, "The Ambivalence of Organizational Leaders," in *Sociological Ambivalence*, p. 80.

19. Josephus Larned, "The Selection of Books for a Public Library" (1895) in his *Books, Culture, and Character*, pp. 43–44.

20. "Sociology Section," *LJ* 21 (December 1896): 134–139, esp. pp. 134, 137.

21. Melvil Dewey, "Address," *LJ* 22 (October 1897): C116–118; John Cotton Dana, "The Line of Exclusion," *PL* 2 (April 1897): 147; editorial, *PL* 2 (June 1897): 271; William M. Stevenson, "Weeding Out Fiction in the Carnegie Free Library of Allegheny, Pa.," *LJ* 22 (March 1897): 133–136.

22. Helen Haines, in "Books of 1896—II," *LJ* 22 (March 1897): 140–142; "Report of Committee on Supplement to 'Catalog of ALA Library,' " *LJ* 22 (October 1897): C109–110.

23. Editorial, *LJ* 22 (March 1897): 127–128.

24. Haines, "Books of 1896," pp. 140–142; "Report on ALA Supplement," p. C112.

25. "Report on ALA Supplement," pp. C110–112.

26. Franklyn Giddings, in "Books of 1896—I," *LJ* 22 (February 1897): 85–86; Josephus Larned, in "Books of 1896—II," *LJ* 22 (March 1897); "Report on Supplement," *LJ* 22 (October 1897): C106.

27. Johnson Brigham, "The Danger Line in Fiction," *PL* 3 (January 1898): 9 (Brigham discussed *Maggie, A Lady of Quality, The Manxman, Tess, David Grieve, Theron Ware,* and *The Christian*); Whitehill, *Boston*, pp. 174–175, 185–186, 219; Wadlin, *Boston*, p. 190; *DAB*, 3d supplement (1973), on Ford.

28. Editorial, *LJ* 24 (November 1899): 607.

29. All references in paragraphs following note 28 are from Lindsay Swift, "Paternalism in Public Libraries," *LJ* 24 (November 1899): 613–617. Quoted passage pp. 614–615.

30. Ibid., pp. 609–613, 618.

31. John Cotton Dana, "Paternalism—An Appreciation!" *LJ* 24 (December 1899): 660.

32. Worthington C. Ford, "The Public Library and the State," *LJ* 25 (June 1900): 275–279.

33. Linda Eastman, *Portrait of a Librarian: William Howard Brett* (Chicago: American Library Association, 1940), pp. 94–96; William H. Brett, "Cooperative Reading," *PL* 5 (June 1900): 250.

34. "Library Meetings," *PL* 2 (March 1897): 99; "Anarchistic Books in Free Libraries," *PW* 52 (7 August, 14 August 1897): 214, 219.

35. "The Library and Dogma," *LJ* 25 (May 1900): 232.

36. Purd B. Wright, "Character of Permitted Access to the Shelves," *LJ* 25 (August 1900): C35–36; William E. Foster, "The Standard Library," ibid., pp. C36–38.

6. CENSORSHIP, FREEDOM, AND PROFESSIONAL AUTONOMY: A THEORETICAL REVIEW

1. Seymour M. Lipset, *Political Man* (New York: Doubleday, 1960), chs. 4 and 5; Arthur Ekirch, Jr., *The Decline of American Liberalism* (New York, London: Longmans, Green, 1955).

2. Hofstadter and Metzger, *Academic Freedom*, pp. 420–451; Furner, *Advocacy*, pp. 150–152.

3. Crunden, "What of the Future?"; editorial, *LJ* 20 (May 1895): 161–162.

4. Furner, *Advocacy*, pp. 171–180, 232–239; Hofstadter and Metzger, *Academic Freedom*, pp. 425–446, 458–467; Laurence R. Veysey, *The Emergence of the American University* (Chicago: University of Chicago Press, 1965), pp. 17–18, 409–414.

5. Hofstadter and Metzger, *Academic Freedom*, pp. 407, 425–435; Furner, *Advocacy*, pp. 3–9, 152–157, 185–191, 205–222; Veysey, *Emergence of the American University*, p. 395.

6. See Wiebe, *Search for Order*, pp. 129–130, 162–163; Merton, *STSS*, pp. 432–433.

7. Goode, "Librarian," pp. 316–317.

8. Merton, "The Normative Structure of Science," in his *Sociology of Science*, pp. 275–276.

9. Rose Laub Coser, "The Complexity of Roles as a Seedbed of Individual Autonomy," in *The Idea of Social Structure: Papers in Honor of Robert K. Merton* (New York: Harcourt Brace, 1975), pp. 237–264.

10. Ibid.; Merton, *STSS*, pp. 422–438; "Sociological Ambivalence," pp. 10–11.

11. Merton, "Science and the Social Order," *STSS*, pp. 260–261.

12. Ibid., p. 263; Weber, "Politics as a Vocation," *From Max Weber*, pp. 115–127; Merton, "Normative Structure," *Sociology of Science*, pp. 267–268, 271.

13. Michael Mulkay, "Norms and Ideology in Science," *Social Science Information* 15, nos. 4–5 (1976): 653–654.

14. Bernard Barber, "Some Problems in the Sociology of the Professions," *Daedalus* 92 (Fall 1963): 669–688; William Goode, "Encroachment, Charlatanism, and the Emerging Profession: Psychology, Sociology and Medicine," *American Sociological Review* 25 (December 1960): 902–914 (hereafter *ASR*); Everett Hughes, *Men and Their Work* (Glencoe, Ill.: Free Press, 1958), p. 131 (here-

after *Work*); See also Howard S. Becker, "Against the Code of Ethics," *ASR* 29 (June 1964): 409–410; Eliot Freidson, "Against the Code of Ethics," *ASR* 29 (June 1964): 410.

15. Merton, "Ambivalence of Organizational Leaders," in *Sociological Ambivalence*, p. 85; William J. Goode, "Protection of the Inept," *ASR* 32 (February 1967): 5–19; Merton and Zuckerman, "Patterns of Evaluation," in *Sociology of Science*; Hughes, *Work*, pp. 94–95.

16. Hughes, *Work*, p. 61 n.12.

7. THE LIBRARIAN AS A CENSOR: 1900–1908

1. Henry May, Introduction to *The End of American Innocence: A Study of the First Years of Our Time, 1912–1917* (1959; reprint, Chicago: Quadrangle, 1964); John D. Buenker, *Urban Liberalism and Progressive Reform* (New York: Scribner's, 1973), esp. ch. 5. Lead quotation from Arthur E. Bostwick, "The Librarian as a Censor," *LJ* 33 (July 1908): 257.

2. William Preston, Jr., *Aliens and Dissenters: Federal Suppression of Radicals, 1903–1933* (Cambridge, Mass.: Harvard University Press, 1963), pp. 14, 19; Paul Brissenden, *The I.W.W.: A Study of American Syndicalism* (New York: Columbia University Press, 1919); Phyllis Dain, "Emma Goldman and Free Speech: A Chapter in the History of Civil Liberty in the United States" (M.S. dissertation, Columbia University, n.d.) (hereafter "Emma").

3. Hofstadter, *Reform*, pp. 154–155, 192–200, 238–241; James Burkhart Gilbert, *Writers and Partisans: A History of Literary Radicalism in America* (New York: John Wiley, 1968), ch. 1; Robert H. Bremner, *From the Depths: The Discovery of Poverty in the United States* (New York: New York University Press, 1956), ch. 12–14; Walter B. Rideout, *The Radical Novel in America, 1900–1954* (Cambridge, Mass.: Harvard University Press, 1956); E. McClung Fleming, *R. R. Bowker, Militant Liberal* (Norman: University of Oklahoma Press, 1952), p. 349; Louis Filler, "The Muckrakers and Middle America," in *Muckraking*, ed. John M. Harrison and Harry H. Stein (University Park: Pennsylvania State University Press, 1973), p. 31.

4. Kazin, *On Native Grounds*, pp. 69–83; Tindall, *Forces*, pp. 27–35, 218; Tebbel, *Book Publishing*, 2:698; Lewis, *Obscenity*, pp. 59–60; Leon Edel and Gordon N. Ray, eds., *Henry James and H. G. Wells: A Record of Their Friendship, Their Debate on the Art of Fiction, and Their Quarrel* (Urbana: University of Illinois Press, 1958), pp. 131–156.

5. Rideout, *The Radical Novel*; Spiller, *Literary History*, 1:993–995; see also note 3, above.

6. Rosemary Konig Dumont, *Reform and Reaction: The Big City Public Library in American Life* (Westport, Conn.: Greenwood Press, 1977), p. 59; Arthur E. Bostwick, *The American Public Library*, 3d ed., rev. and enl. (New York: Appleton, 1928), p. 219; Arthur E. Bostwick, *A Life with Men and Books* (New York: H. W. Wilson, 1939), p. 226; Frank P. Hill, "One Phase of Library Development," *LJ* 31 (August 1906): C8.

7. John Shaw Billings, "Some Library Problems of Tomorrow," *LJ* 27 (July 1902): C5–6; "The Fiction Question Redivivus," *LJ* 27 (March 1902): 119; Arthur

E. Bostwick, "The Uses of Fiction," *American Library Association Bulletin* 1 (May 1907): 186 (hereafter *ALAB*).

8. Nathaniel D. C. Hodges, "An Anathema on Fingerposts," *LJ* 35 (July 1910): C3–8; Henry Legler, "Libraries and the World's Work," *ALAB* 7 (conf. no., 1913): 73–82; Herbert Putnam, "Address by Dr. Putnam," *ALAB* 6 (July 1912): 63–64.

9. Ernest C. Richardson, "The National Library Problem Today," *LJ* 30 (August 1905): C3–8; Herbert Putnam, "The Service of Books in a Democracy," *LJ* 37 (February 1912): 59–62; Legler, "Libraries and the World's Work," pp. 73–82.

10. Hofstadter, *Reform*, pp. 179–180; Dain, *New York Public Library*, pp. 288–306; John Higham, *Strangers in the Land: Patterns of American Nativism*, 2d ed. (New Brunswick, N.J.: Rutgers University Press, 1963), pp. 109, 152–164.

11. *Bill Haywood's Book*, cited in Richard O. Boyer and Herbert M. Morais, *Labor's Untold Story* (New York: United Electrical, Radio & Machine Workers of America, 1965), p. 146.

12. On Edison, see ch. 10, note 50 below; Virginia Hollingsworth, "A Dedicated Life: Electra Collins Doren," in Marshall, *Reader*, p. 276; Oscar Leonard, "Branch Libraries as Social Centers," *Survey* 25 (18 March 1911): 1035; Marilla W. Freeman, "The Relation of the Library to the Outside World," *LJ* 33 (December 1908): 491; Lutie E. Stearns, "An Innovation in Library Meetings," *LJ* 31 (February 1906): 55–57.

13. Dain, *New York Public Library*, p. 296; Wiebe, *Search for Order*, pp. 181–195.

14. Hofstadter, *Reform*, pp. 234–237; Arthur S. Link, with William B. Catton, *American Epoch: A History of the United States Since the 1890's*, vol. 1, *1897–1920*, 3d ed. (New York: Knopf, 1967), pp. 59–65; Bremner, *From the Depths*, pp. 149–151, 204–208; Boyer and Morais, *Labor's Untold Story*, pp. 182–183; Legler, "Libraries and the World's Work."

15. Larson, *Rise of Professionalism*, pp. 146–148.

16. "Restriction of Purchases of Current Fiction," *LJ* 29 (February 1904): 72–74; James Hosmer, "Some Things That Are Uppermost," *LJ* 28 (July 1903): C6; Anna Rockwell, "Fiction Again: Where Shall We Draw the Line of Exclusion?" *PL* 8 (July 1903): 309–312.

17. Billings, "Some Library Problems," p. C6; cf. also Dain, *New York Public Library*, pp. 250–251.

18. Billings, "Some Library Problems," pp. C5–6.

19. Bostwick, "Librarian as Censor," p. 259.

20. Michael Polanyi, "The Potential Theory of Adsorption," *Science* 141 (September 1963): 1010–1013.

21. George Iles, "The Trusteeship of Literature—I," *LJ* 26 (August 1901): C16–22; Richard T. Ely, "The Trusteeship of Literature—II," *LJ* 26 (August 1901): C22–24.

22. Ernest C. Richardson, "The National Library Problem Today," p. 4.

23. Charles W. Eliot, "The Division of a Library into Books in Use, and Books not in Use, with Different Storage Methods for the Two Classes of Books," *LJ* 27 (July 1902): C51–56; "Lord Rosebery and Mr. Gosse on Dead Books," *LJ* 36 (December 1911): 639–641.

24. "Lord Rosebery and Mr. Gosse on Dead Books," *LJ* 36 (December 1911): 639–641.

25. "Andrew Carnegie on Dead Books," *LJ* 37 (February 1912): 74.

26. Editorial, *LJ* 36 (December 1911): 608.

27. Electra Collins Doren, "Action Against Bad Books," *LJ* 29 (April 1903): 167–169.

28. Asa Don Dickinson, "Huckleberry Finn Is Fifty Years Old—Yes, But Is He Respectable?" *Wilson Bulletin* 19 (November 1935): 193 (hereafter *WB*).

29. Edmund L. Pearson, "The Children's Librarian vs. Huckleberry Finn: A Brief for the Defense," *LJ* 32 (July 1907): 312–314; Arthur E. Bostwick, in "Recent Books for Boys," *ALAB* (conf. no., 1909): 263–277; E. L. Pearson, "The Evil That Books Do," *PL* 16 (May 1911): 188–19l, quote on p. 188.

30. William P. Trent, "Address," *ALAB* 1 (May 1907): C30; William Dean Howells, introduction to Thomas Hughes's *Tom Brown's School Days* (New York: Harper, 1910); Caroline Hewins, *Books for the Young* (American Library Association, 1882); Caroline Hewins, ALA conference proceedings, *LJ* 24 (August 1901): C60–61; Alice Miller Jordan, "The Use of Children's Books," *ALAB* 1 (May 1907): 178–179.

31. Bostwick, *Autobiography*, p. 177; *New York Times*, 21 September 1905, p. 9, col. 6; p. 8, col. 3; 26 September 1905, p. 1, col. 7; Lewis, *Obscenity*, pp. 55–56; "Magistrate Poll Tells Comstock to Get Out of Court, Says He Cannot See Obscenity in Shaw," *New York Times*, 7 October 1905, p. 13, col. 1.

32. Kingdon, *Dana*, pp. 85–86; *LJ* 30 (October 1905): 824; "Library Censorship," *LJ* 30 (December 1905): 916; "The Librarian as Censor," *New York Evening Post* editorial, reprinted in *LJ* 30 (December 1905): 929–930. "A Mystery Entitled the Ban Lifted," *New York Times*, 27 September 1905, p. 1, col. 2.

33. Rockwell, "Fiction Again," pp. 311–312.

34. Bostwick, "Librarian as Censor," p. 327.

35. Ibid., pp. 257–261.

36. "Librarian's Responsibility in the Treatment of Bad Literature," *LJ* 33 (July 1908):256–257; see also editorial, *LJ* 33 (September 1908): 347; "What Shall Libraries Do About Bad Books?—I," *LJ* 33 (September 1908): 349–356; "What Shall Libraries Do About Bad Books?—II," *LJ* 33 (October 1908).

37. Lutie E. Stearns, "Magazines and Morals," *Wisconsin Library Bulletin* 7 (December 1911): 172–173.

38. Herbert Gans, *Popular Culture and High Culture* (New York: Basic Books, 1974), p. 54. Gusfield's temperance crusades also resemble these movements.

39. Merton, "The Self-Fulfilling Prophecy," *STSS*, p. 480; Garrison, *Apostles*, pp. 173, 226n., 282 for statistics: by 1920, women would make up 80 percent of all library workers, as against 52 percent for social workers; Edmund Lester Pearson, *The Librarian: Selections from the Column of That Name*, ed. Jane B. Durnell and Norman D. Stevens (Metuchen, N.J.: Scarecrow Press, 1976), pp. 29–30. Cf. also ALA conference proceedings, *LJ* 37 (August 1912): 410; Adelaide R. Hasse, "Women in Libraries," *LJ* 43 (February 1918): 141–142. Garrison, *Apostles*, pp. 190–191, has an approach different from that in this study.

40. *DALB* on Henry Legler and Nathaniel Hodges, pp. 248, 309; "Multitude of Sins Cover Library's Restricted Shelf," *Cincinnati Post*, 29 June 1903, cited in Dumont, *Reform*, ch. 6.

41. Pearson, *Librarian*, pp. 39–40.

42. Corinne N. Bacon, "What Makes a Novel Immoral?" *Wisconsin Library Bulletin* 6 (August 1910): 83–95. Biographical details from bylines on various ar-

ticles; Charles Compton, *Memories of a Librarian* (St. Louis, Mo.: St. Louis Public Library, 1954), p. 29; biographical note, *LJ* 37 (September 1912): 528–529.

43. Library of Congress, *ALA Catalog: 8000 Volumes for a Popular Library, with Notes, 1904*, ed. Melvil Dewey; assoc. eds., May Seymour, Mrs. H. L. Elmendorf (Washington, D.C.: Government Printing Office, 1904) (hereafter *ALA Catalog, 1904*).

44. *Fiction Catalog: A Selected List Cataloged by Author and Title with Annotations* (Minneapolis: The H. W. Wilson Company, 1908).

8. EROSION: 1908–1917

1. May, *End of Innocence*, pp. 219–266, 311–314; Boyer, *Purity*, ch. 2.

2. Preston, *Aliens*, pp. 44–46; Dain, "Emma," pp. 147–157.

3. Rideout, *Radical Novel*, pp. 292–294; Kazin, *On Native Grounds*, p. 140.

4. Tindall, *Forces*, pp. 122–123; Edel and Ray, *James and Wells*, pp. 24, 35.

5. Spiller, *Literary History*, 1:993; Kazin, *On Native Grounds*, pp. 31, 94; Lewis, *Obscenity*, pp. 64–71.

6. Boyer, *Purity*, pp. 41–42.

7. "Library Censorship," *LJ* 30 (December 1905): 916; Owen Wister, "Subjects Fit for Fiction," *LJ* 31 (August 1906): C20–24; Willard Huntington Wright, "Is Library Censorship Desirable?" *ALAB* 5 (conf. no., 1911): 59–60.

8. "As Others See Us," *ALAB* 7 (conf. no., 1913): 90–91.

9. Herbert Putnam, "The Service of Books in a Democracy," *LJ* 37 (February 1912): 61–62.

10. Ethel Sawyer, "Questionable Books," *LJ* 40 (October 1915): 691–699; "The Library World," *LJ* 40 (April 1915): 282.

11. "The Library World," *LJ* 40 (April 1915): 282; "Literary Censorship in the Library," *LJ* 42 (January 1917).

12. *DALB* on Charles Lummis, Jennie Flexner, Marilla Freeman; ch. 7, note 42 above.

13. Corinne Bacon, "A Library That's Alive," *PL* 18 (February 1913): 50–55, and "What Novels?" ibid., pp. 56–57.

14. Rideout, *Radical Novel*, pp. 67–72.

15. Bacon, "A Library That's Alive," pp. 52, 56, 57.

16. James Wyer, "What the Community Owes the Library," *ALAB* 5 (conf. no., 1911): 58.

17. Mary Wright Plummer, "The Public Library and the Pursuit of Truth," *ALAB* 10 (July 1916): 113–115.

18. Lewis, *Obscenity*, p. 68; Boyer, *Purity*, ch. 2; *PW* 90 (8 July 1916): 93–100.

19. American Sociological Society, *Papers and Proceedings, Ninth Annual Meeting, Princeton, New Jersey, December 28–31, 1914*, vol. 9 (Chicago: University of Chicago Press, 1915); Hofstadter and Metzger, *Academic Freedom*, pp. 471–479, 407.

20. Hofstadter and Metzger, *Academic Freedom*, p. 478.

21. Elva Bascom, ed., *ALA Catalog Supplement: 1904–1911* (Chicago: American Library Association, 1912).

22. *Fiction Catalog* (White Plains, N.Y.: H. W. Wilson, 1914).

23. Titles were in print according to the *U.S. Catalog* (1912). Mott, *Multitudes*, pp. 214, 324.

24. Herbert J. Gans, *People and Plans*, pp. 97–98.

25. Not listed because their positions on popular culture were not clear: Isabel Lord, Frances Rathbone, Samuel Ranck, Mary Plummer, Sara Van de Carr. All, however, were liberal, making women even more prominent among liberals.

9. WAR AND PEACE: 1914–1922

1. Edwin H. Anderson, "The Tax on Ideas," *LJ* 39 (July 1914): 499–503; George Bowerman, "How Far Should the Library Aid the Peace Movement and Similar Propaganda?" *LJ* 40 (July 1915): 477–478.

2. "Librarians Trapped in Europe," *LJ* 39 (September 1914): 657; "The Embargo on Books," *LJ* 41 (July 1916): 457.

3. Bowerman, "Peace Movement," p. 477.

4. Ibid., pp. 477–481.

5. Link, *American Epoch*, 1:193, 208–212; Walter Lippmann, *Public Opinion* (New York: Macmillan, 1922), p. 47; Ekirch, *Decline of Liberalism*, pp. 214–215; James R. Mock, *Censorship 1917* (Princeton, N.J.: Princeton University Press, 1941), chs. 2–3.

6. Zechariah Chafee, Jr., *Free Speech in the United States* (Cambridge, Mass.: Harvard University Press, 1941), pp. 51, 58, 98, 104, 247–257, 541.

7. "Calling Down the Writers," *PL* 22 (November 1917): 370; Emil Baesch, "Seditious Publications in the Public Library," *Wisconsin Library Bulletin* 14 (January 1918): 1–2; "The Wisconsin Policy as to the Literature of Disloyalty," *Wisconsin Library Bulletin* 14 (February 1918): 39–40.

8. Peggy Sullivan, *Carl H. Milam and the American Library Association* (New York: H. W. Wilson, 1976), pp. 84–85; Mock, *Censorship 1917*, pp. 153–161.

9. "Books to be Barred from Library," (Indiana) *Library Occurrent* 5 (February 1918): 93–94; Pearson, *The Librarian*, pp. 564–565, 571.

10. Hofstadter and Metzger, *Academic Freedom*, p. 499.

11. Ibid., pp. 501–503; *DALB* on Isom; Donald Johnson, *The Challenge to American Freedoms: World War I and the Rise of the American Civil Liberties Union* (Lexington: University of Kentucky Press, 1963) (hereafter *ACLU*); "Patriotism in Portland," *LJ* 43 (June 1918): 385.

12. "Vigilantes Object to Books in Newark Public Library," *LJ* 43 (February 1918): 117–118; "Seditious Propagandist Publications in Public Libraries," *LJ* 43 (March 1918): 145.

13. Ernest C. Richardson, "The Question of Censorship in Libraries," *LJ* 43 (March 1918): 152–154.

14. Mock, *Censorship 1917*, pp. 164–171.

15. Tebbel, *Book Publishing*, 2:632; "Secretary Baker Censors the Censor," (Indiana) *Library Occurrent* 6 (January 1919): 112, reprinted from *PW*, 16 November 1918.

16. Ekirch, *Decline of Liberalism*, pp. 210, 215; Brissenden, *IWW*; George Creel, *Rebel at Large* (New York: Putnam, 1947), p. 103; Johnson, *ACLU*, pp. 15, 36–38, 79–81.

17. Everett C. Hughes, "Good People and Dirty Work," in *The Other Side: Perspectives on Deviance*, ed. Howard S. Becker (New York: Free Press, 1964), pp. 28, 34.

18. Ekirch, *Decline of Liberalism*, pp. 234–242; Link, *American Epoch*, 1:234–240; Chafee, *Free Speech*, pp. 141, 240, 306–317; Higham, *Strangers in the Land*, pp. 232–233, 282–299, ch. 11; Preston, *Aliens*, pp. 218–258.

19. Ekirch, *Decline of Liberalism*, pp. 216–219; Link, *American Epoch*, 1: 211; Chafee, *Free Speech*, interprets Holmes's decision as deference to majority sentiment.

20. Murray Levin, *Political Hysteria in America: The Democratic Capacity for Repression* (New York: Basic Books, 1971), pp. 74–82; Preston, *Aliens*, pp. 259, 271–272; Brissenden, *IWW*, pp. xv-xvii.

21. Dana, ALA conference proceedings, *ALAB* 13 (July 1919): 368–369; "Mr. Dana's Letter of Resignation from the Enlarged Program," *LJ* 44 (15 May 1920): 459–460.

22. Paul M. Paine, "The Library's Task in Reconstruction," *ALAB* 13 (July 1919): 117–120.

23. Paul M. Paine, "Library Service Is Free," *New York Libraries* 7 (November 1919): 12–13.

24. "Library Board to Decide," *LJ* 46 (August 1921): 652.

25. Rideout, *The Radical Novel*; Boyer, *Purity*, ch. 4; Kazin, *On Native Grounds*.

26. Lewis, *Obscenity*, pp. 73–90.

27. Louis Feipel, "Public Libraries and the New Fiction," *LJ* 46 (15 April 1921): 347; Louis Feipel, "The Fiction of 1920—a Library Survey," *LJ* 46 (15 September 1921): 750; editorial, *LJ* 47 (15 October 1922): 877–878; Louis Feipel, "Questionable Books in Public Libraries—I," *LJ* 47 (15 October 1922): 857–859.

28. Feipel, "Questionable Books in Public Libraries—I," pp. 857–861, and "Questionable Books in Public Libraries—II," *LJ* 47 (15 October 1922): 877–878.

29. Feipel, "Questionable Books—II," p. 911.

30. Editorial, *LJ* 47 (15 October 1922): 878.

31. May Massee, ed., *ALA Catalog, 1912–1921: An Annotated List of 4000 Books* (Chicago: American Library Association, 1923).

32. Corinne Bacon, ed., *Fiction Catalog* (New York: H. W. Wilson, 1923), p. i.

33. Gouldner, "Anti-Minotaur: The Myth of a Value-Free Sociology," in his *For Sociology: Renewal and Critique in Sociology Today* (London: Allen Lane, 1973), p. 10.

34. Merton, "Science and Democratic Social Structure," *STSS*, p. 607.

35. Eliot Freidson, *Professional Dominance*, pp. 152, 153.

36. Charles Knowles Bolton, "The Ethics of Librarianship," *LJ* 47 (15 June 1922): 549–550. For earlier versions, see Charles K. Bolton, "The Librarian's Canon of Ethics," *PL* 14 (June 1909): 203–205; *PL* 17 (May 1912): 169.

37. Della R. Prescott, "What Americanization Is Not," *LJ* 45 (1 March 1920): 218; John Cotton Dana, "The Librarian as a Censor," *LJ* 44 (November 1919): 728.

10. THE CRITICAL SHIFT: 1923–1930

1. Lewis, *Obscenity*, pp. 317–329; Higham, *Strangers*, pp. 317–324.

2. Wiebe, *Search*, pp. 287–288; Hofstadter, *Reform*, pp. 237–239; Reinhard Bendix, *Work and Authority in Industry: Ideologies of Management in the Course of Industrialization* (New York: John Wiley, 1956), pp. 281–286; Link, *American Epoch*, 2:276–280; Kazin, *On Native Grounds*, pp. 18l, 239–241.

3. Sarah K. Vann, *The Williamson Reports: A Study* (Metuchen, N.J.: Scarecrow, 1971), pp. vii, 2, 14–23, 141.

4. William Learned, *The American Public Library and the Diffusion of Knowledge* (New York: Harcourt, 1924).

5. Judson Jennings, "Sticking to Our Last," *ALAB* 18 (August 1924): 150–156; Carl Roden, "Ten Years," *ALAB* 22 (September 1928): 311–328; cf. Ernest Victor Hollis, *Philanthropic Foundations and Higher Education* (New York: Columbia University Press, 1938), pp. 39–55.

6. ALA conference proceedings, *ALAB* 23 (August 1929): 237–240, 260–265; Arthur Bostwick, "Taking Stock in the Library Business," *LJ* 55 (15 April 1930): 361; Bostwick, *Autobiography*, pp. 301–302, 291, 293.

7. Boyer, *Purity*, pp. 97–119.

8. Ibid., pp. 117–123; Thomas Dixon, "Censorship," *PW* 105 (24 May 1924): 1698–1701.

9. Edith Tobitt, "Novels of the Last Two Years" (abstract), *ALAB* 17 (conf. no., 1923): 243–244; Mary U. Rothrock, "Censorship of Fiction in the Public Library," *LJ* 48 (15 May 1923): 454–456; extract in *PW* 103: 1765–1766.

10. ALA conference proceedings, *ALAB* 17 (conf. no., 1923); Mary Ahern, "One Man's Meat Is Another Man's Poison," *PL* 28 (May 1923): 296.

11. Helen Haines, "Modern Fiction and the Public Library," *LJ* 49 (15 May 1924): 458–461.

12. News story, *LJ* 48 (1 December 1923): 1023; Mahlon K. Schnacke, "A Plea for Liberalism in the Selection of Books for Public Libraries," *New York Libraries* 9 (May 1925): 198–200; "Library Censorship of Current Fiction: Some Principles to be Observed," *New York Libraries* 9 (May 1925): 208–209.

13. J. J. Gummerscheimer, "Trustees and Library Extension," *Illinois Libraries* (July 1926): 63–64; Irving Howe and Lewis Coser, *The American Communist Party: A Critical History, 1919–1957* (Boston: Beacon Press, 1957), p. 2.

14. "Massachusetts Library Club," *LJ* 49 (15 February 1924): 182; Frank H. Chase, "What People Are Reading in Boston," *ALAB* 18 (August 1924): 172–173; editorial, *LJ* 50 (15 June 1925): 542; correction, *LJ* 50 (1 July 1925): 606.

15. Charles Belden, "Looking Forward," *ALAB* 20 (October 1926): 274.

16. Dane Yorke, "Three New England Libraries" (excerpted from *American Mercury*), *LJ* 51 (1 October 1926): 830.

17. *DALB* on Belden.

18. Editorial, *LJ* 52 (15 February 1927): 200.

19. Boyer, *Purity*, pp. 168–18l; Lewis, *Obscenity*, p. 98.

20. Lewis, *Obscenity*, p. 181.

21. Editorial, *LJ* 52 (1 April 1927): 360–361.

22. Editorial, *LJ* 52 (15 April 1927): 422.

23. Editorial, *LJ* 62 (1 May 1927): 478–479.

24. Boyer, *Purity*, pp. 187–195, 203; *PW* 111 (18 May 1927): 2118–2120; *PL* 32 (March 1927): 136.

25. Link, *American Epoch*, 2:302; "Patriotism in Chicago," *PW* 112 (29 October 1927): 1630–1631; Milton Fairman, "Superintendent McAndrew and Chicago Textbooks on Trial," *PW* 112 (29 October 1927): 1627–1629; "The History of Censorship in Chicago," *LJ* 52 (1 November 1927).

26. Fairman, "Patriotism," p. 1628; "The Chicago Censorship Question," *LJ* 52 (15 November 1927): 1072; editorial, *LJ* 52 (15 November 1927): 1078; "Library Directors Rebuke Thompson," *PW* 112 (5 November 1927): 1718.

27. *DALB* on Roden, p. 441; "Patriotism in Chicago," *PW* 112 (29 October 1927): 1630.

28. Marilla W. Freeman, "Censorship in the Large Public Library," *LJ* 53 (1 March 1928): 221–224; Elva Bascom, "Education for Book Selection," *ALAB* 22 (conf. no., 1928): 441; Greta Brown, "Buying Books for a New England Library," *LJ* 54 (15 March 1929): 240–241; Marjorie Bedinger, "Censorship of Books by the Library," *WB* 3 (May 1929): 621–626 (originally in *Pacific Northwest Library Association Quarterly*, 1928); Margery Quigley, "Books in Suburbia—the Suburban Library's Book Buying Problems," *LJ* 55 (1 April 1930): 303.

29. George Bowerman, "Censorship and the Public Library," *Libraries* (the old *PL*) 35 (April 1930):127–132.

30. Quigley, "Books in Suburbia," p. 303.

31. Freeman, "Censorship in the Large Public Library," p. 223; Ethel G. Baker, "Selection of Fiction," *WB* 3 (March 1929): 581–584.

32. George Hill Evans, "The Boston Book Review Club," *LJ* 56 (15 November 1931): 945–948.

33. Boyer, *Purity*, pp. 207–234; Lewis, *Obscenity*, pp. 97–133.

34. H.C.W., editorial, *LJ* 54 (1 March 1929): 219.

35. "Editorial Forum," *LJ* 54 (1 May 1929): 395; editorial, *LJ* 54 (15 June 1929): 537.

36. Boyer, *Purity*, pp. 207–234.

37. Carl Cannon, "Who Shall Decide What We Can't Read?" *LJ* 54 (1 December 1929): 1024–1026; "Censorship Resolutions from Rhode Island," *LJ* 54 (15 November 1929): 952; "Censorship Again!" *LJ* 55 (15 February 1930): 169.

38. Bedinger, "Censorship," pp. 621 626; William E. Marcus, "Censorship from the Viewpoint of a Trustee," *Wisconsin Library Bulletin* 27 (June 1931): 152–153; Edward Weber Allen, "What the Public Wants," *LJ* 57 (15 June 1932): 559–560.

39. Bowerman, "Censorship and the Public Library," pp. 127–134; "Part 2," *PL* 35 (May 1930): 184–186.

40. The passage on trustees was added in George Bowerman, *Censorship and the Public Library* (New York: H. W. Wilson, 1931).

41. Carl Cannon, review of George Bowerman, *Censorship and the Public Library*, *LJ* 56 (July 1931): 610–611; William F. Yust, "Censorship—a Library Problem," *LJ* 57 (15 February 1932): 176–179.

42. Paul M. Paine, "The Library Must Be Free," *New York Libraries* 11 (February 1928): 42–45; quotation is from Milton's "Areopagitica."

43. Lutie E. Stearns, "The Great Unreached and Why," *WB* 3 (March 1929): 523–527 (originally in *Wisconsin Library Bulletin*, 1928); *DALB* on Stearns.

44. Stearns, "The Great Unreached," pp. 525–526.

45. Pierce Butler, review of George F. Bowerman, *Censorship and the Public Library*, *Library Quarterly* 2 (April 1932): 168–169; *DALB* on Butler.

46. Isabella M. Cooper, ed., *ALA Catalog, 1926: An Annotated Basic List of 10,000 Books* (Chicago: American Library Association, 1926).

47. *Fiction Catalog Supplement* (New York: H. W. Wilson, 1928).

48. *ALA Catalog, 1926–1931: An Annotated List of Approximately 3000 Titles*, ed. by Marion Horton (Chicago: American Library Association, 1933).

49. Available documentary works included Marion Frankfurter and Gardner Jackson, eds., *The Letters of Sacco and Vanzetti* (New York: Viking, 1930); *Sacco-Vanzetti Case*, transcript edited by Newton D. Baker and others, 6 vols. (New York: Holt, 1928); Governor of Massachusetts, 1925 [Alvan T. Fuller], *Decision* (Boston, Mass.: Secretary of the Commonwealth). More slanted works were also available. Titles from *U.S. Catalog, 1928* and *Cumulative Book Index, 1928–1932*.

50. John Dos Passos, *The Forty-Second Parallel* (New York: Random House [1939]), pp. 297–299 (part of his *U.S.A.* trilogy); on Edison, Anne M. Mulheron, "Examples of Personal Service in Adult Education," *ALAB* 19 (conf. no., 1925): 141.

51. Editorial, *LJ* 55 (15 February 1930): 160; "Suggested Code of Library Ethics," *LJ* 55 (15 February 1930): 164–165.

52. Paine, "The Library Must Be Free." He mentions that his board included a liberal minister, a lawyer, and the president of the University of Syracuse.

53. ALA was engaged in a continuing effort to win trustee support. In 1929, for example, the *ALA Bulletin* launched a series of articles by trustees.

54. Metzger, "Academic Freedom in Delocalized Academic Institutions," in Walter P. Metzger et al., *Dimensions of Academic Freedom* (Urbana: University of Illinois Press, 1969), pp. 8–10, 14–17, 21–28.

55. Paul F. Lazarsfeld and Wagner Thielens, Jr., *The Academic Mind* (New York: Free Press, 1958).

56. Howard Becker, "Normative Reactions to Normlessness," *American Sociological Review* 25 (December 1960): 803–804. Becker changed his initial view because of the reactionary radicalism of the Nazi movement.

57. Chafee, *Free Speech*, pp. 285–354.

11. WITHOUT DUST OR HEAT: 1930–1935

1. Personal interview, Stanley J. Kunitz, July 20, 1982. Quotation from John Dos Passos, *U.S.A.*, p. vii.

2. Rideout, *Radical Novel*, pp. 116–247; Kazin, *On Native Grounds*, pp. 283–328; Lewis, *Obscenity*, pp. 97, 114–122.

3. Asa Don Dickinson, "Uneasy About Bureaucratic Tendencies," *LJ* 56 (15 June 1931): 548–549; Jesse Shera, "Handmaidens of the Learned World," *LJ* 56 (1 January 1931): 21–23; Lutie Stearns, "Tomorrow Is Just Another Day," *LJ* 56

(1 November 1931): 894; editorials, *LJ* 55 (1 June 1930): 504; *LJ* 56 (1 February 1931): 124; Morse A. Cartwright, "The Librarian as a Part of Adult Education," *LJ* 56 (1 October 1932): 802–803.

4. C. Seymour Thompson, "Do We Want a Library Science?" *LJ* 56 (July 1931): 581–587.

5. Douglas Waples, "Do We Want a Library Science? A Reply," *LJ* 56 (15 September 1931): 741–746.

6. Stephen Karetzky, *Reading Research and Librarianship* (Westport, Conn.: Greenwood Press, 1982), pp. 110–117; Douglas Waples, "People and Libraries," in *Current Issues in Library Administration*, ed. Carleton Joeckel (Chicago: University of Chicago Press, 1939), p. 370.

7. "How Libraries Are Meeting Present Problems," *ALAB* 26 (February 1932): 67–73; "The Trustees Service," *ALAB* 26 (October 1932): 760–761; quote from Matthew Josephson, *Infidel in the Temple: A Memoir of the Nineteen-Thirties* (New York: Alfred A. Knopf, 1967), pp. 78–80.

8. Josephine Rathbone, "Creative Librarianship," *ALAB* 26 (May 1932): 310–311.

9. Gratia Countryman, in "How Libraries Are Meeting Present Problems," p. 68; Jennie Flexner, "Shall the Public Library Be for All the People?—Yes!" *ALAB* 26 (July 1932): 411–416; Milton Ferguson, "Shall the Public Library Be for All the People?—No!" *ALAB* 26 (July 1932): 418–419.

10. Carleton B. Joeckel, "Questions of a Political Scientist," *ALAB* 27 (February 1933): 68; *DALB* on Joeckel.

11. Carl Milam, "Secretary's Report," *ALAB* 27 (October 1933): 421.

12. Jesse Shera, "Librarian's 'Changing World,' " *LJ* 58 (15 February 1933): 149–152; Pierce Butler, *An Introduction to Library Science* (Chicago: University of Chicago Press, 1933), p. xi; Arthur Berthold, "Science of Librarianship" (review of Pierce Butler), *WB* 8 (October 1933): 120–12l; Philip O. Keeney, "What About the 1933 Applicants?" *LJ* 57 (15 June 1932): 582–583; Sydney Mitchell, "Personnel in Relation to Significant Trends," *LJ* 59 (July 1934): 554–558.

13. Lyman Bryson, "Public Forums and Readable Books," *ALAB* 27 (15 December 1933): 636–638.

14. Ibid., pp. 638, 641: John W. Studebaker, *The American Way: Democracy at Work in the Des Moines Forums* (New York and London: McGraw-Hill, 1935), pp. 67–71.

15. Gratia Countryman, "Building for the Future," *LJ* 59 (July 1934): 541–547.

16. Editorial, *LJ* 59 (July 1934): 560.

17. Philip Selznick, *TVA and the Grass Roots: A Study in the Sociology of Formal Organizations* (Berkeley: University of California Press, 1949), p. 37; John W. Studebaker, "Public Forums and Libraries," *ALAB* 29 (October 1935): 769.

18. Carl Milam, "National Planning for Libraries," *ALAB* 28 (February 1934): 60–62; Frank Kingdon, "The Public Library and the Federal Treasury," *LJ* 60 (1 May 1935): 388.

19. Sydney Mitchell, "Certification and Federal Aid," *LJ* 60 (15 June 1935): 526; William P. Tucker, "Mr. Thompson's Article Considered," *LJ* 60 (15 September 1935): 721–722; Rachel Anderson, "We Must Read Widely," *LJ* 60 (1 May 1935): 488.

20. Carleton Joeckel, *The Government of the American Public Library* (Chicago:

University of Chicago Press, 1935); Mary Rothrock, ALA conference proceedings, 1936.

21. Arundell Esdaile, "Chicago Highlights," *ALAB* 27 (November 1933): 520; Frederick B. Keppel, "The Responsibility of Writers, Publishers and Librarians in Promoting International Understanding," *ALAB* 27 (15 December 1933): 594–597.

22. Howard Mumford Jones, "The Place of Books and Reading in Modern Society," *ALAB* 27 (15 December 1933): 585–592.

23. Sullivan, *Milam*, p. 222.

24. "German Library of Banned Books" (in Paris), *LJ* 59 (1 June 1934): 470; Arthur Berthold, "The Young Librarian," *WB* 8 (January 1934): 296; Lyman Bryson, "The Treason of the Liberals," *ALAB* 28 (August 1934): 429–438, 474.

25. Gretchen Garrison, "Libraries and the World Mind," *WB* 9 (September 1934): 18–20; Arthur Berthold, "The Young Librarian," *WB* 9 (November 1934): 129–132; Stanley J. Kunitz, "The Roving Eye," *WB* 9 (November 1934): 137.

26. "The Roving Eye," *WB* 9 (November 1934): 138.

27. Leon Carnovsky, "Libraries in Nazi Germany," *LJ* 59 (15 November 1934): 893–894.

28. R. Carmine Ruggiero, letter, "Disagrees with Mr. Carnovsky," *LJ* 59 (15 December 1934): 978.

12. FACING ARMAGEDDON: 1935–1939

1. Link, *American Epoch*, 2:446–449; Adele Martin, letter, *WB* 10 (June 1936): 672–673; MacLeish quoted in Bernard Berelson, "The Myth of Library Impartiality, an Interpretation for Democracy," *WB* 13 (October 1938): 87–90.

2. Oscar Chapman, "Facing the Challenge of Democracy," *ALAB* 29 (September 1935): 536–541.

3. "Jay Otis," "Will Libraries Live?" *WB* 10 (September 1935): 25–29, quotation on pp. 28–29.

4. Charles Compton, "The Opportunity of the Public Library Trustee," *ALAB* 29 (September 1935): 718.

5. "How Shall the Library Treat So-Called Radical Propaganda Periodical Literature?" *ALAB* 29 (September 1935): 645.

6. Ibid., pp. 645–646.

7. Ibid., p. 646.

8. Ibid., pp. 646–647.

9. Wilhelm Munthe, "The Annual Meeting of the German Librarians in Tübingen," *LJ* 60 (15 September 1935): 711.

10. Stanley Kunitz column, "The Roving Eye," *WB* 10 (September 1935): 41–43, November 1935, p. 195, December 1935, p. 257.

11. Marion Harmon, "Tale of Two Cities," *WB* 10 (October 1935): 144.

12. Harold Laski, "The Uses of the Public Library," *WB* 10 (November 1935): 176, 179. Also reprinted in *LJ*.

13. Leroy Merritt, "Assembly Rooms," *LJ* 61 (1 May 1936): 341; Kate Deane Andrew, "Assembly Rooms," *LJ* 61 (1 June 1936): 427; Leon Carnovsky, "The

Worst Periodical Usually Found in Library Reading Rooms," *ALAB* 30 (August 1936): 737–740.

14. Anonymous letter, "The Great Red Hunt," *WB* 10 (June 1936): 672; John Henderson, "Censorship in Montana," *WB* 10 (March 1936): 480–481; Jesse Shera, "Call to Action," *WB* 10 (April 1936): 532–533.

15. Rideout, *Radical Novel*, pp. 225–234; Theodore Norton, letter, *WB* 9 (January 1935): 261; *Reader's Guide to Periodical Literature*, July 1935-June 1937 and July 1937-June 1939 vols., inside front covers.

16. Jesse Shera, "The College Library of the Future," *ALAB* 30 (June 1936): 499–500; Sidney Ditzion, "The Problem of Propaganda Magazines," *WB* 11 (September 1936): 21–24.

17. William H. Carlson, "Preparers of the Mind and Heart," *LJ* 60 (1 March 1936): 183–185.

18. Stanley J. Kunitz, "Specter at Richmond," *WB* 10 (May 1936): 592–593; personal interview, July 20, 1982.

19. Louis R. Wilson, "Restudying the Library Chart," *ALAB* 30 (June 1936): 480–490; Lowell Martin, "What Is This Library Science?" *LJ* 60 (15 December 1935): 974. Martin was a librarian at Lane Technical High School, Chicago. These young followers illustrate "anticipatory socialization"; cf. Merton, *STSS*, pp. 319–322.

20. Harrison Craver, "Unfinished Business," *ALAB* 30 (July 1938); 413–419; Malcolm Wyer, "Enduring Values," *ALAB* 31 (July 1937): 381–386; Ralph Munn, "Library Objectives," *ALAB* 30 (August 1936): 583–586; Milton Ferguson, "Adult Education and the Library," *LJ* 63 (1 September 1938): 624–627.

21. Helen Haines, *Living with Books* (New York: Columbia University Press, 1935); Clarence Sherman, "The Definition of Library Objectives," in *Current Issues in Library Administration*, pp. 44, 45; Clarence Sherman, "Bibliographic Birth Control," *LJ* 61 (1 September 1937): 640.

22. Sherman, "Bibliographic Birth Control."

23. Marian Scandrett, "Studs Lonigan and the Library," *LJ* 61 (15 April 1937): 327–329; "Gleanings from Annual Reports," *LJ* 61 (1 June 1937): 460.

24. Ray Nichols, *Treason, Tradition, and the Intellectual: Julien Benda and Political Discourse* (Lawrence: The Regents Press of Kansas, 1978), pp. 94–108.

25. Bendix, *Work and Authority*, pp. 338–339; Karl Marx, *The Eighteenth Brumaire of Louis Bonaparte*, in *The Marx-Engels Reader*, ed. Robert Tucker (New York: W. W. Norton, 1972), p. 462.

26. Jesse Shera, "College Librarianship and Educational Reform," *ALAB* 31 (March 1937): 142–145.

27. "Should Libraries Unionize?" Ruth Hale, "I. The Librarian and the Open Shop," *LJ* 62 (August 1937): 587–589; Barbara Falkoff, "II. The Librarian and the Closed Shop," *LJ* 62 (August 1937): 590–593. Both were members of the University of Washington library staff.

28. Helen Ziegler, "The Staff Association Picture, 1936," *LJ* 61 (15 September 1936).

29. [Mary] van Kleeck, "New Developments in Workers' Organizations," *ALAB* 31 (15 October 1937): 893–894.

30. Jesse Shera, "An Exchange of Correspondence," *WB* 11 (June 1937): 715.

31. Glenn M. Wyer, in "An Exchange of Correspondence," *WB* 11 (June 1937): 716.

32. Milton Ferguson, "A Case for Careful Investigation," *LJ* 62 (15 June 1937): 512.

33. "Code of Ethics," *ALAB* 31 (September 1937): 537.

34. "ALA—Commendable or Condemnable?" *ALAB* 31 (December 1937): 942–943; on background, "Junior Librarians Section," *WB* 12 (June 1938): 633.

35. "ALA—Commendable or Condemnable?" p. 943. Among those who saw Keeney's dismissal as a freedom to read issue, see Minnie Rubin, "Keeney Case," *WB* 12 (September 1937): 43–44.

36. Philip Keeney, letter, *PNLA Quarterly* 2 (January 1938): 86; AAUP, Committee A, statement on findings, *AAUP Bulletin* 24 (April 1938): 321–348; American Federation of Teachers, National Academic Freedom Committee, *Keeney Case: Big Business, Higher Education, and Organized Labor, Report of an Investigation . . . of the Role Played By Certain Business and Political Interests in the Affairs of the University* (American Federation of Teachers, 1939); "Keeney Ordered Reinstated," *WB* 12 (June 1938): 660–661; "Keeney Resolution," *ALAB* 32 (July 1938): 455.

37. Philip Keeney, "The Public Library—A People's University?" *WB* 13 (February 1939): 369–377, 387; Chalmers Hadley, "Responsible Trustees," *WB* 13 (April 1939): 531.

38. Hadley, "Responsible Trustees," *WB* 13 (April 1939): 664; Roberto Michels, *Political Parties*, tr. Edcon and Adar Paul (New York: Free Press, 1949).

39. Philip O. Keeney, "The Next Case," *WB* 13 (June 1939): 663–666.

40. Marilla Freeman, "The Social Outlook of the Librarian," *LJ* 63 (15 June 1938): 491.

41. "Literary Notes" and other columns, *WB* 12 (1937–1938), for March 1938, p. 424, April, p. 530, May, p. 562, June, p. 628. Only the note on Chinese librarians appeared in the other major library publications.

42. Milton Ferguson, "The Library Crosses the Bridge," *ALAB* 32 (July 1938): 423–424.

43. Maurice Leon, "Disagrees with President Ferguson," *WB* 13 (September 1938): 58; Leroy C. Merritt, "Protest Ferguson Comment on Unions," *ALAB* 32 (August 1938); Elizabeth French, chairman, librarians' committee, Teachers' Union, local 5, N.Y.C., "Courageous Stand on Democracy," *ALAB* (March 1939): 216.

44. Staff Organization Round Table resolutions, *ALAB* 32 (15 October 1938): 968–969.

45. Berelson, "Myth of Library Impartiality," pp. 87–90.

46. Marian Scandrett, "Mr. Berelson's Lost Cause," *WB* 13 (February 1939): 398–400.

47. Stewart Smith, "Propaganda and the Library," *LJ* 64 (1 January 1939): 13–15; Ralph T. Esterquest, "Pressure Groups in Your Pamphlet File," *LJ* 64 (15 March 1939): 226–227; Sydney Mitchell, "The Public Library in the Defense of Democracy," *LJ* 64 (15 March 1939): 209–212; cf. also Lawrence Hyle, "On Boycotting German Books and Periodicals," *ALAB* 33 (April 1939): 331.

48. Leon Carnovsky, "Community Analysis and the Practice of Book Selec-

tion," in *The Practice of Book Selection: Papers Presented Before the Library Institute at the University of Chicago, July 31 to August 13, 1939*, ed. Louis R. Wilson (Chicago: University of Chicago Press, 1940), p. 32.

49. Ibid., p. 29.

50. Stanley J. Kunitz, "The Roving Eye," *WB* 13 (January 1939): 314.

51. Des Moines Public Library, "The Library's Bill of Rights, *ALAB* 33 (January 1939): inside back cover.

52. "Code of Ethics for Librarians," *ALAB* 33 (February 1939): 128–130; "Library's Bill of Rights," *LJ* 64 (1 July 1939): 549; "San Francisco Conference," *LJ* 64 (1 October 1939): 753.

53. "MacLeish Appointment Protested," *ALAB* 33 (July 1939): 467.

54. "Code of Ethics," pp. 128, 129.

55. Des Moines Public Library, "Library's Bill of Rights."

56. Donald K. Campbell, "Let's Keep Our Heads," *ALAB* 33 (December 1939): 728–729; Ralph Munn, "A Message from President Munn," *ALAB* 33 (October 1939): 669; Carl H. Milam, "The Library and Today's Problems," *ALAB* 33 (December 1939): 721–722; Milam, "Outline for Action," *ALAB* 33 (December 1939), esp. p. 725; Milam "Town Meeting: Is the Library Doing Its Job?" *ALAB* 33 (December 1939): 45.

57. William P. Tucker, "Progressive Librarians Council Formed," *WB* 14 (September 1939): 29; Sullivan, *Milam*, p. 136.

58. Editorial, "Whose Responsibility Is It?" *LJ* 61 (1 October 1939): 744.

59. Staughton Lynd, *Intellectual Origins of American Radicalism* (1968; reprint, New York: Random House, Vintage Books, 1969), pp. 67–68, 160–161.

60. Selznick, *TVA and the Grass Roots*, p. 59.

61. Ibid., p. 50.

62. Carl Milam, "Secretary's Report," *ALAB* 33 (September 1939): 537; Jens Nyholm, "The American Way: Notes on Censorship in Libraries," *WB* 14 (April 1940): 555–559; letter, "Impartiality," *WB* 14 (April 1940): 597.

63. Archibald MacLeish, "The Librarian and the Democratic Process," *ALAB* 34 (June 1940): 385–388, 422.

64. Ibid., p. 422.

13. CONCLUSIONS AND THEORETICAL IMPLICATIONS

1. Richard Hofstadter, *Anti-Intellectualism in American Life* (New York: Knopf, 1963), pp. 126–129; Charles Tilly, *The Vendée* (Cambridge, Mass.: Harvard University Press, 1964), classifies rural communities in terms of degree of cosmopolitan intrusion.

2. Lewis, *Obscenity*, pp. 160, 185–187.

3. Coser, *Men of Ideas*, discussed in ch. 2, pp. 22–23 above.

4. Reinhard Bendix, *Nation-Building*, pp. 433–434; Sigmund Diamond, *Immigration, Citizenship, and Social Change: Some Reflections on the American Experience* (Tel-Aviv: Israel Press for the Aranne Foundation, 1977), pp. 20–21.

5. Goode, "Librarianship," discussed in chs. 5 and 11.

6. Cf. Magali S. Larson, *The Rise of Professionalism*; Terence Johnson, *Profes-*

sions and Power (London: Macmillan, 1972), defines professionalism as a form of occupational control.

7. Weber, "Bureaucracy," in Gerth and Mills, *From Max Weber*, pp. 198–200, 237, and Bendix, *Nation-Building*, pp. 139–148.

8. Cf. Robert K. Merton, *Some Thoughts on the Professions in American Society*, Brown University Papers, no. 37 (Providence, R.I.: Brown University, 1960), pp. 11–12, 15, and *STSS*, p. 446 n.6.

9. Cf. Wilbert Moore, *Professions*.

10. Peter Rossi, "Discussion," in *Seven Questions About the Profession of Librarianship*, ed. Philip Enmis (Chicago: University of Chicago Press, 1962), p. 83; Amitai Etzioni, *The Semi-Professions and Their Organization* (New York: Free Press, 1969).

11. Herbert Gans, *Deciding What's News* (New York: Basic Books, 1980), p. 186; Bernard Roshko, *Newsmaking* (Chicago: University of Chicago Press, 1975), pp. 41–47, 132 n.12.

12. Max Weber, "The Social Psychology of the World Religions," in *From Max Weber*, p. 280.

13. Elliott A. Krause, *Sociology of Occupations* (Boston: Little, Brown, 1971), pp. 98–104, 192–193.

14. Paul L. Murphy, *The Constitution in Crisis Times, 1918–1969* (New York: Harper, 1972), pp. 171, 175; Lloyd C. Taylor, Jr., *The Medical Professions and Social Reform, 1885–1945* (New York: St. Martin's Press, 1974), pp. 103–142.

15. Selznick, *TVA*, pp. 47–48.

BIBLIOGRAPHICAL ESSAY

This review outlines only a few of the analyses and sources used in this work. Fuller documentation and an extensive bibliography are included in my original doctoral dissertation in sociology, "Ideals and Ideology: The Freedom To Read in American Public Libraries, 1876–1939" (1980), at Columbia University.

The major sources for this qualitative content analysis, scanned page by page, were the *Library Journal, Public Libraries,* the *Bulletin of the American Library Association,* the *Wilson Bulletin,* and proceedings of the annual conferences of the American Library Association. Other sources, reviewed in lesser detail, were such state publications as the *Wisconsin Library Association Bulletin* and *New York Libraries,* the University of Chicago's *Library Quarterly, Saturday Review of Literature,* and other lay publications. Biographical details were taken from the *Dictionary of American Biography,* ed. Dumas Malone (New York: Scribner's, 1935), and its supplement, from the *Dictionary of American Library Biography,* 1st ed. (Littleton, Colo.: Libraries Unlimited, 1978), from individual biographies, and from histories of individual libraries.

The classic histories of libraries are Jesse Shera's *Foundations of the American Public Library: The Origins of the Public Library Movement in New England, 1829–1853* (Chicago: University of Chicago Press, 1949), and Sidney Ditzion's *Arsenals of a Democratic Culture: A Social History of the American Public Library Movement in New England and the Middle States from 1850 to 1900* (Chicago: American Library Association, 1947). More recent histories include Dee Garrison's *Apostles of Culture: The Public Librarian and American Society, 1876–1970* (New York: Free Press, 1979) and Michael H. Harris, *The Purpose of the American Public Library in Historical Perspective: A Revisionist Interpretation* (Washington, D.C.: ERIC Clearinghouse on Library and Information Science, 1972); Michael H. Harris, "Public Libraries and the Decline of the Democratic Dogma," *LJ* 101 (1 November 1976): 2225–2230; Michael H. Harris, "The Purpose of the American Public Library: A Revisionist Interpretation of History," *LJ* 98 (15 September 1973): 2509–2514. Phyllis Dain, "Ambivalence and Paradox: The Social Bonds of the Public Library," *LJ* 100 (1 February 1975): 261–266, takes issue with Harris's thesis.

Other historiographic discussions include Elaine Fain, "Manners and Morals in the Public Library: A Glance at Some New History," *Journal of Library History* 10 (April 1975): 99–105; Michael H. Harris, "Externalist or Internalist Frameworks for the Interpretation of American Library History—The Continuing Debate," *Journal of Library History* 10 (April 1975): 106–110; Dee Garrison, "Rejoinder," ibid., pp. 111–116; John Calvin Colson, "The Writing of American Library

History, 1876–1976," *Library Trends* 25 (July 1976): 7–21. These works do not discuss library censorship per se, but comment on censorship in debating whether librarians were elitist or not. Surveys of censorship in libraries include little historical discussion, but Marjorie Fiske's *Book Selection and Censorship: A Study of School and Public Libraries in California* (Berkeley: University of California Press, 1959), has a brief discussion of library elitism and a social-psychological interpretation that differs somewhat from the structural approach adopted in this study.

Historical works providing background on censorship issues include, among others, John Tebbel, *A History of Book Publishing in the United States* (New York and London: R. R. Bowker, 1972–1980), vol. 1, *The Creation of An Industry, 1629–1835* (1972), and vol. 2, *The Expansion of An Industry, 1865–1919* (1975); Paul Boyer, *Purity in Print: The Vice Society Movement and Book Censorship in America* (New York: Scribner's, 1968); Felice Flannery Lewis, *Literature, Obscenity, and Law* (Carbondale: Southern Illinois University Press, 1976); Zechariah Chafee, Jr., *Free Speech in the United States* (1920; reprint, Cambridge, Mass.: Harvard University Press, 1948); Walter B. Rideout, *The Radical Novel in America* (Cambridge, Mass.: Harvard University Press, 1956); Richard Hofstadter and Walter B. Metzger, *The Development of Academic Freedom in the United States* (New York: Columbia University Press, 1955); Frank Luther Mott, *Golden Multitudes: The Story of Best Sellers in the United States* (New York: Macmillan, 1947); Robert E. Spiller et al., eds., *Literary History of the United States*, 3d ed., rev. (New York: Macmillan, 1963), vol. 1; Lawrence Cremin, *American Education*, vol. 1, *The Colonial Experience, 1607–1783*, and vol. 2, *The National Experience, 1783–1876* (New York: Harper, 1970 and 1980); and Lewis A. Coser, *Men of Ideas: A Sociologist's View* (New York: Free Press, 1970). More general histories include Richard Hofstadter's *The Age of Reform* (New York: Random House, 1955); and Robert Wiebe's *The Search for Order, 1877–1920* (New York: Hill & Wang, 1968).

Of the vast sociological literature on the subjects of this study, only a few works can be cited here. The great classic approaches to the sociology of knowledge by Marx, Durkheim, Weber, and Mannheim are compared in Robert K. Merton's "The Sociology of Knowledge," in his *Social Theory and Social Structure*, enl. ed. (New York: Free Press, 1968). Talcott Parsons discusses the content of ideology in chapter 8 of *The Social System* (New York: Free Press, 1951). Bernard Barber's "Function, Variability, and Change in Ideological Systems," in *Stability and Social Change*, ed. Bernard Barber and Alex Inkeles (Boston: Little, Brown, 1971), pp. 244–262, takes a functional approach to ideology. See also Max Weber's "Politics as a Vocation," in *From Max Weber: Essays in Sociology*, ed. H. H. Gerth and C. Wright Mills (New York: Oxford University Press, 1946), and Reinhard Bendix, *Max Weber: An Intellectual Portrait* (Garden City, N.Y.: Doubleday, 1960).

Studies of specific occupational and professional ideologies include Max Weber's "Science as a Vocation," in *From Max Weber*; Robert K. Merton's *Science, Technology, and Society in Seventeenth-Century England* (1938; reprint, New York: Howard Fertig, 1970); and Merton's essays on norms in science and technology—the culture or code of science—in his *Social Theory and Social Structure*. The changing legitimacy of these values is discussed by André Cournand and Harriet Zuckerman in "The Code of Science: Analysis and Some Reflections on the

Future," *Studium Generale* 23 (1970): 141–162, and a critical perspective is typified in Michael Mulkay's "Norms and Ideology in Science," *Social Science Information* 15, nos. 4–5 (1976): 637–656. Fruitful discussions of occupational values are also provided in Alvin Gouldner's "Anti-Minotaur: The Myth of a Value-Free Sociology," in his *For Sociology: Renewal and Critique in Sociology Today* (London: Allen Lane, 1973); Mary O. Furner, *Advocacy & Objectivity: A Crisis in the Professionalization of American Social Science, 1865–1905* (Lexington: The University of Kentucky Press, 1965); and Oscar and Mary Handlin, *The Dimensions of Liberty* (1961; reprint, New York: Atheneum, 1966).

On the sociology of professions, see Talcott Parsons, "The Professions and Social Structure," *Social Forces* 17 (May 1939): 457–467; Bernard Barber, "Some Problems in the Sociology of the Professions," *Daedalus* 92 (Fall 1963): 669–688; Wilbert E. Moore, with Gerald W. Rosenblum, *The Professions: Roles and Rules* (New York: Russell Sage Foundation, 1970). For the critical school, see Everett C. Hughes, *Men and Their Work* (Glencoe: Free Press, 1958); Eliot Freidson, *Profession of Medicine: A Study of the Sociology of Applied Knowledge* (New York: Dodd, Mead, 1970) and his *Professional Dominance* (Chicago: Aldine, 1970); Howard S. Becker, "The Nature of a Profession," in *Education for the Professions*, ed. Nelson B. Henry (Chicago: National Society for the Study of Education, dist. University of Chicago Press, 1962), pp. 27–46; Eliot Freidson, "The Impurity of Professional Authority," in *Institutions and the Person: Papers Presented to Everett C. Hughes*, ed. Howard S. Becker et al. (Chicago: Aldine, 1968), pp. 25–34; and Magali S. Larson, *The Rise of Professionalism: A Sociological Analysis* (Berkeley: University of California Press, 1977). Subgroup conflicts are discussed in Rue Bucher and Anselm Strauss, "Professions in Process," *American Journal of Sociology* 66 (January 1961): 325–334. A summary perspective is provided by Joseph Ben-David, "Science as a Profession and Scientific Professionalism," in *Explorations in General Theory in Social Science: Essays in Honor of Talcott Parsons*, ed. Jan J. Loubser et al. (New York: Free Press, 1976), vol. 2; and by Terence Johnson, *Professions and Power* (London: Macmillan, 1972).

Not dealing with the issue of professionalism as such, but illustrating conflicts within scientific professions are Thomas Kuhn's *The Structure of Scientific Revolutions*, 2d ed. enl. (Chicago: University of Chicago Press, 1970); and Schmuel N. Eisenstadt with M. Curelau, *The Form of Sociology—Paradigms and Crises* (New York: John Wiley, 1976).

Among the rare discussions of librarians in the sociological literature are the essays by William J. Goode, "Librarianship: From Occupation to Profession?" in *Library Quarterly* 31 (October 1961): 300–318, and references in several essays in Amitai Etzioni, ed., *The Semi-Professions and Their Organization: Teachers, Nurses, Social Workers* (New York: Free Press, 1969).

On the broader conceptual framework of role-conflict and value-conflict, see Robert K. Merton's discussion of the role-set in his *Social Theory and Social Structure*, pp. 422–438; his essay, with Elinor Barber, on "Sociological Ambivalence" in his *Sociological Ambivalence and Other Essays* (1963; reprint, New York: Free Press, 1976), pp. 30–31; and Rose Laub Coser, "The Complexity of Roles as a Seedbed of Individual Autonomy," in *The Idea of Social Structure: Papers in Honor of Robert K. Merton*, ed. Lewis A. Coser (New York: Harcourt Brace, 1975), pp. 237–264.

INDEX

About the Author

EVELYN GELLER, an investment broker with D. H. Blair Investors, holds a master's degree in library service and a Ph.D. in sociology from Columbia University. She collaborated with J. Morton Davis, president of D. H. Blair, in the writing of *Making America Work Again* and has contributed numerous articles to *Library Journal, School Library Journal, Wilson Library Bulletin,* and *American Libraries.*

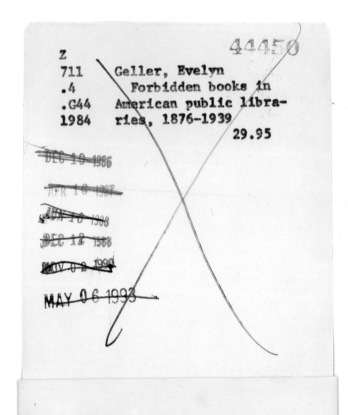